The
POWER
of
Economic
Thinking

How the New Imperial Science of ECONOMICS
Has Invaded and Transformed
POLITICS, FINANCE, HISTORY, LAW, RELIGION,
and Other SOCIAL SCIENCES

BY MARK SKOUSEN

Foundation for Econom
Irvington-on-Hudson,

The Power of Economic Thinking
Copyright © 2002 by Mark Skousen.

Foundation for Economic Education
30 South Broadway
Irvington on Hudson, New York 10533
(914) 591-7230 / www.fee.org / fee@fee.org

Cataloging in Publication Data on file with the Library of Congress

ISBN 1-57246-201-9

Manufactured in the United States of America

The
POWER
of
Economic
Thinking

To
Jo Ann,
Who made it all possible.

Contents

Contents

Correcting Fallacies and Debunking Myths

Breakthroughs in Economics

Changing People's Lives

Changing the Course of History

Predicting the Future

Acknowledgments

Economics as the new imperial science has caused me to extend my research and contacts to many other disciplines—political science, law, finance, history, religion, philosophy, and sociology, among others. I wish to thank the following individuals for their help: P.T. Bauer, Gary Becker, Peter Bernstein, Mark Blaug, Walter Block, John Blundell, Peter Boettke, Ken Boulding, Bill Breit, Peter Brimelow, Todd Buchholz, Eamonn Butler, David Card, David Colander, Michael Cox, John Patrick Diggins, Jim Dorn, Peter Drucker, Dinesh D'Souza, Richard Ebeling, Lanny Ebenstein, Al Ehrbar, Ken Elzinga, Milton Friedman, Roger Garrison, Martin Gilbert, George Gilder, Jim Gwartney, Robert Heilbroner, Paul Heyne, Robert Higgs, Larry Iannoccone, Roy Jastram, Paul Johnson, Steven Kates, Israel Kirzner, Paul Krugman, Robert Lawson, Stanley Lebergott, Bjørn Lomborg, John Lott, Jr., Burt Malkiel, Yuri Maltsev, Greg Mankiw, Hyman Minsky, Barun Mitra, Mark Mobius, Robert Mundell, Charles Murray, Robert H. Nelson, Bill Nordhaus, Gary North, Gerald P. O'Driscoll, Jr., Norman Pearlstine, Bill Peterson, Madsen Pirie, Charley Reese, Paul Craig Roberts, Sherwin Rosen, Richard Salsman, Paul A. Samuelson, Juliet Schor, Anna Schwartz, Amartya Sen, Hans Sennholz, Parth Shah, William Shipman, Julian Simon, Robert Skidelsky, W. Cleon Skousen, Gene Smiley, Tom Stanley, John Stossel, Vito Tanzi, John Templeton, Gordon Tullock, Richard Vedder, Jude Wanniski, Larry White, Walter Williams, Larry Wimmer, Leland Yeager, Daniel Yergin, and Muhammad Yunus.

Among the staff here at the Foundation for Economic Education, I'd like to thank Sheldon Richman, Mary Ann Murphy, and Beth Hoffman for their editing and selection skills, and intern Adrienne Stark for help with research. I would also like to thank my wife, Jo Ann, who has edited and often rewritten my material over these many years and crafted them into the King's English.

Mark Skousen
Irvington-on-Hudson, New York

Introduction:
The Power of
Economic Analysis

"The ideas of economists and political philosophers, both when they are right and when they are wrong, are more powerful than is commonly understood. Indeed the world is ruled by little else."

—JOHN MAYNARD KEYNES[1]

When John Maynard Keynes wrote these famous words at the end of his magnum opus in 1936, he did not realize how far-reaching and influential the new frontiers of economics would climb. (He had no idea that in the long run, beyond his lifetime, economists would be telling investors to reduce their risk and maximize their returns through stock index funds, that government officials could save millions by changing the way they auction off their debt, that churches are better off through free competition among a large number of rival faiths, that legislators can reduce crime by permitting concealed weapon permits, or clean up the environment by auctioning off pollution permits, and murder-mystery novelists can solve their crimes by using elementary economic principles!

---

[1]*The General Theory of Employment, Interest, and Money* (London: Macmillan, 1936), p. 383.

1

All of these new forms of economic research and analysis are discussed in this book.

In writing about economics over the past decades, I've been amazed at the wide and diverse ways in which economic analysis can have such a powerful influence in the world of finance, business, law, religion, politics, history, and the other social sciences. Economics can change people's and nation's lives, for better or for worse, depending on whether they adhere to or violate these basic principles. It can change the course of history.

Seven Principles of the Market

What are these basic concepts? Below are seven essential principles that can be applied to a wide variety of problems.

1. Accountability: Economics is all about accountability. In a market economy, those who benefit from the fruits of labor pay for them. If someone else pays, you don't pay much attention to the cost. When consumers don't pay for the products they use, the results are high costs, waste, and fraud. Property rights are essential to accountability. Nobody spends someone else's money as carefully as he spends his own. What belongs to you, you tend to take care of; what belongs to someone else or no one tends to fall into disrepair. As William Graham Sumner states, "A fool is wiser is his own house than a sage in another man's house."

2. Economy: In a world of scarcity and choice, one must economize. The most successful households, businesses and governments are those that invest for a better tomorrow, live within their means, and avoid excessive debt. Thrift is a virtue. Competition and the profit motive are the best system ever devised to keep costs low and avoid losses. Measuring costs and benefits help determine the best, most efficient use of resources.

3. Investment: Saving and investment are critical elements in achieving long-term success in business and life in general. As a sign posted outside a business states, "You can't do today's work with yesterday's machines if you expect to be in business tomorrow."

4. Incentives. Incentives matter. The law of the downward sloping demand curve means that if you encourage something, you get more of it; if you discourage something, you get less of it. The profit motive promotes economic growth by creating better products at cheaper prices. A freely competitive price system is also the best solution to an economic crisis. Shortages are eliminated quickly because higher prices reduce consumption and expand new supplies naturally, without government interference. Taxes can also have a significant impact on incentives. As Calvin Coolidge states, "You can't increase prosperity by taxing success."

5. **Opportunity and freedom of choice:** Economic freedom means choices and opportunity—the freedom to move, obtain a better education, start a new business, find a new job, hire and fire, and buy and sell. The best way to achieve prosperity is to produce what people want. In Latin the phrase is *do ut des*, "I give in order that you should give." The faster way to earn more is to produce more of what the customer wants, as a worker or business entrepreneur. The key to greater consumption in the long run is greater production (known as Say's Law). The secret to ending poverty is equal opportunity, not state-mandated equality of wealth or income. Free people are not equal in wealth or income, and equal people are not free.

6. **Non-discrimination, or the principle of "one price."** Under a market system, there is a tendency toward one price for the same product or service. No matter whether you are black or white, male or female, Protestant or Catholic, rich or poor, you pay the same price for bread. The market actually discourages discrimination—those who discriminate usually have to pay more.

7. **Welfare:** The welfare principle states that you should only help those who really need help. This policy applies to all charitable organizations, private and public. If you institute a welfare program for everyone, irrespective of their financial condition, you open yourself up to costly and inefficient operations. Imagine if everyone in a parish, rich or poor, were eligible for church welfare. If a government program offers benefits to everyone, it discourages self-discipline and destroys initiative. It also creates waste and inefficiency, a clear violation of Occam's Razor.

One more point: The principles of accountability, economy, incentives, investment, opportunity and welfare apply to all peoples and all nations. As Leonard E. Read, founder of FEE, states, "Let everyone do what they please as long as it's peaceful." The role of government in every nation is to keep the peace and defend everyone's right to liberty and property. Good government should limit itself to enforcing contracts, prevent injustice, provide a stable monetary and fiscal system, and encourage good relations with its neighbors. Benjamin Franklin correctly observes, "No nation has ever been ruined by trade."

A sound economy cannot be founded on an unsound monetary system. Keynes rightly states, "There is no subtler, no surer way of overturning the existing basis of society than to debauch the currency." Sound policy also requires that government officials consider the impact of legislation on all people in the long run, and not just some people in the short run. Finally, Frederic Bastiat observes, "Countries which enjoy the highest level of peace, happiness and prosperity are the ones where the law least interferes with private affairs." And the great Chinese philosopher Lao-tzu wisely notes, "Governing a large country is like frying a small fish. You spoil it by too much poking."

In these series of essays, I demonstrate repeatedly the virtues of these seven great principles. They constitute the power of economic thinking. The future belongs to sound economics.

The Imperial Science

The Imperial Science

"I think it is quite likely that we are entering an era of much
more interaction among the sciences."
                                    —KENNETH E. BOULDING[1]

During the 20th century it was popular to label economics the
"dismal science," a term of derision coined by the English
critic Thomas Carlyle in the 1850s. Carlyle lashed out against laissez-faire capitalism, which he defined as "anarchy plus the consta-
ble," for, among other things, being inconsistent with slavery.[2]

But attitudes are rapidly changing as we enter the 21st century.
Economics, no longer dismal, has come a long way toward
reinventing itself and expanding into new territories so rapidly
that another descriptive phrase is needed. Like an invading army,
the science of Adam Smith is overrunning the whole of social science—law, finance, politics, history, sociology, environmentalism,
religion, and even sports. Therefore, I have dubbed 21st-century
economics the "imperial science."

Boulding's Dream Comes True

The father of economics as an interdisciplinary movement is
Kenneth E. Boulding, long-time professor at the University of Colorado in Boulder, who died in 1993. He published over 1,000 articles on more than two dozen eclectic subjects, ranging from capital theory to Quakerism. But Boulding's vision of every discipline
borrowing ideas from other disciplines isn't exactly what has hap-

pened. Instead, economics has started to dominate the other professions.

The first breakthrough came in finance theory. Harry Markowitz, a graduate economics student at the University of Chicago, wrote an article on portfolio theory in the March 1952 issue of *The Journal of Finance*. It was the first attempt to quantify the economic concept of risk in stock and portfolio selection. Out of this work came modern portfolio theory and the "efficient market theory," which argues that short-term changes in stock prices are virtually unpredictable and that it is extremely difficult if not impossible to beat the market averages over the long run.

These ivory-tower theories were greeted with scorn by Wall Street professional managers, but eventually confirmed by numerous studies. Index funds, the economists' favorite investment vehicles, are now the largest type of mutual fund sold on Wall Street.[3]

Public Choice Theory

James Buchanan and Gordon Tullock, both at the University of Virginia, published *The Calculus of Consent* in 1962 and forever changed how political scientists view public finance and democracy. Today public-choice theory has been added to every economics classroom's curriculum.

Buchanan and other public-choice theorists contend that politicians, like businessmen, are motivated by self-interest. They seek to maximize their influence and set policies in order to be re-elected. Unfortunately, the incentives and discipline of the marketplace are often missing in government. Voters have little incentive to control the excesses of legislators, who in turn are more responsive to powerful interest groups. As a result, government subsidizes vested interests of commerce while it imposes costly, wasteful regulations and taxes on the general public.

The public-choice school has changed the debate from "market failure" to "government failure." Buchanan and others have recommended a series of constitutional rules to require the misguided public sector to act more responsibly, including requiring super-majorities to raise taxes, protecting minority rights, returning power to local governments, and imposing term limits.[4]

Economics Enters the Courtroom

In 1972 Richard A. Posner, an economist who teaches at the University of Chicago Law School and serves as chief judge of the U.S. Seventh Circuit of Appeals, wrote *Economic Analysis of Law,* which synthesized the ideas of Ronald Coase, Gary Becker, F. A. Hayek, and other great economists at the University of Chicago. Today centers of "law and economics" are found on many campuses. Judge Posner states, "Every field of law, every legal institution, every practice or custom of lawyers, judges, and legislators, present or past—even ancient—is grist for the economic analyst's mill."[5] Economists apply the principles of cost-benefit and welfare analysis to all kinds of legal issues—antitrust, labor, discrimination, environment, commercial regulations, punishments and awards. In my essay "Chicago Gun Show" (see page 38), I report on Chicago law professor John R. Lott, Jr.'s extensive work on the relationship between gun ownership and crime. He applied the incentive principle to demonstrate that well-armed citizens deter crime.

Chicago's Gary Becker has been in the forefront of applying price theory to contemporary social problems, such as education, marriage and divorce, race discrimination, charity, and drug abuse. Not surprisingly, he called his book for the general public *The Economics of Life.* But Becker warned, "This work was not well received by most economists," and the attacks from his critics were "sometimes very nasty."[6]

There are many other cases where economists have made significant improvements in other disciplines—in accounting (see my July 1999 *Ideas on Liberty* column on "Economic Value Added," or EVA), history (see the work of Robert Fogel and Douglass North), religion (Lawrence Iannaccone and Edwin West have shown that increased competition in religions increases attendance at churches), management (the Center for Market Processes at George Mason University), and sociology (see the writings of Richard Swedberg). They've even changed the way Treasury bills are auctioned.

In the 21st century, false theories still prevail in politics, law, history, sociology, and other disciplines. As Lord Acton once stated, "There is no error so monstrous that it fails to find defenders among the ablest men." The sooner the principles of market economics enter the fray and attack false doctrines, the better off we'll all be.

---

1. Kenneth E. Boulding, *The Skills of the Economist* (Cleveland: Howard Allen, Inc., 1958), p. 134.

2. For the complete background of Carlyle's racism and vile attack on market capitalism, see David M. Levy, "150 Years and Still Dismal!," in *Ideas on Liberty*, March 2000, and chapter 3 of my book *The Making of Modern Economics* (Armonk, N.Y.: M.E. Sharpe, 2001).

3. Two excellent books on modern portfolio theory are Burton Malkiel, *A Random Walk Down Wall Street*, 6th ed. (New York: W. W. Norton, 1996) and Peter L. Bernstein, *Capital Ideas* (New York: Simon & Schuster, 1992).

4. Buchanan and Tullock's *The Calculus of Consent* (Ann Arbor: University of Michigan Press, 1962) is still worth reading. For an excellent summary, see chapter XI, "The Public Choice School: Politics as a Business," in Todd G. Buchholz, *New Ideas from Dead Economists* (New York: Penguin Books, 1989).

5. Richard A. Posner, *Law and Literature*, 2nd ed. (Cambridge, Mass.: Harvard University Press, 1998), p. 182. A comprehensive summary of the "law and economics" movement can be found in Nicholas Mercuro and Steven G. Medema, *Economics and the Law: From Posner to Post-Modernism* (Princeton, N.J.: Princeton University Press, 1997).

6. Gary S. Becker and Guity Nashat Becker, *The Economics of Life* (New York: McGraw-Hill, 1997), p. 3.

Solving Domestic Issues

How Many of You Are on Food Stamps?

"There is a strong case for reducing the role of the government budget in providing health services beyond a minimum."

—Vito Tanzi and Ludger Schuknecht[1]

At a recent San Francisco Money Show, I asked an audience of several hundred investors, "By a show of hands, how many of you are on food stamps?" Not a single hand went up. Then I asked, "How many of you are on Social Security or Medicare?" A third of the audience raised their hands.

Finally, I asked, "How many of you think you will be on the food stamp program during your lifetime?" Again, not a single hand went up. But when I asked how many would eventually go on Social Security or Medicare, almost everyone raised his hand.

My point was simple. The food stamp program is a social welfare program limited to the very poor; there's a means test to qualify, and most Americans attending investment conferences don't need food stamps. On the other hand, Social Security and Medicare are universal social insurance plans. All people pay taxes for the programs, and at age 65 (sometimes earlier) they all collect benefits, even though most Americans can afford their own pension program and health insurance. Is there any wonder voters are more worried about Social Security and Medicare than they are about food stamps?

13

The following table shows the stark contrast between the food stamp program and Social Security and Medicare.

U.S. Social Welfare Systems

Program	Total Coverage (in millions)	Current Recipients (in millions)	Total Annual Expenditures
Social Security	180.0	44.2	$375 billion
Medicare	180.0	38.4	$215 billion
Food Stamps	19.8	19.8	$17 billion

Source: *Statistical Abstract of the United States* (Washington D.C.: U.S. Dept. of Commerce, 1999), Tables 173, 614, 616, 636. Figures for Social Security and Food Stamps are for 1998; Medicare for 1997, the latest available.

Why Not "Foodcare"?

Suppose the President of the United States proposes a new welfare program called "Foodcare." Since food is even more vital to each American citizen than health or retirement, he argues, the food stamp program should be expanded and universalized, like Social Security and Medicare, so that everyone qualifies for food stamps and pays for the program through a special "food stamp" tax. Congress agrees and passes new welfare legislation. Thus, instead of 19.8 million Americans on food stamps, suddenly 180 million or more begin paying the "food stamp" tax and collecting food stamps, representing perhaps 10 percent of household budgets.

What effect do you think this universal "Foodcare" plan would have on the food industry? Would we not face unprecedented costs, red tape, abuse, and powerful vested interests demanding a better, more comprehensive "foodcare"? And suppose snacks were not covered by "Foodcare"—wouldn't the general public start demanding that they be covered by the government because their costs were rising too fast? Ludwig von Mises was right: "Middle of the road policies lead to socialism."[2]

Fortunately, there is no nightmarish "foodcare" program.

Granted, there have been abuses and waste in the food stamp program, but the problems of efficiency are few compared to, say, Medicare. In fact, since 1995 the number of Americans on food stamps has declined from almost 27 million to under 20 million, and the costs have fallen from $22.8 billion to $16.9 billion.[3]

Yet have the size and cost of Social Security or Medicare declined? Never.

Safety Net or Dragnet?

The conclusion is clear. Government welfare systems—if they should exist at all—should be limited to those who really need assistance. They should be safety nets, not dragnets that capture everyone. It was a tragic mistake to create a Social Security and Medicare system where everyone at some point became a ward of the state. I'm convinced that if President Roosevelt had conceived Social Security in 1935 as a retirement plan for only the less fortunate who could not plan ahead financially, it would be a relatively inexpensive welfare program that would require taxpayers to pay at most 2–3 percent of their wages and salaries in FICA "contributions," not 12.4 percent as they do today. If President Johnson had proposed Medicare in 1965 as a supplemental medical/hospital plan limited to the needy, taxpayers would be paying 0.5 percent of their wages and salaries to Medicare, not 2.9 percent as they do today. Instead, the systems were made universal, and the duplication is horrendous—and unnecessary.

Because we all pay in and we all benefit, we don't always think straight about these "entitlements." Example: A stockbroker recently told me about a client who called and complained bitterly about attempts by Congress to revamp Medicare. He angrily said, "They can cut spending all they want, but don't touch my Medicare!" While the stockbroker listened patiently to this man's tirades, he pulled up the client's account on his computer screen. He had an account worth $750,000! If anyone could afford his own medical insurance plan, it was this man. He didn't need Medicare. Yet he saw Medicare as his right. He had paid into it all his life, and he deserved the benefits.

Imagine what this man would be saying about Congress and food prices if we had "Foodcare."

1. Vito Tanzi and Ludger Schuknecht, *Public Spending in the 20th Century; A Global Perspective* (Cambridge, U.K.: Cambridge University Press, 2000), p. 201.

2. Ludwig von Mises, *Planning for Freedom,* 4th ed. (South Holland, Ill.: Libertarian Press, 1980), pp. 18–35. This argument applies equally to today's efforts to include pharmaceutical drugs in Medicare coverage.

3. "Federal Food Stamps Program, 1995 to 1998," Table 636, *Statistical Abstract of the United States* (Washington, D.C.: U.S. Department of Commerce, 1999).

Wards of the State?

"Skeptics focus on the drawbacks to [Social Security] privatization . . . its potential for unraveling support for a social safety net."

— *New York Times*, MARCH 21, 1997

"No ordered community has callously allowed the poor and incapacitated to starve. There has always been some sort of institution designed to save from destitution people unable to sustain themselves. As general well-being has increased hand in hand with the development of Capitalism, so too has the relief of the poor improved."

— LUDWIG VON MISES, *Socialism* (1932)

The ongoing debates over the future of Social Security and Medicare raise a fundamental question about almost all social programs in industrial nations. Why is the government involved in financing and distributing benefits to virtually *all* its citizens? The original intent of national welfare programs may have been to provide a "social safety net" for the needy, but instead they cover the entire population, rich and poor. (Of course, the only moral safety net is the one that depends on voluntary charity—not coercive transfer payments.) In the industrial world, the vast majority of workers make mandatory payments into a government retirement system, which will provide monthly income to these same workers when they retire. Millions are involved in a government retirement program which significantly restricts their freedom to save and invest on their own. Medicare works the same way. All U.S. workers pay Medicare taxes (now 2.9 percent on unlimited income), qualifying these same workers to receive benefits when they reach 65.

Everybody pays in, everybody benefits, no matter whether he's John Doe or David Rockefeller. That's the underlying philosophy of the modern welfare state.

Defenders of the Welfare State

Such a ubiquitous system leads to a pernicious effect. It makes virtually every citizen a ward of the state. Even the most diehard critic of government becomes a defender of the welfare state if and when he signs up for Medicare and Social Security. There are, of course, those who have the courage to follow the example of Leonard E. Read, FEE's founder, who refused to take a penny of government money. May their tribe increase.

For many years, my uncle, W. Cleon Skousen, author of several conservative bestsellers (*The Naked Communist, The Miracle of America*) and known for his strong anti-government views, said he would never take Social Security. But he could not resist when he turned 65. (Social Security never comes automatically—you must declare your allegiance.)

From time to time, I've written in my investment letter arguing that Social Security is a welfare program. I always get several irate letters from subscribers vehemently denying it. "I paid in, I deserve it," they say. "And don't try to change it!"

Forcing all of us to become part of a social welfare system weakens our resistance and our self-reliance. We become benefit-corrupted. Social Security and Medicare are articles of faith—we are "entitled" to them. Is it no wonder that Congress will not touch these entitlement programs?

The Solution

As Milton Friedman wrote over 40 years ago, "The 'social security' program is one of those things on which the tyranny of the status quo is beginning to work its magic. Despite the controversy that surrounded its inception, it has come to be so much taken for granted that its desirability is hardly questioned any longer. Yet it involves a large-scale invasion into the personal lives of a large fraction of the nation without, so far as I can see, any justification that is at all persuasive, not only on liberal principles, but on almost any other."[1]

There's simply no reason why the vast majority of citizens should rely on Social Security for retirement or Medicare for hospital and medical expenses. Most people have enough in company and private pension plans to finance their own retirement. Most have sufficient resources to pay for their own medical bills or buy their own medical policies. Private charity can assist those who cannot help themselves.

An example at our church demonstrates this point: On the first Sunday of each month, each member of the congregation is asked to donate the cost of two meals as a "fast offering" to the poor. The fast offering is used to pay for the welfare needs of members of our congregation needing assistance—food, utilities, and rent if necessary. Each family usually contributes $20 to $50 a month, depending on family size. It's not a burden, but it's sufficient to handle normal emergency needs.

Now suppose our church leaders required all of us to obtain *all* our basic food supplies from the church storehouse. Not only would we have to donate much larger amounts of money to the "fast offering" fund, but we would all demand our fair share of food. It would be a nightmare.

Limiting social programs would not solve our welfare problem, but it would be a step in the right direction.[2] It would sharply reduce our tax burden and give people the freedom to choose where to spend or invest their money.

---

1. Milton Friedman, *Capitalism and Freedom* (Chicago: University of Chicago Press, 1962), pp. 182–183.

2. Charles Murray has advanced a number of proposals to resolve social problems in his books, *Losing Ground: American Social Policy, 1950–1980* (New York: Basic Books, 1984) and *What It Means to Be a Libertarian* (New York: Broadway Books, 1997).

$4,000 a Month from Social Security?

"Social Security will remain nicely in balance for at least the next 20 years . . . If it ain't broke, don't tinker."
—Professor Robert Kuttner[1]

Professor Kuttner, the American Association of Retired Persons (AARP), and other apologists for the current Social Security system don't get it. The real issue is not whether the national pension program is solvent or not. It is not a question of whether to reduce Social Security payouts, defer retirements, assess a means test or raise FICA taxes again. Congress has attempted all of the above, and the system is still fundamentally unsound.

The real problem is simple: Social Security is a lousy retirement program and, as a result, imposes a huge drag on the U.S. economy and every other nation with a similar plan. FICA taxes cut deep into the pockets of every worker and every business. Payroll taxes have increased 17 times, from 2 percent of wages, up to a maximum of $60, in 1937, to 12.4 percent, up to a maximum $6,438.00 today. To cover future payouts beyond 2015, experts predict taxes will have to rise to 17 percent of gross income. When is this craziness going to stop?

The tragic irony of Social Security is that it is a forced savings plan that doesn't contribute one dime to real savings. That's because Social Security is a pay-as-you-go system. Contributions are immediately paid out in benefits. FICA taxes go either to (a)

20

pay current Social Security retirees, who use the money to pay bills, or (b) the Social Security Trust Fund, which invests entirely in T-bills, in other words, government spending. In short, payroll taxes are consumed, not saved. As Professor Joseph Stiglitz states, "the Social Security program is a tax program, not a savings account."

Social Security vs. Individual Retirement Accounts

Imagine what would happen if Social Security taxes were invested in Individual Retirement Accounts, so that wage earners could invest in stocks and bonds. In other words, what would be the effect if Social Security funds were invested in free-enterprise capitalism, rather than government transfer programs.

Such a study was done in the mid-1990s by William G. Shipman, principal at State Street Global Advisors in Boston, Massachusetts. He analyzed two workers, one earning half the national average wage (approximately $12,600 in today's wages), and the other making the maximum covered earning ($61,200 today). A low-income earner who retires this year will receive $551 a month from Social Security. But if he had been allowed to invest his contributions in conservative U.S. stocks over his working years, he would be receiving an annuity of $1,300 a month for the rest of his life, almost three times his Social Security income.

A high-income earner would do even better. If he retired today, he would receive $1,200 a month from Social Security. Had he invested the money in stocks, he would be receiving an annuity of $4,000 a month.[2] Now that's what I call retiring with dignity.

In sum, Social Security is a lousy retirement plan and a tragic waste of resources. This year approximately $350 billion will be paid into Social Security. In addition, the Social Security Trust Fund, held for future payouts, is valued at $436 billion and rising. Imagine if all that money had been invested in the capital markets. Imagine if the Social Security Trust Fund could be managed by Peter Lynch, Warren Buffett, or another top money manager and invested in the financial markets. (However, I do not favor government control of American companies. I'm simply demonstrating the profit potential when funds are invested rather than consumed.)

Chile Sets the Example

Wishful thinking is reality in a small nation south of us—Chile. Its Social Security system puts America to shame. In 1981, under the influence of free-market economists, Chile privatized its failing Social Security system and replaced it with private pension fund accounts for new workers. Middle-aged workers were given the option of using the new privatized pensions, or remaining in the state system, while the government plans for existing retirees and those within a few years of retirement remained untouched.

The results have been astounding. Today 93 percent of the labor force is enrolled in 20 separate private pension funds. Annual real returns on pension investments averaged 13 percent from 1981 to 1993. Chile's private pension plan deepened the nation's capital market and stimulated economic growth. Its domestic savings rate has climbed to 26 percent of gross domestic product, and economic growth rate averaged 5.4 percent annually from 1984 to 1992.

Retirees still on the state pension system are being paid from general revenues, boosted by tax revenues from privatizations of state companies and the expanding economy.

In short, Chile provides a role model for a successful privatization of the U.S. Social Security system. Converting the pay-as-you-go-system into a genuine saving program will dramatically increase capital formation and economic growth in the United States.

Reform Is Coming

Until recently, discussion of privatizing Social Security or highlighting the Chile model has been muted. The typical college economics textbook ignores the possibility of privatizing Social Security, and overlooks Chile's alternative.

However, resistance to reform has been crumbling. *Time* magazine even ran a cover story, "The Case for Killing Social Security," and virtually endorsed the Chile model. Business writers have penned favorable columns about Chile and Social Security reform. Politicians have even tentatively put forth measures to allow workers to pay 2 percent less in payroll taxes if they invest it in their own IRAs. It's a beginning. As Lao-tzu says, "To resist change is like holding your breath—if you persist, you will die."

---

1. *Business Week,* February 20, 1995.
2. William G. Shipman, "Retiring With Dignity: Social Security's Harmful Role, Capital Markets' Helpful Solution," Cato Institute Policy Analysis, August 1995.

Single Policy Change—
Double Economic Growth?

"Shifting to a pro-savings, pro-investment economic policy can lift the economy over the next few years to a long-term growth rate of 3% or more."
—*Business Week, JULY 8, 1996*

The establishment journal *Business Week* is typically pro-government and skeptical of free markets, but in the July 8, 1996, cover story, "Economic Growth: A Proposal," it shocked the world by highlighting a single change in a major social program that, it claims could dramatically increase the U.S. economic growth rate: Convert Social Security to a fully funded pension plan, complete with individual savings accounts. "Privatizing Social Security would boost national savings and increase U.S. plant and equipment by 25 percent by 2020. The massive flow of funds into the equity markets would substantially reduce the cost of capital and encourage investment." *Business Week's* endorsement of privatized Social Security followed a *Time* magazine's cover story on March 20, 1995, entitled "The Case for Killing Social Security." The article wrote favorably about Chile's privatized social pension program.

The Social Security Fraud

Free-market economists have been highly critical of national social insurance ever since the Social Security Act of 1935 was

24

signed into law. Milton Friedman wrote in the early 1960s that Social Security is "without justification"; he was partly responsible, through his Chicago students, for creating the Chilean model.[1] Twenty-five years ago, New York attorney Abraham Ellis dissected the pay-as-you-go-system as "conceptually flawed" and an offshoot of "the something-for-nothing philosophy, the free lunch syndrome."[2]

The continuing crisis of Social Security—growing deficits, higher taxes, poor payouts—has led many policymakers to seek fundamental reforms. The reforms instituted by the 1983 Commission on Social Security, led ironically, by Alan Greenspan, are no longer viable. (Oddly enough, Greenspan refused even to consider privatization as an option!) Privatization has grown in popularity as the Chilean private alternative has proven so successful, especially for low-income workers. (See the previous chapter.) Private worker pensions are particularly popular in Latin America— Peru, Bolivia, and, most recently, Mexico—as well as Great Britain.

Right now, Social Security is a drag on America's economy. It funnels workers' savings into consumption—in the form of transfer payments to retirees or into a trust fund that is invested entirely in Treasury securities (thus funding the deficit and government spending). Imagine what the result would be if everyone's FICA taxes were invested in a true retirement program, into the capital markets instead of consumption? It could turbocharge the U.S. economy, just as it has done in Chile, where the economic growth rate is more than double the U.S. rate. The Cato Institute, a free-market think tank in Washington, D.C., has been in the forefront of advocating radical reform of Social Security. It has released numerous reports written by pension experts, including Peter Ferrara, William J. Shipman, and José Piñera, the official responsible for establishing Chile's privatized pension system. Recently, Cato issued a study showing that low-wage workers would gain the most from privatized Social Security. The poor, who rely almost exclusively on Social Security for retirement income, would earn "as much as three times the income available under the current system."[3] According to a Cato Institute poll, two-thirds of American voters, and more than three-quarters of young voters, support privatization.

What's truly amazing is there is wide-ranging support for this kind of positive reform—from the libertarian Cato Institute to the establishment World Bank, from Republican Steve Forbes to Democrat Sam Beard, author of *Restoring Hope in America, The Social Security Solution* (ICS Press, 1996), which claims that with privatization, the middle class could retire as millionaires. MIT Professor Rudi Dornbusch, no friend of supply-side economics, has even endorsed privatizing Social Security and education as two key sources of growth. "The resulting capital formation will support rising real wages and therefore offer a long-term answer to the eroding standard of living."[4]

---

1. Milton Friedman, *Capitalism and Freedom* (Chicago: University of Chicago, 1982 [1962]), p. 182.

2. Abraham Ellis, *The Social Security Fraud*, 2nd ed. (Irvington-on-Hudson, N.Y.: The Foundation for Economic Education, 1996 [1971]), pp. 105, 201.

3. Michael Tanner, "Privatizing Social Security: A Big Boost for the Poor," Cato Institute, July 26, 1996.

4. Rudi Dornbusch, "Dole Blew a Chance to Be Bold," *Business Week*, September 2, 1996.

Social Security Reform: Lessons from the Private Sector

"Of all social institutions, business is the only one created for the express purpose of making and managing change. . . . Government is a poor manager."

—Peter F. Drucker[1]

In the ongoing debate over the privatization of Social Security, one story has been overlooked: The private business sector in the United States has already faced the pension-fund problem and resolved it.

Here's what happened. After World War II, major U.S. companies added generous pension plans to their employee-benefit programs. These "defined benefit" plans largely imitated the federal government's Social Security plan. Companies matched employees' contributions; the money was pooled into a large investment trust fund managed by company officials; and a monthly retirement income was projected for all employees when they retired at 65.

Management guru Peter F. Drucker was one of the first visionaries to recognize the impact of this "unseen revolution," which he called "pension fund socialism" because this Social Security lookalike was capturing a growing share of investment capital in the United States.[2] Drucker estimated that by the early 1990s, 50 percent of all stocks and bonds were controlled by pension-fund administrators.

But Drucker (who doesn't miss much) failed to foresee a new revolution in corporate pensions—the rapid shift toward individualized "defined contribution" plans, especially 401(k) plans. Corporate executives recognized serious difficulties with their traditional "defined benefit" plans, problems Social Security faces today. Corporations confronted huge unfunded liabilities as retirees lived longer and managers invested too conservatively in government bonds and blue-chip "old economy" stocks. Newer employees were also angered when they changed jobs or were laid off and didn't have the required "vested" years to receive benefits from the company pension plan. Unlike Social Security, most corporate plans were not transferable. The Employment Retirement Income Security Act (ERISA), passed in 1974, imposed regulations on the industry in an attempt to protect pension rights, but the headaches, red tape, and lawsuits grew during an era of downsizing, job mobility, and longer life expectancies.

The New Solution: Individualized 401(k) Plans

The new corporate solution was a spinoff of another legislative invention—the Individual Retirement Account (IRA). The 401(k) rapidly became the business pension of choice, and there is no turning back. These "defined contribution" plans solve most of the headaches facing traditional corporate "defined benefit" plans. Under 401(k) plans, employees, not company officials, control their own investments (by choosing among a variety of no-load mutual funds). Corporations no longer face unfunded liabilities because there is no guaranteed projected benefit. And workers and executives have complete mobility; they can move their 401(k) savings to a new employer or roll them over into an IRA.

According to recent U.S. Labor Department statistics, there are about nine times more defined-contribution plans than defined-benefit plans. Almost all of the major Fortune 500 companies have switched to defined-contribution plans or hybrid "cash-balance" plans. Companies that still operate old plans include General Motors, Procter and Gamble, Delta Airlines, and the New York

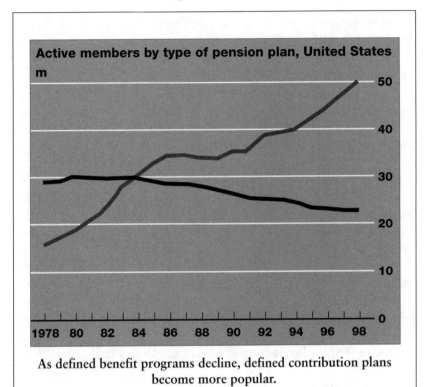

Active members by type of pension plan, United States

m

50

40

30

20

10

0

1978 80   82   84   86   88   90   92   94   96   98

As defined benefit programs decline, defined contribution plans
become more popular.

Times Company. IBM, a company that once guaranteed lifetime
employment, switched to a "cash-balance" plan several years ago,
giving its 100,000 employees individual retirement accounts they
can take with them in a lump sum if they leave the company before
retirement (long-service workers are still eligible for IBM's old
defined-benefit plan). But virtually all "new economy" companies,
such as Microsoft, AOL, and Home Depot, offer 401(k) plans
only.

Why Social Security Needs Reform

Congress could learn a great deal studying the changes corporate America has made in pension-fund reform. In fact, Social
Security is in a worse position than most corporate plans were.

Since less than a fourth of all contributions go into the Social Security "trust fund," the government program is more a pay-as-you-go system than a defined-benefit plan, where most of the funds go into a corporate managed trust fund. As a result, the unfunded liability, or payroll-tax shortfall, exceeds $20 trillion over the next 75 years. To pay for so many current recipients, Congress has had to raise taxes repeatedly to a burdensome 12.4 percent of wages, and payroll taxes will need to be raised another 50 percent by the year 2015 to cover the growing shortfall.[3] Few corporate plans require such high contribution levels.

Moreover, the Social Security trust fund is poorly managed, so much so that experts indicate that the annual return on Social Security is 3.5 percent for single-earner couples and only 1.8 percent for two-earner couples and single taxpayers.[4]

Clearly, converting Social Security into personal investment accounts would be a step in the right direction, a policy change already achieved in Chile and other nations.

Unfortunately, government—unlike business—is not prone to innovation. As Drucker notes, "Government can gain greater girth and more weight, but it cannot gain strength or intelligence."[5]

---

1. Peter F. Drucker, "The Sickness of Government," in *The Age of Discontinuity* (New York: Harper, 1969), pp. 229, 236.

2. Peter F. Drucker, *The Unseen Revolution: How Pension Fund Socialism Came to America* (New York: Harper & Row, 1976). This book was reprinted with a new introduction as *The Pension Fund Revolution* (New Brunswick, N.J.: Transaction, 1996).

3. Andrew G. Biggs, "Social Security: Is It a Crisis that Doesn't Exist?" Cato Social Security Privatization Report 21 (www.cato.org), October 5, 2000, p. 3.

4. Ibid., p. 32.

5. Peter F. Drucker, *The Age of Discontinuity*, p. 241.

The Free Market Works Fine, Except . . .

"In health care today, fundamental principles of the market-place do not apply. Prices are not determined by supply and demand. . ."

—"America's Economic Outlaw:
The U.S. Health Care System,"
New York Times
OCTOBER 26, 1993

In the early 1990s, as health care became a national issue, the *New York Times* ran a cover story contending that America's health-care system "operates with almost total disregard for basic economic principles" and therefore deserves special treatment by government. "Prices are not determined by supply and demand or by competition among producers. Comparison shopping is impossible. Greater productivity does not lower costs."

But are medical services really that different from soap, cars, or baseball tickets?

Let's go back to Economics 101 to analyze the health-care debate. We shall see that, contrary to the *Times*'s statement, supply and demand are working all too well in the health-care industry. Here is a graph of supply and demand for product x.

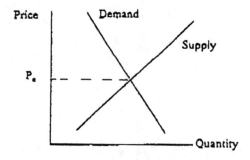

This simple graph teaches us three grand principles which, if followed, will easily explain (and resolve) the health-care crisis.

Market Principle #1: Supply and Demand

First is the principle of supply and demand. When supply is free to adjust for changes in demand, prices move quickly toward equilibrium without creating shortages or surpluses. As demand increases, prices rise; as supply increases, prices decline.

Why is the cost of health care rising so rapidly? Two reasons: first, increasing demand from Medicare and Medicaid, which today accounts for 65 percent of all medical expenses; second, restrictions by the American Medical Association on the number of students admitted to medical school and limitations on what services nurses and paramedics are permitted to perform.

Market Principle #2: Non-Discrimination

Second is the principle of non-discrimination. Note in the graph that everyone tends to pay the same price for product x. No matter what your income, religious beliefs, or color of skin, you pay the same price as everyone else. Republicans and Democrats pay the same amount, P_e, for the same product. So do rich and poor, Christians and atheists, secretaries and engineers. In the free market, as customers compare prices and producers compete, price discrimination is minimized and products are universally available.

Maintaining the principle of non-discrimination in the marketplace is essential. If prices were based on income, there would be little incentive to work harder and earn more income, or for businesses to compete and shoppers to compare prices.

However, this principle is being eroded. Private insurance premiums are still the same for each participant, but an increasing share of medical costs is being borne by taxpayers based on income level. The Medicare tax is now an unlimited tax on income (2.9 percent).

Market Principle #3: Accountability

Third is the principle of accountability. The graph suggests you, the customer, pay a specified price, P_e, for each product you buy, or for each unit of service you use. In other words, there is a direct link between beneficiaries and payers. Those who benefit from a service should pay for it. That's a cardinal principle of sound economics. If you buy one loaf of bread, you pay $1. If you buy two loaves, you pay $2.

When people don't pay for the services or products they are using, there is a tendency to overuse the benefits and less incentive to keep costs down. The connection is obvious: If you use a doctor's services, you should pay for them. If you use more, you pay more. And if you use less, you shouldn't have to pay the same amount as someone who uses more.

The principle of accountability is also disintegrating. The link between payers and beneficiaries is breaking down. In more and more cases, Medicare users are not paying the bill, taxpayers are.

Another major source of trouble is the pervasive use of employer-paid medical insurance to pay for even routine doctor visits. When employees know that someone else—the insurance company—is going to foot the bill, there is less incentive to shop around and to limit the number of visits to the doctor or the hospital's emergency room. Fortunately, the insurance companies do attempt to maintain some form of cost control on hospitals and doctor services, but the current system is less than optimal.

Who's to Blame

The author of the *Times*'s article blames the market for America's health-care problems, but the real cause is the government's failure to let the market operate fully. Even employer-paid medical insurance is, in a way, a government creation. High corporate taxes encourage businesses to offer a wide variety of supplemental benefits, which are tax-deductible to corporations and tax-free income to employees.

Contrast the health-care industry with the dental industry. The dental market does not suffer from the problems facing the medical industry (spiraling costs, bureaucracy, long waits at medical facilities) largely because (1) most dental services are paid for directly by the patients, and (2) the number of dental students is not restricted. These two factors, patient accountability and expanding supply, have worked to keep the price of dental care down. Despite the *Times*'s dire pronouncement, market principles do work.

How to Resolve the Health-Care Problem

What should be done to improve the situation? Imitating national health programs in Canada and Europe won't do because they violate market principles. If you want to know the weaknesses in each country's health-care system, analyze each according to the three market principles. For example, the kind of health-care plan proposed by the Clinton administration in the early 1990s would have had disastrous effects. The cost of medical services would vary according to income, beneficiaries wouldn't pay directly for medical services, and a new federal agency would impose cost controls on drugs and other medically related services. The result would be shortages, bureaucracy, higher costs, reduced services, and less research and development.

The solution to the so-called health-care crisis is to get government out of the picture. Private insurance would be able to solve the problem on its own through flexible deductibles and co-payment arrangements. This would encourage competition and comparison shopping to control costs, stimulate further medical advances, and encourage preventive care and exercise. The United States would then be reassured of its position as the nation with the world's best health-care system.

Back to Basics: Economists Enter the Classroom

"Were the students . . . left free to choose what college they liked best, such liberty might perhaps contribute to excite some emulation among different colleges."

—ADAM SMITH[1]

The consummate diplomatic Adam Smith always avoided insulting his readers. But he made an exception in the most famous putdown in *The Wealth of Nations*. Referring to "sham-lectures" at his alma mater, the prestigious Oxford University, he declared with obvious disdain, "In the University of Oxford, the greater part of the public professors have, for these many years, given up altogether even the pretence of teaching. . . . It must be too unpleasant to him [the Oxford professor] to observe that the greater part of his students desert his lectures; or perhaps attend upon them with plain enough marks of neglect, contempt, and derision."[2]

Why was Smith so agitated? In eighteenth-century Britain, teachers and tutors were paid mostly from student fees and therefore had to compete among themselves to maintain the interest of their pupils and parents. But Oxford was so richly endowed that professors were largely paid by the college. As a result, a student was not allowed to choose the college he liked best, and classes were developed for the benefit of the instructors not the student. Without incentives, the quality of education at Oxford deteriorated.

35

Adam Smith opposed all forms of monopoly, which he felt would create a political system characterized by high cost, waste, bureaucracy, and privilege. The invisible hand of natural liberty only functions successfully under conditions of competition. He applied his theory of competitive enterprise to a wide variety of markets—commerce, religion, and even education. He felt that students would enjoy a better education if they could choose between schools and teachers at all levels of training.

Milton Friedman and Vouchers

Milton Friedman, a modern-day Adam Smith, first applied the economic principle of competition to primary and secondary education in chapter 6 of his famous book, *Capitalism and Freedom*. He criticized today's government educational system as a rigid, uniform, expensive, and highly centralized quasi-monopoly where the program benefited teachers and administrators more than students and parents. His solution? Give parents a fixed-dollar amount, known as "vouchers," redeemable at any public or private school of their choice. "The injection of competition would do much to promote a healthy variety of schools. It would do much, also, to introduce flexibility into school systems. Not least of its benefits would be to make the salaries of school teachers responsive to market forces."[3]

The idea of school choice—whether through vouchers, tax credits, or charter schools—has gradually gained momentum and is now being tested in several states, mainly because primary and secondary education has performed so poorly since Friedman wrote about vouchers in 1962. Public-spirited citizens and parents are demanding change, including minority groups who feel their children are being short-changed in government schools. At the same time, the public school systems have become more centralized and unionized, and the teachers unions are strongly opposed to any form of radical change. Charter schools and tax credits for education are a growing alternative in many states. Vouchers are being tested in Milwaukee, Cleveland, and Florida, and so far the results are encouraging. Test scores are higher and the competition has improved the public schools. But the teachers unions are fighting change all along the way, even to the Supreme Court.

Milton Friedman says the experience has been "both rewarding and frustrating." But he hasn't given up. In fact, in the twilight of his career, he and his wife have established the Milton and Rose D. Friedman Foundation with the sole mission of promoting support for school choice. (Go to www.friedmanfoundation.org.)

---

1. Adam Smith, *The Wealth of Nations* (New York: Modern Library, 1965 [1776]), p. 719.
2. Ibid., pp. 718, 720.
3. Milton Friedman, *Capitalism and Freedom* (Chicago: University of Chicago Press, 1982 [1962]), p. 93.

Chicago Gun Show

"According to the economic approach, criminals, like everyone else, respond to incentives."

—Gary Becker[1]

The Chicago boys keep at it! The economists at the University of Chicago have made headlines again in the hotly disputed ongoing debate about gun control. Milton Friedman set the general standard a generation ago by insisting on rigorous empirical work to support sound (though often unpopular) theory and policy. More recently, Gary Becker extended Chicago-style economic analysis into such contemporary social problems as education, marriage, discrimination, professional sports, and crime.

John R. Lott, Jr., who did his research as the John M. Olin Law and Economics Fellow at Chicago, has made the case that a well-armed citizenry discourages violent crime. Lott analyzed the FBI's massive yearly crime statistics for all 3,054 U.S. counties over 18 years, the largest national surveys on gun ownership, and state police documents on illegal gun use. His surprising conclusions, published in his 1998 book, *More Guns, Less Crime:*

- States experiencing the largest drop in crime are also the ones with the fastest-growing rates of gun ownership.
- The Brady five-day waiting period, gun buy-back programs, and background checks have little or no impact on crime reduction.

- States that have allowed concealed weapon permits have witnessed significant reductions in violent crime.
- Guns are used on average five times more frequently in self-defense than in committing a crime.[2]

According to Lott, recent legislative efforts to restrict gun ownership may actually keep many law-abiding citizens from protecting themselves from attack. (There's that Law of Unintended Consequences again.)

The Incentive Principle

Underlining Lott's findings is a basic economic concept, the law of demand: If the price of a commodity goes up, people use less of it. In the case of criminal activity, if the cost and risk of committing a crime rises, less crime will be committed. This is often referred to as the market's incentive principle.

Gary Becker has showed that increasing the cost of crime through stiffer jail sentences, quicker trials, and higher conviction rates effectively reduces the number of criminals who rob, steal, or rape.[3]

Similarly, Lott argues that state laws permitting concealed handguns deter crime. "When guns are concealed, criminals are unable to tell whether the victim is armed before striking, which raises the risk to criminals."[4] He produces a variety of statistics and graphs to support his case. For example, the graph on the next page compares the average number of violent crimes in states before and after the adoption of a concealed-handgun law.

Lott's crime figures also remind me of Frédéric Bastiat's brilliant essay "What Is Seen and What Is Not Seen." In 1850, this great French journalist wrote, "In the economic sphere,. . . a law produces not only one effect, but a series of effects. Of these effects, the first . . . is seen. The other effects emerge only subsequently; they are not seen."[5]

According to Lott, Bastiat's principle applies in crime statistics. "Many defensive uses [of guns] are never reported to the police."[6] Lott gives two reasons. First, in many cases of self-defense, a handgun is simply brandished, the assailant backs off, and no one is harmed. Second, in states that have stringent gun laws, citizens

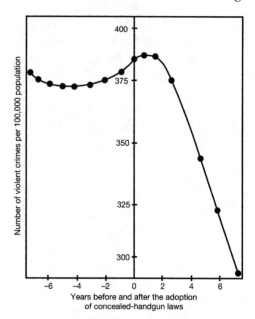

The effect of concealed-handgun laws
on violent crimes

who use a gun for protection fail to report the incident for fear of being arrested by the police for illegal use of a weapon. Thus, Lott confirms (through extensive surveys) the initial work of Gary Kleck, professor of criminal justice at Florida State University, that guns are used far more frequently in self-defense than in committing crimes. Kleck, by the way, used to have a strong anti-gun bias until he uncovered this revealing statistic.

All this confirms a long-standing constitutional principle: People have the right to own a gun for self-protection.

---

1. Gary S. Becker and Guity Nashat Becker, *The Economics of Life* (New York: McGraw-Hill, 1997), p. 143.

2. John R. Lott, Jr., *More Guns, Less Crime* (Chicago: University of Chicago Press, 1998).

3. Becker and Becker, p. 137.

4. Lott, p. 5.

5. Frédéric Bastiat, "What Is Seen and What Is Not Seen," *Selected Essays on Political Economy* (Irvington-on-Hudson, N.Y.: Foundation for Economic Education, 1995 [1850]), p. 1.

6. Lott, p. 5.

If You Build It—Privately—
They Will Come

"Government provides certain indispensable public services without which community life would be unthinkable and which by their nature cannot appropriately be left to private enterprise."

—PAUL A. SAMUELSON

If you take a course in public finance, you will invariably encounter the "public goods" argument for government: Some services simply can't be produced sufficiently by the private sector, such as schools, courts, prisons, roads, welfare, and lighthouses.

The lighthouse example has been highlighted as a classic public good in Paul Samuelson's famous textbook since 1964: "Its beam helps everyone in sight. A businessman could not build it for a profit, since he cannot claim a price for each user."[1] Really? Chicago economist Ronald H. Coase revealed that numerous lighthouses in England were built and owned by private individuals and companies prior to the nineteenth century. They earned profits by charging tolls on ships docking at nearby ports. The Trinity House was a prime example of a privately owned operation granted a charter in 1514 to operate lighthouses and charge ships a toll for their use.

Samuelson went on to recommend that lighthouses be financed out of general revenues. According to Coase, such a financing system has never been tried in Britain: "the service [at Trinity House]

41

continued to be financed by tolls levied on ships."[2] What's even more amazing, Coase wrote his trailblazing article in 1974, but Samuelson continued to use the lighthouse as an ideal public good only the government could supply. After I publicly chided Samuelson for his failure to acknowledge Coase's revelation,[3] Samuelson finally admitted the existence of private lighthouses "in an earlier age," in a footnote in the 16th edition of his textbook, but insisted that private lighthouses still encountered a "free rider" problem.[4]

Private Solutions for Public Services

The lighthouse isn't the only example of a public good that can be provided for by private enterprise. A privately run toll road operates in southern California. Wackenhut Corrections manages state prisons. Catholic schools provide a better education than public schools. The Mormon church offers a better welfare plan than the USDA food stamp program. Habitat for Humanity builds houses for responsible poor people.

And now, for the first time since the early 1960s, there is a privately built major league baseball stadium—Pacific Bell Park, new home of the San Francisco Giants. After Bay area voters rejected four separate ballot initiatives to raise government funds to replace the windy and poorly attended Candlestick Park, Peter Magowan, a Safeway and Merrill Lynch heir, teamed with local investors, to buy the club and, with the help of a $155 million Chase Securities loan, built the new stadium for $345 million. The owners also got huge sponsorships from Pacific Bell, Safeway, Coca-Cola, and Charles Schwab.

So far the private ballpark has been a super success, selling a league-leading 30,000 season tickets for the 41,000-seat stadium. The team's 81 home games are nearly sold out. Other team owners, whose stadiums are heavily subsidized, are skeptical, but a dozen team owners have visited the new operation to study what they've done. They include George Steinbrenner, who is considering a $1 billion new Yankee stadium.[5]

Economists Attack Public Financing

Perhaps private funding of major league sports facilities has been influenced by two recent in-depth studies by professional economists attacking publicly subsidized sports arenas. In *Major League Losers*, Mark Rosentraub of Indiana University (and a big sports fan) studied stadium financing in five cities and meticulously demonstrated that pro sports produce very few jobs with little ripple effects in the community, take away business for suburban entertainment and food venues, and often leave municipalities with huge losses.[6] A Brookings Institution study came to similar conclusions. After reviewing major sports facilities in seven cities, Roger G. Noll (Stanford) and Andrew Zimbalist (Smith College) found they were not a source of local economic growth and employment, and the net subsidy exceeded the financial benefit to the community.[7]

These empirical studies confirm a long-standing sound principle of public finance: Beneficiaries should pay for the services they use. In my free-market textbook I call this "The Principle of Accountability," also known as the "benefit principle." It's amazing how often politicians violate this basic concept. For example, John Henry, a commodities trader worth $300 million and owner of the Marlins baseball team, tried to push through the Florida state legislature a bill to tax cruise-ship passengers to help fund a new Miami ballpark. (Fortunately, Governor Jeb Bush vetoed it.)

Mr. Henry needs to read my free-market textbook, *Economic Logic.*

1. Paul A. Samuelson, *Economics*, 6th ed. (New York: McGraw Hill, 1964), p. 159.

2. Ronald H. Coase, "The Lighthouse in Economics," in *The Firm, the Market, and the Law* (Chicago: University of Chicago Press, 1988), p. 213. Coase's article originally appeared in *The Journal of Law and Economics*, October 1974.

3. Mark Skousen, "The Perseverance of Paul Samuelson's *Economics*," *Journal of Economic Perspectives*, Spring 1997, p. 145.

4. Paul A. Samuelson and William D. Nordhaus, *Economics*, 16th ed. (New York: McGraw Hill, 1998), p. 36n.

5. Peter Waldman, "If You Build It Without Public Cash, They'll Still Come," *Wall Street Journal*, March 31, 2000, p. 1.

6. Mark S. Rosentraub, *Major League Losers: The Real Cost of Sports and Who's Paying for It* (New York: Basic Books, 1997).

7. Roger G. Noll and Andrew Zimbalist, *Sports, Jobs, and Taxes: The Economic Impact of Sports Teams and Stadiums* (Washington, D.C.: Brookings Institution, 1997).

Why Wages Rise

"For low-paying jobs that already exist, public policy must aim at supplementing the income of the working poor. . . . One way would be to raise gradually the minimum wage."
—WALLACE C. PETERSON, *Silent Depression*[1]

Whenever the debate heats up over the minimum wage and the working poor, I think of a little book, *Why Wages Rise,* by F. A. Harper (The Foundation for Economic Education, 1957). In his book, Harper made an important distinction between legitimate ways to raise the average wage and artificial means of raising workers' income.

Genuine Means of Raising Wages

First, let's discuss the genuine ways that wages can rise. Here Harper focused on the critical role of production and worker productivity. "Production comes first," he explains. "Higher wages come from increased output per hour of work." (p. 19) Harper produces a graph (see the next page) showing a close relationship between wages per hour and output (GDP) per hour, expressed in constant dollars, between 1910 and 1960.

Harper's theory of wages is not new—it is the classical theory of labor taught in college economics. John B. Taylor, economics professor at Stanford, produces graphs that show a similar relationship in his latest textbook (see page 46 for a graph showing the rise in hourly compensation since 1955). Even Wallace Peterson, an

44

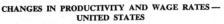

CHANGES IN PRODUCTIVITY AND WAGE RATES —
UNITED STATES

SOURCE: This chart is designed so that a constant percentage increase would appear as a straight line. The values of product and wages are both expressed in dollars of constant buying power. The data for product are for the private sector, and are from the series by John W. Kendrick in his paper, *National Productivity and Its Long-Term Projection* (National Bureau of Economic Research, May 1951), brought up to date by the National Industrial Conference Board. For the data on wage rates, see Chapter 1, p. 11.

economist who favors increasing the minimum wage and other forms of government intervention in the labor market, supports the view that, in the long run, "productivity gains are the ultimate source of . . . increases in real living standards."[2]

Two Benefits of Higher Profits

How is it that workers tend to receive higher wages as output increases? The key is profitability. When firms increase their profits, there are dual benefits to workers: (1) more and better products and services are sold to consumers, and (2) more funds are made available from retained earnings to pay workers and to improve tools, equipment, and training. When firms are successful, company officers aren't the only ones who benefit. Workers also receive higher wages and more services, including training, better equipment, and fringe benefits. The advantages of giving higher compensation are: (1) less job turnover, (2) better workers, and (3) higher incentives to work more productively.

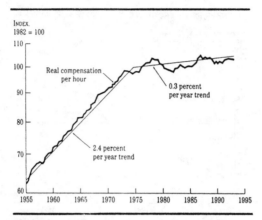

FIGURE 12.2
Growth of Real Hourly
Compensation
In the United States, average real
hourly compensation (including
fringe benefits) grew rapidly from
the mid-1950s to the mid-1970s.
Starting in the mid-1970s, the
growth rate slowed down.
Source: U.S. Department of Commerce.

The Ford $5-a-Day Story

The Henry Ford $5-a-day story is a classic example. As a result of the huge success of the Model T, in 1913 the Ford Motor Co. doubled its profits from $13.5 million to $27 million. With these profits, Ford decided to share the wealth with his employees and overnight doubled the minimum wage at his Detroit plant from $2.50 to $5 a day. It made Henry Ford an industrial messiah.

The effect of the instant pay raise was dramatic: a tremendous surge in output and skyrocketing morale among Ford workers. Thousands of potential employees moved to Detroit in hopes of getting a job. Ford argued that the higher wage had two great benefits, increased efficiency at the automobile plant, and increased buying power of his workers. Importantly, the $5 wage permitted Ford workers to buy their own cars for the first time. Indeed, sales of Model T's continued to soar as wages went up and prices declined. By 1916, over half a million cars were sold.[3]

Ludwig von Mises adds the following point to Harper's original argument: it is marginal productivity, not just total productivity, that has raised average wages over the past hundred years. He points out that many jobs have not changed over the years (barbers, butlers, etc.), yet they benefit from higher wages due to labor competition. "It is not any merit on the part of the butler that causes this rise in his wages, but the fact that the increase in capital invested surpasses the increase in the number of hands." Mises concludes, "there is only one means to raise wage rates permanently . . . namely, to accelerate the increase in capital available as against population."[4]

Do's and Don'ts

Harper, Mises, and other free-market economists warn politicians not to seek artificial ways to increase income, such as:

—minimum-wage legislation,
—welfare programs,
—labor union power, and
—anti-immigration laws.

All of these measures either cause unemployment or economic inefficiency.

On the other hand, there are a few policies the government can undertake to encourage productivity and higher wages, such as tax cuts on business and investment. Reducing corporate income taxes will increase net income and thereby increase the capability to pay workers more and provide greater benefits. Cutting capital gains taxes will encourage private savings, reduce interest rates, and stimulate capital formation.

Minimum-Wage Millionaires

But the most dramatic improvement in the lives of the working poor could be achieved by converting Social Security into a genuine private pension system. Privatizing Social Security would increase the nation's saving rate and, most importantly, provide a high retirement income for all American workers. Even minimum-wage earners could have over $1 million in pension assets under a privately funded Social Security at retirement.[5]

These measures are far superior to raising the minimum wage and other counterfeit proposals to help the working poor.

1. Wallace C. Peterson, *Silent Depression: Twenty-five Years of Wage Squeeze and Middle-Class Decline* (New York: Norton, 1994), p. 232.

2. Ibid., p. 232.

3. For a retelling of the $5-a-day story, see Jonathan Hughes, *The Vital Few* (New York: Oxford, 1986), pp. 301–304.

4. Ludwig von Mises, *The Anti-Capitalistic Mentality* (South Holland, Ill.: Libertarian Press, 1972), pp. 88–89.

5. Sam Beard calculates that Social Security contributions of minimum-wage earners ($1,240 a year) would make them millionaires in 45 years if their Social Security contributions earned 8 percent a year. See his book *Restoring Hope in America* (ICS Press, 1996). Also, see "$4,000 A Month From Social Security?," pp. 20–23 of this book.

Having Their Cake

"The duty of 'saving' became nine-tenths of virtue and the
growth of the cake the object of true religion."
—JOHN MAYNARD KEYNES[1]

In his 1920 bestseller, *The Economic Consequences of the Peace*,
John Maynard Keynes made a profound observation about the
success of capitalism before the Great War. He lauded "the
immense accumulations of fixed capital" built up by the "new
rich" during the half century before the war and compared the
huge capital investment of this golden era to a "cake," noting how
"vital" it was that the cake "never be consumed," but continue to
"grow."

Keynes was intensely optimistic about the prospects of humanity, "if only the cake were not cut but was allowed to grow in the
geometrical proportion predicted by Malthus for population."
Rapid capital accumulation would result in the elimination of
"overwork, overcrowding, and underfeeding," and workingmen
"could proceed to the nobler exercises of their faculties."

Alas, it was not to be. The First World War destroyed Keynes's
dream of universal progress. The cake was consumed. "The war
has disclosed the possibility of consumption to all and the vanity
of abstinence to many."[2]

War isn't the only enemy of capital accumulation. Since World
War II, the greatest threat to capital formation (the growth of the
cake) has been the direct and indirect taxation of capital.

Take, for example, the federal estate tax. The estate tax is often

49

viewed as an "inheritance" tax and even a "death" tax. But it's much worse than that. It's also a tax on capital. An estate's taxable property includes stocks, bonds, business assets, real estate, coins, and collectibles—all after-tax, after-consumption investments.

Capital is the lifeblood of the economy. Capital investment finances new technology, new production processes, quality improvements, jobs, and economic growth in general. When those investment funds are taxed, the funds are removed from the investment pool and transferred to Washington, where they are consumed. For the most part the funds are consumed through government expenditures and "transfer payments" (welfare, salaries of government workers, and so on).

The estate tax also creates economic distortions. It encourages individuals to engage in "estate planning," expensive legal exercises to avoid the death tax. It forces individuals to buy insurance policies they would not otherwise buy and create tax-exempt trusts and foundations that they would not ordinarily create. Undoubtedly, millions of funds are transferred every year into foundations and charities just to avoid estate taxes. Charitable giving and public foundations have become big business, but what is the price? Mismanagement and waste are common features in these nonbusiness organizations.

Another Inefficient Tax: Capital Gains Taxes

Perhaps an even more sinister tax is the capital gains tax. If you sell an asset (stock, bond, commodity, real estate, or collectible), the profits are taxed between 20 and 40 percent, depending on how long you held the asset. (If you hold for more than a year, the maximum rate is 20 percent.) This is a terrible penalty on capital. It means that every time a stock or other asset is traded outside a tax-exempt vehicle, 20 to 40 percent of the profits are removed from the private economy and sent to Washington, never to be invested again. During the recent bull market on Wall Street, annual capital gains taxes exceeded $100 billion. What a terrible drain on the economy.

Capital gains taxes also result in economic inefficiency. Because of the high tax on capital gains, many investors refuse to sell their assets. They may prefer to switch into a potentially more profitable investment, but they stay with their original investment because they hate the idea of paying Uncle Sam. Clearly, capital would be more efficiently allocated to its more productive use without this burdensome profits tax.

The United States can learn a lot from foreign nations. Hong Kong has a flat 15 percent personal income tax, a 16.5 percent corporate income tax, and no tax at all on capital gains. In fact, most of the New Industrial Countries in Southeast Asia do not tax capital gains. Thus capital can move freely throughout Hong Kong and around the world without distortion. And the cake has grown rapidly because of capital's tax-free status. Hong Kong does have an estate tax on values exceeding HK$7 million, but the maximum rate is only 18 percent.[3]

Eliminating taxes on estates and capital gains has been criticized as a break for the rich. Moreover, critics say, estate taxes should be kept in order to establish a level playing field. They argue, "Children and grandchildren of wealthy people didn't earn inherited money. They should have to work for it, just as their parents did. Inheritances create disincentives to work."

Broader Implications

But these critics fail to understand the broader implications of a large tax-free estate and tax-free capital gains. Everyone—not just the rich—benefits from eliminating these taxes because wealthy people's capital would be left intact, invested in the stock market, businesses, farms, banks, insurance companies, real estate, and other capital assets, thus insuring strong economic growth and a high standard of living for everyone. As Ludwig von Mises once stated, "Do they realize that every measure leading to capital decumulation jeopardizes their prosperity?"[4]

As an investment adviser, I share the concern that unrestricted inheritances to children or grandchildren can be morally corrupting, but there are other solutions besides a confiscatory tax. For example, a will can limit the use of inherited funds until a certain age of responsibility is reached, or a trust can offer matching funds as a way to encourage work and responsibility.

1. John Maynard Keynes, *The Economic Consequences of the Peace* (New York: Harcourt, Brace, 1920), p. 20.

2. Ibid., pp. 20–21.

3. For an excellent summary of tax policies throughout the world, see *International Tax Summaries*, published annually by Coopers & Lybrand (New York: John Wiley & Sons).

4. Ludwig von Mises, *Planning for Freedom*, 4th ed. (South Holland, Ill.: Libertarian Press, 1980), p. 208.

The Economics of Ecology: Angry Planet or Beautiful World?

"The bright promise of a new millennium is now clouded by unprecedented threats to humanity's future."
—WORLDWATCH INSTITUTE, 2000[1]

"We know that the environment is not in good shape. . . . My claim is that things are improving . . ."
—BJØRN LOMBORG[2]

Bjørn Lomborg is a Danish professor of statistics who was an environmental activist and member of Greenpeace for years. "I, like most others, care for our Earth and care for the future health and well-being of its succeeding generations." He accepted at face value the Malthusian views, expressed by Paul Ehrlich, Lester Brown, and groups such as the Worldwatch Institute, Greenpeace, and the Sierra Club, that the world is running out of renewable resources, clean water, and forestland, and that the earth is becoming more polluted and that population growth is exploding.

Then, along came Julian Simon, an American economist from the University of Maryland, who challenged Lomborg's thinking. Simon had published several books and papers filled with data supporting his view that life is actually getting better, that air in

53

the developed world is becoming less polluted, that fewer people are starving, and that the population growth is slowing.

Simon made two devastating arguments against the pessimists: First, on the supply side, natural resources are virtually unlimited in the long run because higher prices, reflecting scarcity, encourage the discovery of additional reserves and the use of substitutes. In addition, entrepreneurs and inventors are developing new technologies and cost-cutting techniques allowing more resources to be discovered and developed. Second, on the demand side, a large and growing population is beneficial and leads to a higher standard of living because it increases the stock of useful knowledge and trained workers. "Human beings are not just more mouths to feed, but are productive and inventive minds that help find creative solutions to man's problems, thus leaving us better off over the long run."[3]

At first Lomborg considered Simon's optimistic data mere "American propaganda." But he decided to test Simon's statistics. In the fall of 1997, he and a group of students examined Simon's data. Their conclusion: Simon was right! It was a turning point in Lomborg's career. He reversed course and, in publishing his findings in *The Skeptical Environmentalist*, has created a furor within the environmentalist community, with vicious one-sided attacks from *Scientific American* and other pro-environmental publications.

Lomborg joins Simon in refuting most of the claims of the perma-bear environmentalists: global forests have increased since World War II; the world's population growth rate peaked in 1964 and has since declined; only 0.7 percent of species have disappeared in the past 50 years; fewer people in the world are denied access to water; incidence of infectious disease is still on the decline worldwide; the number of extremely poor/starving people is also declining; air pollution is falling in many parts of the world.

But what about global warming, the overriding concern that our capitalistic lifestyle is changing the climate and could do permanent damage to our ecosystem? The evidence is clear that temperatures have been rising in the past century, but the questions remain: how much of the temperature increase in due to global carbon-dioxide emissions and what is the best course of action? Economic analysis shows it will be far more expensive to cut CO_2

emissions radically than to pay the costs of adapting to global warming.[4]

Economists have also debunked the popular myth that economic development is responsible for environmental degradation, that there is a tradeoff between higher economic growth and a greener environment. The truth is largely the opposite. As Lomborg states, "environmental development often stems from economic development—only when we get sufficiently rich can we afford the relative luxury of caring about the environment."[5] The graph below makes this point.

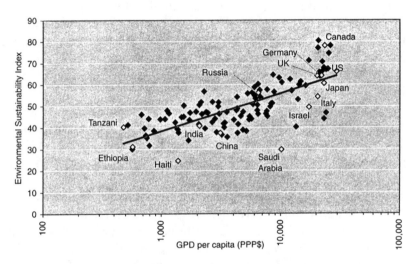

Figure 9 The connection for 117 nations between GDP per capita (current 1998 PPP$) and the 2001 Environmental Sustainability Index, measuring 22 environmental dimensions on 67 variables.[254] A best-fit line is displayed and various nations have been marked out. Source: WEF 2001a&b, World Bank 2000c.

The Polluted State

Economists have also publicized "government failure" in the debate about the environment. As Albert O. Hirschman states, "There's a tendency to blame capitalism for environmental damage, but now we find that in the socialist bloc the situation is much worse."[6] Recent studies have revealed how less-developed countries, including the former Soviet Union, have more pollution, lower health standards, and more environmental hazards than industrialized nations. Economists Terry Anderson and Donald

Leal point to several examples of government mismanagement: National parks such as Yellowstone are in major disrepair, the U.S. Park Service is notoriously wasteful (it built a $330,000 outhouse), the Canadian government destroyed the cod industry, and Brazil and Indonesia forced migrants to burn once-pristine rain forests to plant crops.[7]

Economics has provided real solutions to pollution and environmental degradation. One problem is what is known as the "tragedy of the commons." In a 1968 issue of *Science,* Garrett Hardin, professor of human ecology at the University of California at Santa Barbara, wrote a seminal article arguing that a resource tends to be overexploited when owned by the public and not private individuals. If no one owns a piece of grazing land, each herdsman has an incentive to add another animal to the herd until the land is overgrazed. As a result, "Freedom in a common brings ruin to all."[8]

Hence, the lack of property rights and market prices creates a "tragedy of the commons"—unnecessary pollution, extinction of animals, destruction of forests, strip mining, and more. At first government favored regulation as a solution, but economists have encouraged the establishment of clearly specified property rights and accompanying price signals in water, fishing, and forestland, so that owners can preserve these resources in a balanced way. Private conservation trusts, such as the Nature Conservancy (which owns over four million acres in the United States and half a million in Latin America and the Caribbean), are flourishing. Today there are more than 1,200 such conservation organizations.

Economists traditionally have rejected rationing, regulations, and the fickle whims of legislators. Instead, they have relied on market mechanisms. For example, they favor user fees in national and state parks, individual transferable quotas (ITQs) in fisheries, and in the case of air pollution, pollution fees and marketable permits to pollute. While the idea of "permits to pollute" sounds strange, it has actually worked successfully in Europe. Pollution fees are taxes on polluters that penalize them in proportion to the amount they discharge. Marketable permits allow polluters to sell their permits to other firms and have successfully reduced the rate of pollution in the United States.[9]

In sum, free-market environmentalism has come a long way in

showing how to replace the regulatory fist of command with a greener invisible hand. Many free-market think tanks, such as PERC and the Competitive Enterprise Institute, have challenged the supremacy of the Sierra Club and Greenpeace.[10] Earth Day will never be the same.

1. Worldwatch Institute, *The State of the World 2002* (New York: Norton, 2002), p. xvii.

2. Bjørn Lomborg, *The Skeptical Environmentalist: Measuring the Real State of the World* (Cambridge: Cambridge University Press, 2001), pp. 30, 32.

3. Julian L. Simon, *The Ultimate Resource 2* (Princeton: Princeton University Press, 1996), p. 376.

4. Lomborg, p. 318.

5. Ibid., p. 33.

6. Interview by Carl Ravaioli, *Economists and the Environment* (London: Zen, 1995), p. 32.

7. Terry L. Anderson and Donald R. Leal, *Free-Market Environmentalism,* revised ed. (New York: Palgrave, 2001), pp. 47–58.

8. Garrett Hardin, "The Tragedy of the Commons," reprinted in Garrett Hardin and John Baden, ed., *Managing the Commons* (San Francisco: W.H. Freeman, 1977), p. 20.

9. Anderson and Leal, pp. 130–31.

10. Two additional sources written from a free-market perspective are Michael Sanera and Jane S. Shaw, *Facts, Not Fear: A Parent's Guide to Teaching Children About the Environment* (Washington, D.C.: Regnery, 1996) and Ronald Bailey, ed., *Earth Report 2000* (New York: McGraw Hill, 2000).

Solving International Issues

A Private-Sector Solution
to Worldwide Poverty

"The able bodied poor don't want or need charity. . .
All they need is financial capital."

— MUHAMMAD YUNUS

For years free-market economists have protested the waste and
abuse of foreign aid programs, International Monetary Fund
loans, and World Bank projects.[1] P.T. Bauer has been in the forefront as a dissenter against government development programs.
For the past 50 years, he has argued forcefully that government
assistance in developing nations only retards economic growth.[2]

But if IMF lending, foreign aid, and the World Bank are abolished, what should be done to alleviate poverty? Bauer and other
classical liberals advocate reducing trade barriers; increasing foreign investment; establishing property rights, the rule of law, and
a stable monetary policy; and encouraging free markets and limited government domestically.

Private-Sector Micro Lending

Yet market advocates have been surprisingly silent on a bur-
geoning private-sector success story known as "micro lending,"
the lending of extremely small amounts of money to self-employed
entrepreneurs in the Third World by independent banks and institutions. The most famous of these micro-lenders is the Grameen
Bank, founded by Muhammad Yunus in Bangladesh, the world's

poorest country, in 1983. Yunus is an economics professor at Chittagong University in Bangladesh.

When I say "small loans," I mean minuscule. The Grameen Bank lends only $30 to $200 per borrower. Applicants don't have to read or write to qualify. No collateral or credit check is required. Amazingly, the Grameen Bank has made these micro loans to millions of poverty-stricken people in Bangladesh, $2.5 billion so far. These loans are not interest-free. The Grameen Bank is a for-profit private-sector self-help bank that charges 18 percent interest rates. The default rate? Less than 2 percent. This remarkable record is due to the requirement that borrowers must join small support groups. If anyone in the group defaults, no one else can borrow more.

The bank lends to entrepreneurs, overwhelmingly female, who need only a few dollars to buy supplies and tools. Borrowers might be makers of bamboo chairs, sellers of goat's milk, or drivers of rickshaws. By avoiding the outrageous rates charged by other money-lenders (often 20 percent a month), these people are finally able to break the cycle of poverty. Their small businesses grow, and some use their profits to build new homes or repair existing ones (often using a $300 Grameen house loan). Thousands of Grameen borrowers now own land, homes, and even cell phones. And they are no longer starving. Yunus has plans to issue private stock and eventually go public with his antipoverty program.

His bank has been so successful that other micro-lending institutions have sprung up throughout the world. The concept has gained credence everywhere, to the point that even the World Bank and other government agencies have gotten into the million-dollar micro-loans business.

Saying No to the World Bank

But Yunus won't have anything to do with the World Bank. In his new autobiography, *Banker to the Poor* (highly recommended), Yunus decries the World Bank: "We at the Grameen Bank have never wanted or accepted World Bank funding because we do not like the way the bank conducts business." Nor does he much like foreign aid: "Most rich nations use their foreign aid budgets mainly to employ their own people and to sell their own goods, with poverty reduction as an afterthought. . . . Aid-funding projects create massive bureaucracies, which quickly become corrupt and inefficient, incurring huge losses. . . . Aid money still goes to expand government spending, often acting against the interests of the market economy. . . . Foreign aid becomes a kind of charity for the powerful while the poor get poorer."[3] Peter Bauer couldn't have said it better.

From Marxism to Marketism

Yunus's statements are all the more amazing given that he grew up under the influence of Marxist economics. But after getting a Ph.D. in economics at Vanderbilt University he saw firsthand "how the market [in the United States] liberates the individual" and rejected socialism. "I do believe in the power of the global free-market economy and in using capitalist tools. . . . I also believe that providing unemployment benefits is not the best way to address poverty." Believing that "all human beings are potential entrepreneurs," Yunus is convinced that poverty can be eradicated by lending poor people the capital they need to engage in profitable businesses, not by giving them a government handout or engaging in population control.

His former Marxist colleagues call it a capitalist conspiracy. "What you are really doing," a communist professor told him, "is giving little bits of opium to the poor people. . . . Their revolutionary zeal cools down. Therefore, Grameen is the enemy of the revolution."[4] Precisely.

---

1. The latest examples are Paul Craig Roberts and Karen LaFollette Araujo, *The Capitalist Revolution in Latin America* (New York: Oxford University Press, 1997) and James A. Dorn, Steve H. Hanke, and Alan A. Walters, eds., *The Revolution in Development Economics* (Washington, D.C.: Cato Institute, 1998).

2. See P. T. Bauer, *The Development Frontier* (Cambridge, Mass.: Harvard University Press, 1991), *Equality, the Third World and Economic Delusion* (Cambridge, Mass.: Harvard University Press, 1981), and *Dissent on Development* (Cambridge, Mass.: Harvard University Press, 1976).

3. Muhammad Yunus, *Banker for the Poor* (New York: Public Affairs, 1999), pp. 145–46.

4. Ibid., pp. 203–205.

Japan and the
Macroeconomic Debate

"Economics is a very dangerous science."
—JOHN MAYNARD KEYNES[1]

"Economics is haunted by more fallacies than any other study known to man."

—HENRY HAZLITT[2]

There is no better example of today's heated debate over macroeconomics than Japan. What policy should this nation—economically the second largest in the world—adopt to start growing again after a decade of sluggish performance?

It seems that Japan has tried all the traditional remedies since it collapsed into recession in the early 1990s and lost out as a world economic model. The Bank of Japan lowered short-term interest rates to zero. Tokyo raised taxes, ran huge deficits, and spent billions on public-works projects. But neither an easy-money policy nor an aggressive fiscal policy has done the trick. Japan is still mired in recession and rising unemployment, and now faces the largest debt burden among industrial nations.

In the late 1980s, Japan was considered the model of prosperity. Economists predicted that it would surpass the U.S. economy in 2000; the next century belonged to this Asian giant. Its lifetime-employment and bonus system was considered a superior business-labor management strategy. But the weaknesses of the Japan-

64

ese economy became apparent in the 1990s—its model was too static and homogeneous for the dynamic global new economy. In 1990 the Fraser Institute's economic freedom report ranked Japan ninth in the world. Now it is ranked only 20th primarily due to the growth of government and the mismanagement of the banking system.[3]

I witnessed firsthand this endless story of economic frustration when my wife and I spent a few days in Tokyo in June 2001. The government has spent several trillion yen building a massive underwater highway called Aqualine. Now Tokyo residents have a fast alternate route outside the city. But the government charges $50 one way to go five miles under water and, as a result, even the Japanese are reluctant to use Aqualine.

Classical economists long taught that the government should produce only viable public works, where the benefits clearly outweigh the costs. But John Maynard Keynes turned the world upside down when he proclaimed that in a downturn, "To dig holes in the ground, paid out of savings, will increase, not only employment, but the real national dividend of useful goods and services."[4] Apparently several Japanese prime ministers have fallen under the Keynesian spell, but to no avail.

New Medicine: Print More Yen!

Several prominent economists have urged the charismatic new prime minister, Junichiro Koizumi, to adopt a more radical proposal—flood the country with yen. "Japan needs to spur demand," argue Jeffrey Sachs of Harvard and Paul Krugman of Princeton. Even Milton Friedman, the celebrated free-market economist (famous for his refrain, "There's no such thing as a free lunch"), has joined forces with top Keynesians to promote aggressive easy money as a way to jump-start a weak economy and counter deflation. Friedman has supported a rapid increase in the money supply in Japan since late 1997.[5]

At the Mont Pelerin Society meetings in September 1999, I confronted Friedman on this issue. He and his wife had organized the program under the topic "Can Creeping Socialism Be Stopped?" In one of the breakout sessions I asked him about his easy-money solution to Japan's economic problems. I held up his article in the

Wall Street Journal and noted how it made no reference to cutting taxes, deregulation, or opening up the Japanese economy; only inflation was proposed as a solution. "Isn't printing more money another example of creeping socialism?" I asked. He was not amused. Friedman said that historically increasing the money supply stimulates economic growth, and fast monetary growth was necessary given Japan's fragile condition. "Then there is a free lunch?" I asked. "A free disaster!" responded Friedman. Afterwards, Professor Jim Gwartney came up to me and said, "You attacked God today!" Indeed. Yet even free-market icons can make mistakes.

Fortunately, Prime Minister Koizumi has rejected this artificial stimulus and favors a supply-side agenda. He supports a regimen of capping government spending, requiring banks to write off and restructure their mammoth $1.2 trillion in bad loans, and privatizing the massive postal saving system, which funded much of the misconceived public works of the 1990s. Tax cuts would also be highly beneficial. Koizumi would be wise to follow the lead of the Obuchi administration (1998–99), which pushed through moderate tax cuts in personal and corporate income taxes. But he has postponed this vital supply-side ingredient until the crushing government-debt burden can be reduced.

Structural reform, as opposed to easy money and public spending, can work wonders in getting the Japanese economy back on track. For example, in 1994, when Japan deregulated the cellphone industry, prices dropped and sales skyrocketed, and this year cellular-related revenues are expected to exceed $72 billion, nearly 2 percent of economic output.

The lesson is clear: Free the economy and prosperity will follow.

---

1. John Maynard Keynes, *Essays in Biography* (New York: Norton, 1951), p. 107.

2. Henry Hazlitt, *Economics in One Lesson,* 3rd ed. (New York: Arlington House, 1979), p. 15.

3. James Gwartney et al., *Economic Freedom of the World Annual Report 2001* (Vancouver, B.C.: Fraser Institute, 2001), p. 182.

4. John Maynard Keynes, *The General Theory of Employment, Interest and Money* (London: Macmillan, 1936), p. 220.

5. Milton Friedman, "Rx for Japan," *Wall Street Journal,* December 17, 1997.

Poverty and Wealth: India Versus Hong Kong

"The government of India regulates nearly everything, so there's very little progress; whereas in Hong Kong the government keeps its hands off . . . and the standard of living has multiplied."

—JOHN TEMPLETON[1]

The mutual fund magnate John Templeton traveled around the world during the 1930s, noting in particular the extreme poverty in two Asian nations under British control, India and Hong Kong. Forty years later, in the 1970s, Templeton returned. Once again he witnessed the incredible poverty in India. But Hong Kong had changed tremendously. "The standard of living in Hong Kong had multiplied more than tenfold in forty years, while the standard of living in Calcutta has improved hardly at all."[2]

Today neither country is under British rule, but the contrast is even more clear. Hong Kong enjoys the greatest concentration of wealth in the world. India suffers the greatest concentration of poverty in the world.[3]

Twenty years ago, development economist P.T. Bauer wrote a famous little essay in which he pondered, "How would you rate the economic prospects of an Asian country which has very little land (and only eroded hillsides at that), and which is indeed the most densely populated country in the world; whose population has grown rapidly, both through natural increase and large-scale

67

immigration; which imports all of its oil and raw materials, and even most of its water; whose government is not engaged in development planning and operates no exchange controls or restrictions on capital exports and imports; and which is the only remaining Western colony of any significance?"[4]

Indeed, the prospects for Hong Kong were dismal. Yet by making cheap products for export to the faraway West, it managed to become the powerhouse of Southeast Asia. Today its citizens' incomes rival the Japanese, despite its teeming seven million people crowded into 400 square miles. What broke the vicious cycle of poverty? According to Bauer, Hong Kong's economic miracle did not depend on having money, natural resources, foreign aid, or even formal education, but rather on the "industry, enterprise, thrift and ability . . . of highly motivated people."[5] Hong Kong's "overpopulation" turned out to be an asset, not a liability.

Equally important, Britain did not interfere in private decision-making. It adopted a laissez-faire economic policy, except in the area of subsidized housing and education. Communist China has pursued a largely noninterventionist approach since it took over in 1997. Hong Kong continues to flourish with a stable currency, free port, and low taxes. Its maximum income tax rate is 18 percent, and it imposes no capital-gains tax. In its economic freedom index, the Fraser Institute has always ranked Hong Kong number one in the world.[6]

Tragic India

India is an entirely different story. Its population of one billion remains relatively poor. Unlike Hong Kong, India has valuable natural resources—forests, fish, oil, iron ore, coal, and agricultural products, among others. It has achieved self-sufficiency in food since independence in 1947, yet deep poverty persists.

Many pundits blame India's anti-capitalist culture, its fatalistic caste system, its overpopulation problem, and its hot and humid climate (it reached 117 degrees when we visited the Taj Mahal last June). But Milton Friedman identified the real culprit when he wrote, "The correct explanation is . . . not to be found in its religious or social attitudes, or in the quality of its people, but rather in the economic policy that India has adopted."[7]

Indeed, in the decade after independence, Nehru and other Indian leaders were heavily influenced by Harold Laski of the London School of Economics and his fellow Fabians, who advocated central planning along Soviet lines. India adopted five-year plans, nationalized heavy industries, and imposed import-substitution laws. Worse, they perpetuated the British civil-service tradition of exercising controls over foreign exchange and requiring licenses to start businesses.

Even today, India is a bureaucratic nightmare.[8] Parth Shah, an economist and head of the Centre for Civil Society (www.ccsindia.org),[9] describes how he recently returned to India and toiled to find an apartment in New Delhi (thanks to rent controls), then spent half a day standing in line to pay his first telephone bill and another half a day to pay his electricity bill. "Corruption has become the standard among those who are in public service at every level," reports Gita Mehta, a well-known Indian writer.[10] India has ranked around number 100 over the years on the Fraser Institute's index of economic freedom.

Yet there is hope. In 1991, facing default on its foreign debt, India abandoned four decades of economic isolation and planning, and freed the nation's entrepreneurs. It sold off many of its state companies, cut tariffs and taxes, and eliminated most price and exchange controls. As a result, India became one of the world's fastest-growing economies in the 1990s, averaging nearly 10 percent growth per year. Most important, while the rich have gotten richer, poverty rates fell sharply in India.

What can the new prime minister, A. B. Vajpayee, do now? Can India ever catch up to Hong Kong? India must cut its government deficits (currently 10 percent of GDP); cut tariffs and taxes further; privatize state enterprises; eliminate red tape; and restore honesty in government. It's a tall order but the only way to achieve what Adam Smith called "universal opulence which extends itself to the lowest ranks of the people."[11]

---

1. Quoted in William Proctor, *The Templeton Prizes* (New York: Doubleday, 1983), p. 72.

2. Ibid.

3. For an excellent updated survey of India, see "Unlocking India's Growth," *The Economist*, June 2, 2001.

4. P. T. Bauer, "The Lesson of Hong Kong," in *Equality, the Third World and Economic Delusion* (London: Weidenfeld and Nicolson, 1981), p. 185.

5. Ibid., p. 189.

6. James Gwartney and Robert Lawson, *Economic Freedom of the World, Annual Report 2001* (Vancouver, B.C.: Fraser Institute, 2001), p. 172.

7. Milton Friedman, *Friedman on India* (New Delhi: Centre for Civil Society, 2000), p. 10.

8. See John Stossel's amazing example in his ABC special "Is America #1?" available on videotape from Laissez Faire Books, 800–326–0996.

9. The other free-market think tank, the Liberty Institute, is run very capably by Barun Mitra. Shah and Mitra hosted my visit to India in June 2001.

10. Gita Mehta, *Snakes and Ladders: A Modern View of India* (London: Minerva, 1997), p. 16.

11. Adam Smith, *The Wealth of Nations* (New York: Random House, 1965 [1776]), p. 11.

Whatever Happened to the Egyptians?

"Governments are generally reluctant to admit mistakes and
to change mistaken policies until much harm has been done."
—P. T. BAUER AND B. S. YAMEY[1]

In *Whatever Happened to the Egyptians?* (American University
in Cairo Press, 2000), a popular book in Egypt, author Galan
Amin raises a good question. Thousands of years ago Egypt was
the birthplace of one of the world's greatest civilizations, with
remarkable advances in architecture, astronomy, mathematics,
and economics. The pharaohs ruled the world for centuries.

But today Egypt is a fallen nation. On our arrival earlier this
year at the port of Alexandria, once the "city of dreams," we saw
garbage and dust scattered profusely on the public highways.
Arriving in Cairo to see the ancient pyramids, we saw filthy canals,
undrinkable water, dire poverty, noisy traffic, teeming millions,
incessant vendors, and more dust.

I picked up a copy of a guidebook on what it's like for a West-
erner to live in Cairo. Author Claire Francy lists so many shortages
that she urges foreign residents to bring the following with them:
answering machine, major appliances, computers, modems, print-
ers, telephones, fax machines, cosmetics, flashlights, pantyhose,
wines, books in English, clothes, and shoes. Yes, shoes. "In a city
with nearly as many shoe stores as feet, it is almost impossible to
find decent shoes."[2] Oh, the joys of import-substitution laws!

And yet Egypt has tremendous resources: oil, cotton, some of the best fertile land in the world along the Nile Valley, a first-rate irrigation system, the Suez Canal, and a huge labor force (nearly 70 million and growing rapidly). Yet true unemployment is 20 percent, and underemployment is endemic. Egypt suffers from a huge "brain drain," with 2.5 million Egyptians working abroad. The nation has illiteracy rates of 66 percent among women and 37 percent among men. It imports half of its food. After Israel, this Arab-African nation is the highest recipient of U.S. foreign aid in the world.

Islamic Economics

What's the cause of this economic collapse? A few blame their Islamic religion for their troubles. Over 90 percent of Egyptians are Sunni Muslims who, critics say, pray too much (five times a day), are overly generous to the poor (and thus support a socialistic welfare state), bear too many children (Egypt has one of the highest birthrates in the world), and suffer an excessive financial burden (in the practice of providing housing for their children as a marital dowry). Egyptians are constantly celebrating holidays, among them the month-long Ramadan consisting of daytime fasting and nighttime feasting, when business activity becomes erratic.

But religion is not the true cause of Egypt's struggles. The real culprit is socialist interventionism in the economy. As one unnamed economist states, "The Egyptian economy bears the legacy of economic policies dating from the 1950's which were motivated by concern for equity and assistance to the poor. These policies were characterized by price regulation, subsidization of consumer goods, a dominant public sector and state control."[3] When Gamal Abdel Nasser gained power in 1954, he established a "democratic socialist state," nationalized everything under the sun (including the local beer company), and dramatically increased government control of the economy. Moreover, under a Napoleonic code, Egypt suffers from a regulatory nightmare of paperwork and bureaucracy.

One of the most harmful policies in Egypt has been import-substitution laws—the use of tariffs, quotas, subsidies, and restrictions to protect and promote local production of all kinds of consumer goods, from shoes to toothpaste to automobiles. This form of protectionism has been popular in Third World countries since development economists such as Gunnar Myrdal and Paul Rosenstein-Rodan claimed that import restrictions would stimulate domestic industry and employment. In Egypt, for example, the U.S. government spent roughly $200 million to help Egypt create a domestic cement industry, even though cement could be obtained more cheaply abroad.

Such policies have proven counterproductive. Today Cairo is covered with dust caused by the local cement factories. Egypt's import-substitution laws have created shoddy workmanship and above-market prices in shoes, appliances, and consumer products. Today most economists have changed their mind about import-substitution laws, admitting that they stifle growth. They point to the rapid expansion of East Asian nations, which eschewed import substitution and have concentrated on producing inexpensive exports.[4]

Fortunately, Nasser's successor, Anwar el-Sadat, began a program of reducing the role of government. After his tragic assassination in 1981, Hosni Mubarak accelerated market policies of privatization and foreign investment, and eliminated price and exchange controls. The local beer company is now in private hands. Yet even today, 36 percent of the labor force is employed by the government and the economy continues to suffer from over-regulation and controls.

Egypt has made substantial progress since 1990, when the Fraser Institute ranked it 88th in the institute's economic freedom report. Today it is ranked 52nd.[5] But clearly the Egyptian leaders have a long way to go to fulfill the Koran's promise of "wealth and children" as the "adornments of this present life."

---

1. P. T. Bauer and B. S. Yamey, *The Economics of Underdeveloped Countries* (Cambridge: Cambridge University Press, 1957), p. 157.

2. Claire E. Francy, *Cairo: The Practical Guide*, 10th ed. (Cairo: American University in Cairo Press, 2001), p. 68. This guidebook is both shocking and indispensable for anyone moving to or studying this strange Arab nation. I placed exclamation points on practically every page.

3. Cited in W. W. Rostow, *Theorists of Economic Growth from David Hume to the Present* (New York: Oxford University Press, 1990), p. 423.

4. Doug Bandow, "The First World's Misbegotten Economic Legacy to the Third World," in James A. Dorn, Steve H. Hanke, and Alan A. Walters, *The Revolution in Development Economics* (Washington, D.C.: Cato Institute, 1998), pp. 217, 222–23.

5. James Gwartney and Robert Lawson, *Economic Freedom of the World, Annual Report 2001* (Vancouver, B.C.: Fraser Institute, 2001), pp. 9–10.

How Real Is the Asian Economic Miracle?

"Singapore grew through a mobilization of resources that would have done Stalin proud."

—PAUL KRUGMAN

In the November/December 1994 issue of *Foreign Affairs*, Stanford economist Paul Krugman wrote a controversial article titled "The Myth of Asia's Miracle."

The postwar Asian economic miracle came as a great shock to the economics profession. In my review of the top-ten textbooks (*Economics on Trial*, Irwin, 1993), I found that few economists tell the wonders of Japanese prosperity and none reveals the secrets of the Four Tigers (Hong Kong, Singapore, Korea, and Taiwan) or the newly industrialized economies (Indonesia, Malaysia, and Thailand).

A desperate, starving, shattered Japan of 1945 was one of the poorest countries on earth. There were no skyscrapers, no wealthy banks, no automobile and electronics industries. Yet within a single human lifespan, Japan became an economic superpower, ranking second behind the United States among the world's richest nations.

Hong Kong has faced gigantic problems: six million people jammed into 400 square miles, with no oil or other natural resources, most of its water and food imported, and its trading partners thousands of miles away. Yet this small British colony has broken the vicious cycle of poverty and become the second most prosperous country in the Pacific Basin.

Since 1965, the 23 economies of East Asia have grown faster than all other regions of the world. The high-performing Asian economies have experienced extremely rapid growth and rising incomes. The proportion of people living in absolute poverty has dropped sharply. Life expectancy increased from 56 years in 1960 to 71 years in 1990.[1]

The Cause of the Miracle

Why have American economists ignored until recently these economic success stories? Perhaps because the Asian development model does not fit neatly into the Keynesian framework and policy prescriptions, which favor high levels of consumption, debt, and government spending. In almost all of the rapidly growing economies in East Asia, the degree of government taxation and central planning has been relatively low, savings rates excessively high by Keynesian standards, government budgets normally in surplus, and the welfare state relatively small. As the World Bank concluded in its 1993 study, "the rapid growth in each economy was primarily due to the application of a set of common, market-friendly economic policies, leading to both higher accumulation and better allocation of resources."[2]

Krugman contended that East Asian leaders have been just as authoritarian, pushing more of the population to work, upgrading educational standards, and making an awesome investment in physical capital. In short, East Asia is just like the Soviet Union, "growth achieved purely through mobilization of resources."

Moreover, like the Soviet Union, growth in East Asia is likely to diminish, due to limits on labor and capital. Krugman stated, "it is likely that growth in East Asia will continue to outpace growth in the West for the next decade and beyond. But it will not do so at the pace of recent years."[3] Asia is subject to the law of diminishing returns.

Indeed, Krugman proved to be right following the Asian financial crisis of 1997–98. But the reasons for the Asian crisis were more complex than either one of us realized.

As I see it, there were two factors at work that led to the collapse in the Asian markets and recession. First, overinvestment, and second, the strength of the U.S. dollar. Let's review each of these factors and the lessons we can learn from each.

Malinvestment and the Boom-Bust Cycle

First, it is clear that most of the Southeast Asian economies, including Singapore, Thailand, Malaysia, the Philippines, and South Korea, suffered from overinvestment, or what Ludwig von Mises called "malinvestment." The authoritarian regimes engaged in a "forced savings" program, demanding its citizens and businesses to overinvest. When voluntary savings were deemed insufficient to build up the nation's infrastructure and capital formation, the state promoted industrial planning. Moreover, it created cheap credit policies and encouraged foreign investment at low interest rates. In sum, Southeast Asia created a classic inflationary boom.

The Austrian school has warned time and time again that an inflationary boom in capital investment not only causes prices to rise, but also makes unsustainable projects look attractive. Eventually, interest rates must rise and the economy is hit by a recession.[4]

The Dollar as a Quasi-Gold Standard

What brought about the crash in Asia? Strangely enough, it was the strength of the U.S. dollar. Most of the Southeast Asian currencies were tied to the dollar, and that was their demise. In some ways, it reminds me of the specie-flow mechanism under the gold standard. Under a classic gold standard, when a nation inflates, gold flows out of the inflationary country, forcing the economy to contract. That's more or less what happened in Southeast Asia, except that instead of gold, the standard was the U.S. dollar.

When the dollar rose 30 percent against the other major currencies, Southeast Asian economies that were export-oriented and linked to the dollar, were placed at a disadvantage. Their exports suddenly became 30 percent more expensive, and demand for their goods declined. Exports dropped, profits fell, and debts couldn't be repaid at current exchange rates. Consequently, their governments were forced to delink from the dollar and their currencies collapsed. The boom turned into a bust.

Silver Lining: Free-Market Reforms Coming

There was a silver lining in the Asian crisis. It forced Southeast Asian countries and their governments to adopt market capitalism. No longer can these authoritarian regimes afford to subsidize favored corporations or play political favorites. Inefficient or corrupt businesses must be allowed to go bankrupt. Easy credit is not the solution to a shortage of capital. In the midst of the crisis, *Business Week* sounded the alarm and warned Asia not to fall back to angry nationalism or anti-capitalism. This was all the more amazing because *Business Week* has long had the reputation for being anti-free market. But it has changed for the better. To quote an editorial: "There is a strong chance that the Asian crisis can act as a solvent, dissolving authoritarian governments and economic practices while spreading democratic market capitalism" (January 26, 1998). Amen.

---

1. For an excellent survey of the region, see *The East Asian Miracle* (The World Bank, 1993).

2. Ibid., p. vi.

3. Paul Krugman, "The Myth of Asia's Miracle," *Pop Internationalism* (Cambridge, Mass.: MIT Press, 1996), p. 173. Originally published in *Foreign Affairs* (November/December 1994).

4. The best summary of the Austrian position can be found in *The Austrian Theory of the Trade Cycle and Other Essays*, Richard Ebeling, ed. (Auburn, Ala.: The Ludwig von Mises Institute, 1996 [1983]).

I'm All for Free Trade, But . . .

"The dogma [of free trade] does not stand up. . . . Import relief in the 1980s saved America's industrial base—and countless jobs—at tiny cost."
—Pat Buchanan, "How the Rust Belt Was Revived," *Washington Times*, July 20, 1994

Conservative columnist and political commentator Pat Buchanan needs to take a refresher course in Econ 101. He cites a study by economist Alan Tonelson in *Foreign Affairs* magazine (July/August 1994) supporting his "America First" doctrine of economic protectionism. "The United States ought not to surrender any weapon in its arsenal of defense for vital U.S. economic interests," says Buchanan.

Tonelson concurs: "Five major American industries—automotive, steel, machine tool, semiconductor, and textile—received significant relief from imports through intelligently structured trade laws. Those industries have confounded the predictions of laissez-faire economic ideologies by gaining market share at home and in some cases abroad, contributing to job creation and reinvigorating American competitiveness."

Thus, after Tokyo agreed to voluntary import limits in 1981, American auto makers achieved an astonishing comeback. The Big Three came out with new products such as the minivan and compact utility vehicles. Investment in new plant and equipment resulted in a substantial increase in productivity and quality of U.S. cars.

After Reagan negotiated bilateral agreements limiting imports of finished steel in 1984, investment and worker productivity in the U.S. steel industry soared, making the United States one of the lowest-cost producers in the world. Import curbs on machine tools, semiconductors, and textiles saw similar results—increased research and development, investment, cost-cutting, job creation, and retooling. The United States improved its competitiveness in all these markets.

Buchanan concludes: "The conventional wisdom was wrong."

Is This the Whole Story?

Before we reject two centuries of sound economic wisdom, let us consider all the relevant factors. Messrs. Buchanan and Tonelson conveniently forget to mention the environment in which these five industries performed so well. The reality is that virtually all industrial groups expanded sharply during the "Seven Fat Years" of the Reagan era, as Robert Bartley calls it. The free-trade critics have committed the classic *post hoc, ergo propter hoc* argument. Just because an event (import restrictions) occurs simultaneously to another event (economic recovery) does not mean that one is the primary cause of the other. There may be other, more powerful forces at work. Indeed, in the midst of a sharp recession (1981), Congress cut tax rates substantially for individuals, corporations, and investors, thus stimulating a "supply-side" revolution. Furthermore, in the summer of 1982, the Federal Reserve reversed its tight money, high-interest-rate policy in favor of easy money and lower interest rates. The low-interest rate, tax-cutting era continued almost throughout the 1980s, factors which most likely dwarfed the impact of import restrictions.

One should also not ignore the impact of a falling dollar since 1985 on the improvement in U.S. exports and foreign competition.

In short, the Rust Belt was revived primarily because of the "supply-side" revolution of tax cuts, deregulation, and an accommodating monetary policy—not protectionism. At least Messrs. Buchanan and Tonelson provide little evidence that the protected industries outperformed all other industries.

Global Trade Is Inevitable

This is not to say that U.S. producers didn't benefit from import relief. Undoubtedly, they did benefit. After all, tariffs and quotas aren't the measles. Yet the benefits may not have been all that great. The auto, steel, and textile industries would probably have done almost as well without the import restrictions.

Even before the import quotas were imposed in the 1980s, most of the leaders in these industries had recognized that the world was rapidly moving toward global free trade. Ford, for example, had already decided to take the Japanese and the Germans head on in building high-tech automobiles. Gradually more and more of the components of "American" products are made in foreign countries. Despite all kinds of restrictions and regulations in the textile and apparel industries, more and more shoes and clothing are being made in Asia and Latin America—by American-based companies. Global free trade is a simple fact of life and any manufacturer in the United States who doesn't recognize its inevitability is headed straight for bankruptcy court.

Cost-Benefit Analysis

In his great book *Economics in One Lesson,* Henry Hazlitt says that a good economist looks at how a policy affects all groups, not just one group. His story of the broken window is a classic.

We need to apply his "one lesson" to the free-trade debate. Yes, import relief helps the 21 highly protected sectors of the U.S. economy. It maintains thousands of American jobs in these industries. It keeps prices and wages higher than what they would be.

But what about the other groups in the economy—are they helped or hurt by import restrictions? According to the latest study by the Institute for International Economics, American consumers paid $70 billion more for goods and services as a direct result of import protection in 1990. In a $6 trillion dollar economy, that may not seem like much. And, in fact, it demonstrates the high degree of free trade which already exists in the United States.

Nevertheless, the consumer cost per job saved averages about $170,000. Economists Hufbauer and Elliott conclude: "This is far higher than the average annual wage in the protected industries and far more than any current or proposed labor adjustment program would cost."[1]

Tariffs and quotas affect the U.S. economy in many obscure, subtle ways. For example, the voluntary import quotas on Japan resulted in a substantial increase in the importing of higher-priced, larger Japanese cars. Import limits on finished steel forced U.S. automobile companies to pay higher prices on their inputs.

Clearly, most producers benefit from tariffs and quotas, while consumers are hurt. Why don't consumers complain more loudly? Probably because of the nature of the political system. As public-choice economists demonstrate, industry and labor are much better lobbyists than consumers. Moreover, consumers are also producers and may work in protected industries as well. The protectionist story is the same everywhere, in the U.S., Japan, or Germany. Everyone favors promoting exports, but not imports.

A Better Idea

While the debate over protectionism rages on, economists and journalists should consider a far better alternative to import relief—tax and regulatory relief for domestic business. One of the primary reasons the auto, steel, and textile industries have had difficulty competing in the world economy is because they lack the capital investment to adopt the latest technology and rebuild their markets. Imagine the impact on American industry if the corporate income tax and the capital gains tax were eliminated? If red tape and regulations were streamlined? Economic growth would be so rapid that we wouldn't even think twice about the need for "import relief" and "fair trade."

---

1. Gary Clyde Hufbauer and Kimberly Ann Elliott, *Measuring the Costs of Protection in the United States* (Washington, D.C.: Institute for International Economics, 1994), back cover.

European Unemployment
and the Age of Ignorance

> "This persistence of high unemployment in the European Community is a major puzzle."
> —CHARLES R. BEAN, "EUROPEAN UNEMPLOYMENT: A SURVEY,"
> *Journal of Economic Literature*, JUNE 1994

In the June 1994 issue of *The Freeman*, I wrote "Is this the Age of Ignorance—Or Enlightenment?," my most controversial column. It revealed how a growing number of well-trained economists plead ignorance on the most fundamental aspects of the budget deficit, taxes, inflation, the stock market, and the business cycle. Those cited included Herbert Stein, Robert J. Barro, and Paul Krugman.

My column was not well received by the profession. None of the economists cited in my column responded, perhaps because they were too embarrassed. But Milton Friedman wrote, "Herbert Stein underestimates his knowledge; you overestimate yours." Brigham Young University professor Larry Wimmer said, "Ignorance is preferable to arrogance." So the battle of ideas continues.

Now along comes Charles R. Bean, a bright economist at the London School of Economics, writing in the *Journal of Economic Literature*. After engaging in 47 pages of citations, graphs, charts, cross-country regression analysis, and econometric studies, he bravely concludes that nobody really knows why unemployment is so high in Europe. None of the numerous technical models works. It's all a "major puzzle."

Obviously, if economists can't explain why a major problem such as European unemployment exists, they can't be expected to prescribe a policy to rectify the situation. Hence, the growing impotence of the economics profession. It has blunted Occam's Razor: Complexity is preferable to simplicity. Economists know so much that they now know so little.

Fortunately, not all economists subscribe to this new form of economic nihilism. Some economists see through the clouds of complexity, realizing that econometric modeling often obscures rather than elucidates the real nature of the problem. It's time to return to basic economic principles.

The Real Cause of Unemployment

For example, Richard K. Vedder and Lowell E. Gallaway, economists at Ohio University, demonstrate quite powerfully that government policies cause widespread and persistent unemployment by raising real wages above equilibrium levels. Labor laws significantly increase labor costs and hence discourage businesses from hiring workers. In addition, the federal government's inflationary fiscal and monetary policies create a boom-bust business cycle, causing much temporary unemployment of labor and resources. Their important study, Out of Work, applies their thesis to the United States during the twentieth century and concludes that unemployment is primarily due to "government activism."[1]

Applying the Thesis to Europe

The unemployment rate has been gradually rising in Europe and now exceeds 11 percent, compared to under 6 percent in the United States and 3 percent in Japan. It's the highest since the oil-shock years of the 1970s. But today there is no oil crisis. Through much of the 1980s, virtually no new jobs were created in the private sector. Fifty percent of the 16 million unemployed in Western Europe are considered long-term unemployed—without work for a year or longer. Only 11 percent of U.S. jobless are long term.

What is the cause of European joblessness? Despite the machinations of econometricians, the answer is not that difficult to discover. First, high payroll taxes—personal income tax withholding, social security, and unemployment compensation—discourage businesses from hiring. As Edmund S. Phelps, economics professor at Columbia University, declares, "Nearly every European country has brought much of its unemployment on itself—through its punishing taxation of labor. . . . Big increases in payroll and personal income taxes in most countries have been mass job-killers."[2] Last year, in an effort to close the national deficit, France raised income taxes by 10 percent. Not surprisingly, the unemployment rate in France rose by about a point and a half to 12.6 percent.

A second cause of unemployment in Europe is its labor laws and regulations, such as minimum wages, collective bargaining, and labor-management restrictions. Other mandatory benefits, including health care, pensions, unemployment and disability compensation, and paid vacations, raise labor costs.

The minimum wage in Belgium is $7 an hour, compared to $4.25 in the United States. Even now, German labor unions are pushing for a four-day workweek, amounting to an immediate 20 percent increase in real wages. In Italy, an employer must give up to six months notice before dismissal. In order to protect workers from sudden unemployment, Spain passed legislation making it virtually impossible for employers to fire workers. These are disguised methods of raising labor costs. But the actual effect is unemployment: If you can't fire workers, why hire? Spain's labor law dealing with employers' obligations to the work force is 600 pages long. It should come as no surprise that, as a result of this legislation, Spain's unemployment rate has gradually risen to depression levels, 25 percent. Portugal, on the other hand, has a less encumbered labor market and an unemployment rate of only 5.5 percent.

Third, generous welfare benefits to the unemployed, encourages the jobless to avoid work.

The existence of the European Union Market will undoubtedly force high-cost nations to liberalize their labor laws, or else face a major talent drain. Not surprisingly, many jobless Europeans are headed to other parts of the EU, or to Asia, where jobs are plentiful and labor markets are unfettered.

The answer to Europe's unemployment problem is simple. Sharply reduce payroll taxes and the rules and regulations governing labor-management relations to allow market forces to work more effectively. This means less mandated job security and fewer government benefits, but more jobs and greater productivity. It is a difficult choice for EU governments to make, but if they don't, unemployment can only get worse.

---

1. Richard K. Vedder and Lowell E. Gallaway, *Out of Work* (New York: Holmes & Meier, 1993).

2. Edmund S. Phelps, "Summiteers: Your Taxes Kill Jobs," *Wall Street Journal,* March 14, 1994.

Freedom for Everyone . . .
Except the Immigrant

"We cannot continue to admit millions of legal and illegal
immigrants if we wish to maintain our standard of living and
our national identity."
                    —PETER BRIMELOW, AUTHOR, *Alien Nation*

How often have we heard the refrain, "Well, I'm all for the free
market except . . ."? It's particularly sad to hear it from Peter
Brimelow, an otherwise friend of liberty in high places. Peter is a
senior editor of *Forbes* magazine, the most influential business
magazine in the nation. He has written eloquently about the
bloated federal government and the demise of public education.
He even wrote an article in *Forbes* praising Mr. Libertarian, the
late Murray Rothbard.

But now Peter Brimelow has joined those who are calling for a
drastic curtailment if not entire elimination of new immigrants
entering the United States. Peter demands sanctions and even criminal penalties against U.S. employers who hire undocumented
workers. He also supports the establishment of a national identity
card, which he says "is hardly more an encroachment on personal
freedom than the income tax."[1] He recommends another crack-
down (Operation Wetback) on illegals by the much-hated Immigration and Naturalization Service (INS), including the use of
police attack dogs. Finally, he endorses building a huge barrier
along the U.S.-Mexico border, something akin to a Berlin Wall.

(How about solving the problem right away by putting up signs along the border, "Trespassers Will Be Shot"?) All these plans, of course, would mean thousands of new federal agents and billions in taxpayer dollars, but no matter. America's "lax" immigration policy is a "disaster," Peter says, and something must be done.

Isn't it amazing how a single issue can lead to so much government intervention?

The Benefits of Immigration

Currently, approximately one million legal immigrants are allowed to enter the United States each year (recent legal aliens included, ironically, Peter Brimelow and his wife). Estimates of illegal immigrants run as high as two million a year. Half the world's immigrants come to America. Is this an alarming trend?

Far from a disaster, a liberal immigration policy can be quite beneficial. A cardinal principle of economic liberty is the free movement of goods, capital, and people. As Mises states, "In a world of perfect mobility of capital, labor, and products there prevails a tendency toward an equalization of the material conditions of all countries."[2] Without this freedom, some areas are overpopulated, others are underpopulated. Wage rates and interest rates differ dramatically.

An article in the New York Times, appropriately published on Independence Day, reflects the dynamics of immigration in the United States: "Dead-End Jobs? Not for These Three. Immigrants Flourish in the McDonald's System."[3] It testifies to the energy and talent immigrants can bring to America.

In January 1993, the European Community of 12 nations adopted free immigration. Any citizen of the EC can live and work in any other EC country without a work permit. The effect will be a transfer of labor from low-wage countries (Spain, Portugal, Greece) to high-wage countries (Germany, France, England). Who will benefit in the long run? All members of the EC.

The Cuban Miracle

One of the best cases in favor of immigration is the Cuban miracle in Miami, Florida. Here was potentially one of those disasters that Peter Brimelow talks about. In the early 1960s some 200,000 penurious immigrants thronged this stagnant urban community, more than the total black unemployed youths in all America's urban areas at the time. It was the most rapid and overwhelming migration to one American city. Few spoke English and virtually none had jobs or housing. Yet in less than a decade, these Cuban immigrants revived Miami's stagnant inner city and transformed the entire Miami economy. Even with another 125,000 boat people fleeing to Miami in the early 1980s, Dade County continued to have one of the lowest rates of unemployment in the state of Florida. George Gilder, who has chronicled the Cuban miracle, concludes, "As long as the United States is open to these flows from afar, it is open to its own revival."[4]

There are many examples in other parts of the world where refugees and immigrants have transformed their new homes. Hong Kong, Taiwan, and Singapore come to mind. Foreign tyranny has led to much economic and social progress in exile.

Don't get me wrong. Immigration is not without its side effects, well documented in Peter Brimelow's book. Burdens on local government's educational, health, and welfare services can be immense. But free people and free markets can adjust surprisingly well if they are allowed to. Certainly, no one should object to any immigrant who is in good health, has a guaranteed job, and refuses to take welfare.

The Best Foreign Policy

Unfortunately, most emigrants leave their homeland not because they want to, but because they have to. If governments were less corrupt and onerous in their economic policies, fewer of their citizens would desire to emigrate. If they adopted free-market reforms (slashing taxes, regulations, inflation, and boondoggles), fewer of their citizens would move to America. Perhaps the greatest foreign assistance America could give to Mexico, China, and other countries whose citizens are moving to America in droves is a copy of Mises's *Human Action* or a subscription to FEE's publications. Putting up barriers at our borders is a much more expensive and dangerous alternative.

Jefferson said, "All men are created equal." They shouldn't be penalized just because they happened to be born in the wrong place.

1. Peter Brimelow, *Alien Nation* (New York: Random House, 1994), p. 260.

2. Ludwig von Mises, *Money, Method and the Market Process* (Kluwer, 1990), p. 141

3. "Dead End Jobs?" by Barnaby J. Feder, *New York Times*, July 4, 1995, p. 27.

4. George Gilder, *The Spirit of Enterprise* (New York: Simon & Schuster, 1984), p. 111. See also Julian L. Simon, *The Economic Consequences of Immigration* (Basil Blackwell, 1989).

Peace on Earth, Good Will Toward Men—Through Capitalism and Freedom!

"A great multitude of religious sects . . . might in time [become] free of every mixture of absurdity, imposture, of fanaticism."

—ADAM SMITH[1]

Leonard Read, founder of the Foundation for Economic Education, wrote that freedom of choice is one of the essential agents of peace and harmony. According to Read, true freedom means practicing the Golden Rule and preserving the God-given rights of the individual as declared in the Declaration of Independence. "Everyone is completely free to act creatively as his abilities and ambitions permit; no restraint in this respect—none whatsoever."[2]

The latest edition of the *Index of Economic Freedom*, published by the Heritage Foundation and the *Wall Street Journal*, shows that many parts of the world are "mostly unfree" or "repressed," as judged by the level of corruption, taxation, protectionism, inflation, black markets, and government interventionism. Of the 155 nations surveyed, over half (81) receive a negative grade. Most telling, the area of the world with the highest concentration of "repressed" freedom is the Middle East, particularly Iran, Iraq, and Libya (Afghanistan was not ranked).[3] Judging from recent events, the Middle East confirms Read's thesis. Most of the Arab world continues to suffer from economic dislocation, political turmoil, and military conflict. "When the wicked rule, the people mourn" (Proverbs 29:2). Henry Hazlitt summed it up well: "It is socialist governments, notwithstanding their denunciations of imperialist capitalism, that have been the greatest source of modern wars."[4]

Commerce and Trade Breaks Down Barriers— and Intolerance

The Middle East is also known for dictatorships and religious intolerance. It seems that economic repression goes hand in hand with political and religious repression, just as economic freedom leads to political and religious freedom.[5] Montesquieu, Adam Smith, and other classical-liberal thinkers made the case that liberalized trade and the spirit of capitalism break down cultural and social monotheism and destroy fanaticism and intolerance. Montesquieu saw many virtues in *doux commerce,* stating that the pursuit of profit-making serves as a countervailing bridle against the violent passions of war and abusive political power. "Commerce cures destructive prejudices," Montesquieu declared. "It polishes and softens barbarous mores. . . . The natural effect of commerce is to lead to peace."[6] Adam Smith seconded Montesquieu and taught that the commercial society moderates the passions and prevents a descent into a Hobbesian jungle.

Business encourages people to become educated, industrious, and self-disciplined. As economist Albert Hirschman observes, "The spirit of commerce brings with it the spirit of frugality, of economy, of moderation, of work, of wisdom, of tranquility, of order, and of regularity."[7] Business people are the ultimate in practicality—they are by nature compromisers and tolerant of other viewpoints. They will wheel and deal to sell and produce a product. As John Maynard Keynes once said, "It is better that a man should tyrannise over his bank balance than over his fellow-citizen."[8]

The Case for Religious Competition

The Middle East is also famous for its lack of religious freedom and diversity. A few Protestant Christians live and worship there, but proselyting is prohibited, even in Israel. Egyptians are divided into only two Muslim sects; there are virtually no Jews in the country, and no missionaries. Islamic fundamentalists hate the West's idea (as expressed originally by John Locke) of a free religious society where churches compete for members. According to Andrew Sullivan, America has achieved "one of the most vibrantly religious civil societies on earth," and America "is living, tangible rebuke to everything they [Taliban and bin Laden] believe in."[9]

Adam Smith contends that a state religion breeds fanaticism, intolerance, and persecution. There are numerous examples of holy wars waged by state-supported Christianity, Islam, and other religions that demonstrate Smith's thesis. But Smith goes further. He argues that creating a free, competitive environment in religions would be beneficial. Natural liberty, he said, favors "a great multitude of religious sects" which would generate interest in religion and encourage higher attendance at church. "In little religious sects, the morals of common people have been almost remarkably regular and orderly: generally much more so than in the established church."[10] According to Smith, religious competition would reduce zeal and fanaticism and promote tolerance, moderation, and rational religion.

In short, a good dose of open markets and competition in all walks of life could go a long way toward bringing peace, prosperity, and good will in this dangerous part of the world. Until that happens, many will shout "peace, peace, when there is no peace" (Jeremiah 8:11).

1. Adam Smith, *The Wealth of Nations* (New York: Modern Library, 1965 [1776]), p. 745.

2. Leonard Read, *Anything That's Peaceful,* 2nd ed. (New York: Foundation for Economic Education, 1998), p. 30.

3. Gerald P. O'Driscoll, Jr., Kim R. Holmes, and Melanie Kirkpatrick, *2001 Index of Economic Freedom* (Washington, D.C.: Heritage Foundation and the *Wall Street Journal,* 2001), pp. 2, 4.

4. Henry Hazlitt, *The Foundations of Morality,* 3rd ed. (New York: Foundation for Economic Education, 1998 [1964]), p. 339.

5. See Milton Friedman, *Capitalism and Freedom* (Chicago: University of Chicago Press, 1962), chapter 1.

6. Charles Montesquieu, *The Spirit of the Laws* (Cambridge: Cambridge University Press, 1989 [1748]), pp. 338.

7. Albert O. Hirschman, *The Passion and the Interests,* 2nd ed. (Princeton:

Princeton University Press, 1997), p. 72. I highly recommend this brilliant book. For more discussion of the peaceable nature of capitalism, see Mark Skousen, *The Making of Modern Economics* (New York: M.E. Sharpe, 2001), chapter 1.

8. John Maynard Keynes, *The General Theory of Interest, Money and Employment* (London: Macmillan, 1936), p. 374. Today we might say, "Better that a person tyrannize over his favorite sports team or his favorite stock than over his fellow citizen."

9. Andrew Sullivan, "This Is a Religious War," *New York Times Magazine,* October 7, 2001, p. 53. I highly recommend this article.

10. Smith, op. cit., pp. 747–48.

Correcting Fallacies and Debunking Myths

Sorry, Charley, But That's Not Capitalism!

"All economic transactions involve a win-lose proposition. Every gain involves a loss."
—CHARLEY REESE, *Orlando Sentinel*

Lord Acton once said, "There is no error so monstrous that it fails to find defenders among the ablest men." That was my reaction to a series of articles written a few years ago by national columnist Charley Reese. Over the years, Reese has made a reputation as a strong defender of individual rights against a growing Leviathan, the federal government. So it was all the more perplexing when I read some of his claims about free-market capitalism:

"Two people can't eat the same bean. That's the essence of economics."

"All economic transactions involve a win-lose proposition."

"The historically visible trend [in capitalist societies] is always for the rich to get richer and the poor to get poorer."

"Only the youngest, the strongest can put stock in pure capitalism."

Statements like these were demolished years ago in Leonard Read's classic little book *Clichés of Socialism,* which has been reprinted under the new title, *Clichés of Politics* (Foundation for Economic Education, 1994). Unfortunately, some clichés die slowly.

Let me respond to each one of these commonly held criticisms of the free market.

Voluntary Exchange Is Win-Win

First, is the free market similar to a sporting event, where one team wins and the other loses? Not at all. In every voluntary transaction, both the buyer and seller gain. Here's a simple proof: Suppose I sell an apple to a student for $1. The student buys the apple because he would rather have the apple than the dollar bill. Thus, by purchasing the apple, he improves his situation. On the other hand, I sell the apple because I'd rather have the dollar bill than the apple. I too am better off.

In *Das Capital,* Karl Marx popularized the view that all exchanges under free enterprise capitalism involved an equality of values and therefore one person's gain must be another person's loss. But now we see that just the opposite is true: All transactions in a voluntary exchange involve an inequality of values. In fact, without an inequality of values, no voluntary exchange would ever occur.

Because of an inequality of values, both the buyer and seller gain in every transaction. The only exception to this law is when fraud or deception is involved. When that happens, one party gains at the other's expense. But in a voluntary exchange, where full and honest information is revealed, everyone benefits.

The Essence of Capitalism

Reese says that the essence of capitalism is contained in the statement, "Two people can't eat the same bean." Not so fast, Charley. A free market is not just an "either or" proposition. Capitalism is also a highly cooperative system. If there are two people and only one bean, the free market provides a better alternative: plant the bean and harvest enough beans to feed both people! That's the true essence of capitalism.

Granted, natural resources are limited. But the beauty of free enterprise is its ability to *multiply* these resources into goods and services that people can use to increase their standard of living. What really matters is not so much the amount of resources in their natural state but the supply of *economically useable* natural resources, which are limited only to the extent of our know-how and physical ability to transform these inputs into useable wealth. In that sense, there is virtually no limit to further advances in our standard of living. In reality, nature isn't scarce, only the productive capacity of labor to change nature into real wealth is.

Capitalism Can Improve Everyone's Standard of Living

Finally, Charley Reese is wrong in suggesting that capitalism breeds inequality, that the rich get richer and the poor get poorer. Under the free market, the rich get richer and the poor get richer too. Historically, citizens of capitalistic nations have enjoyed higher real wages and steady advances in the quantity, quality, and variety of goods and services. Only government, the politics of coercion, causes a decline in the standard of living.

Moreover, the free market does not only benefit the young and the strong, as Charley Reese suggests, but the weak, the poor, and the discriminated. Contrary to popular belief, capitalism is not a dog-eat-dog jungle where only the fittest survive. As the classical economist David Ricardo demonstrated, the market is characterized by comparative advantage, not just absolute advantage in the division of labor. Therefore, opportunities abound for people of all abilities, talents, religions and races. The less fortunate may not earn a high wage, but they can and do benefit from the blessings of a technologically advanced capitalistic society. Today practically everyone, rich and poor, enjoys the benefits of electrical power, the telephone, the automobile, television and radio, books and newspapers, and a myriad other goods and services. Such everyday products were available only to the wealthy less than a century ago.

A free society is by no means perfect. People make mistakes, employers sometimes take advantage of workers, sometimes workers shortchange their employers, and salesmen may deceive the public. But the strength of the market is that bad business, deceptive practices, and shoddy merchandise are constantly being overwhelmed by good business, accurate information, and quality products. On net balance, there is no substitute for the free-enterprise system.

The Rich Get Richer, And the Poor Get . . .

> "The modern market economy accords wealth and distribution income in a highly unequal, socially adverse and also functionally damaging fashion."
>
> —John Kenneth Galbraith

The allegation is appearing everywhere: Real average wages are stagnating and the distribution of wealth and income in the United States is becoming more unequal. In his latest *The Good Society: The Humane Agenda,* Galbraith cites recent Federal Reserve statistics: "By 1992, the top 5 percent were getting an estimated 18 percent, a share that in more recent years has become substantially larger, as that of those in the poorest brackets has been diminishing. This, the good society cannot accept."[1] According to the Bureau of Labor Statistics, average real wages have been declining since the mid-1970s. If benefits are included, total real compensation has been rising, but only modestly. Finally, *Business Week* (February 25, 1996) declared, "Is America Becoming More of a Class Society?" The magazine cited several academic studies indicating less upward mobility for less-educated Americans. Several months later the *Wall Street Journal* added, "Inequality may grow for lifetime earnings."

Critics of market capitalism are often misled by conventional measures of economic well-being, in particular the Lorenz curve, which measures income distribution.

100

The Lorenz curve measures the percentage of a nation's total income as earned by various income classes. Typically, it is divided into five income groups. In the United States, the highest fifth (the highest income earners) usually receive 40 percent of the nation's income, while the lowest fifth (the lowest income earners) receive around 5 percent. Using the Lorenz curve, U.S. income appears to be seriously maldistributed, "now the extreme case among the major industrial countries," says Galbraith.

However, the Lorenz curve establishes an unfair and misleading guide for measuring social welfare. Suppose, for example, that an "ideal" line of "perfect" equality is achieved on the Lorenz curve, i.e., the highest fifth (top 20 percent of income earners) only receive 20 percent of the nation's income, while the bottom fifth (lower 20 percent) increase their share to 20 percent. What does this ideal mean? Everyone—the teacher, the lawyer, the plumber, the actor—earns the same amount of income![2]

Since few economists think equal wages for everyone is an ideal situation, why do they think moving toward "perfect equality" on the Lorenz curve is appropriate? Moreover, the Lorenz curve is unable to show an increase in a country's standard of living over time. It merely measures distribution of income.

To measure changes in social welfare, economists often rely on a second measure—average real income. This, too, has its shortcomings. A single statistic may mask improvements in an individual's standard of living over time.

For example, average real income shows hardly any change since the mid-1970s. Yet other measures of well-being, such as consumer expenditures and the quantity, quality, and variety of goods and services, show remarkable advancement over the past 20 years. Consumer spending rose a dramatic 40 percent per person in real terms during this period. As Professor Richard Vedder asks, "How many Americans in 1975 had VCRs, microwaves, CD players, and home computers?"

The Work of Stanley Lebergott

Stanley Lebergott, professor emeritus of economics at Wesleyan University, has probably done more work in this area than anyone else. Instead of relying on general measures such as average real income, he uses a more commonsense approach—looking at individual consumer markets in food, clothing, housing, fuel, housework, transportation, health, recreation, and religion. His work is fascinating.

For example, he developed the following table to measure improvements in living standards from 1900 to 1970:

Living Standards, 1900–1970

Percentage with . . .	Among All Families in 1900	Among Poor Families in 1970
Flush toilets	15	99
Running water	24	92
Central heating	1	58
One (or fewer) occupants per room	48	96
Electricity	3	99
Refrigeration	18	99
Automobiles	1	41

Source: Stanley Lebergott, *The American Economy* (Princeton University Press, 1976), p. 8.

In *Pursuing Happiness,* Lebergott demonstrates repeatedly how American consumers have sought to make an uncertain and often cruel world into a pleasanter and more convenient place. Medicines and medical facilities, artificial lighting, refrigeration, transportation, communication, entertainment, finished clothing—all have advanced living conditions.

Regarding women's work, Lebergott notes that weekly hours for household and family chores fell from 70 in 1900 to 30 by 1981. The 1900 housewife had to load her stove with tons of wood or coal each year and fill her lamps with coal oil or kerosene. "Central heating also reduced the housewife's tasks. She no longer had to wash the carbonized kerosene, oil, coal, or wood from clothes, curtains, and walls, nor sweep floors and vacuum rugs as persistently. Automated and mechanical equipment reduced her labor further. . . . By 1950, over 95 percent of U.S.

families had the facilities [of] central heating, hot water, gas, electric light, baths, and vacuum cleaners."[3]

Regarding water, Lebergott comments, "The average urban resident consumed about 20 gallons of water per day in 1900. Rural families had virtually no piped water; 55 percent did not even have privies. . . . By 1990, American families devoted two days' worth of their annual income to get about 100 sanitary gallons every day, piped into the home."[4]

Benefits to the Poor, Too

This kind of historical perspective is refreshing and eye-opening. The increase in the standard of living as measured by the quantity, quality, and variety of goods and services has increased dramatically and profoundly in the twentieth century, for people of all incomes. In many ways, the poor have advanced the most and are now capable of living in decent housing, owning an automobile, and enjoying many of the pleasures previously afforded by the wealthy. Cheap airline services allow them to travel extensively. Television gives them the chance to see sports events and musical shows previously limited to the rich and the middle class. Compared to yesteryear, every house today is a castle, every man is a king.

---

1. John Kenneth Galbraith, *The Good Society: The Humane Agenda* (Boston: Houghton Mifflin Co., 1996), p. 50.

2. For a critique of the Lorenz curve, see my work *Economics on Trial* (Homewood, Ill.: Irwin, 1991), pp. 187–197.

3. Stanley Lebergott, *Pursuing Happiness: American Consumers in the Twentieth Century* (Princeton, N.J.: Princeton University Press, 1993), p. 58.

4. Ibid., pp. 117–118. See also Lebergott's latest work, *Consumer Expenditures* (Princeton, N.J.: Princeton University Press, 1996).

Overworked and Underpaid?

"Most blue-collar workers and midlevel white-color managers are overworked and overwhelmed."

—ROBERT REICH

In the mid-1990s, then-Labor Secretary Robert Reich claimed that eight million Americans held two or more jobs, the highest figure since the early 1970s, when data were first collected. Work time was on the rise, while leisure time was on the decline.[1] Median wages had fallen from $479 a week to $475 a week (factoring in inflation). In fact, according to the Bureau of Labor Statistics, average real wages had been declining since the mid-1970s. "There is something terribly wrong, terribly un-American, about the fact that the economy's prosperity is bypassing so many working people," Reich asserted.

Has the American dream fallen on hard times? Free-market economists dispute Reich's claims. Ohio University professor Richard Vedder points out that Reich's real-wage data do not include fringe benefits, such as medical insurance, paid vacations, and pension plans. When benefits are added, total real compensation per hour has been rising, albeit modestly since the mid-1970s. Moreover, by using another measure of human economic welfare, consumer spending rose a dramatic 40 percent per person in real terms. As Professor Vedder says, "How many Americans in 1975 had VCRs, microwaves, CD players, and home computers?"

In short, measuring the quantity, quality, and variety of goods and services is often a better measure of economic progress than average real wages.

The Dramatic Slowdown in Productivity

Still, there is much to be concerned about. Statistics from the U.S. Commerce Department clearly show that worker productivity has slowed considerably since the mid-1970s. And productivity is the key to rising or falling wages.

Many years ago, F. A. Harper, an economist and staff member of FEE, wrote a grand little book entitled *Why Wages Rise*. He demonstrates that wages aren't high because of unionization or government-imposed minimum wages. Rather, "Higher wages come from increased output per hour of work."[2] Ludwig von Mises adds, "if you increase capital, you increase the marginal productivity of labor, and the effect will be that real wages will rise."[3] Training, new production methods, and updated machinery and technology make workers more efficient and valuable.

How does a nation increase its capital invested per worker? A clue may be found in another interesting statistic: Government debt as a percentage of GDP started rising in the mid-1970s, at the same time real wages stopped growing significantly. Coincidence? I don't think so. Deficit spending crowds out saving and private capital investment and reduces the funds available for training, new tools, and new technology.

Deficit spending isn't the only factor that has slowed the rate of capital formation in the United States. Other determinants are (a) heavy taxation and regulation of business, (b) Social Security and other employment taxes, and (c) the tax burden on saving and investment, specifically capital gains, interest, and dividends. All of these factors have kept the U.S. savings rate at a low level, creating a serious capital shortage and slowing productivity gains.

The Hong Kong Model

Hong Kong provides an interesting case study of how the United States might increase productivity and thereby reignite the rise in average real wages for Americans. Real earnings in this small Asian colony have been rising steadily and rapidly over the past half-century. Immigration has been high and union member-ship low in Hong Kong over the years. Yet worker income keeps rising. Why? There are several reasons: A high rate of personal and business savings. Heavy emphasis on education and training. No perennial government deficits. No trade barriers. And most impor-tantly, a flat minimum tax on personal income (15 percent) and corporate income (16.5 percent), a minimal Social Security pro-gram, and no tax on capital gains or dividends. In short, there are virtually no limits on the ability of the residents of Hong Kong to save and thus increase the capital per worker. Consequently, wages keep rising.

Here in the United States, many pundits will continue to blame our lackluster performance in real wages on big corporations, for-eigners, women in the workforce, and lack of union power. But the root cause is the anti-growth policies of government.

Recently there has been a strong movement to overhaul the bud-get and tax system in the United States. One proposal favors a flat tax system similar to Hong Kong's. Such a policy change would cause a sharp rise in saving, investment, economic growth, and the standard of living of the American wage-earner.

---

1. Juliet B. Schor, *The Overworked American: The Unexpected Decline of Leisure* (New York: Basic Books, 1991), pp. 1–5.

2. F. A. Harper, *Why Wages Rise* (Irvington-on-Hudson, N.Y.: Foundation for Economic Education, 1957), p. 19.

3. Ludwig von Mises, *Economic Policy: Thoughts for Today and Tomorrow* (Chicago: Regnery Gateway, 1979), p. 88.

Leisure, The Basis of Culture

"How inscrutable is the civilization where men toil and work
and worry their hair gray to get a living and forget to play!"

—Lin Yutang[1]

Ever since moving to the Bahamas in 1984, I have been
intrigued by the idea of leisure—shedding the workaholic rat
race to be "free and easy" and "letting oneself go," to quote the
German philosopher Josef Pieper. To Pieper, leisure is more than
merely getting off work at the end of the day or taking a vacation;
rather "the soul of leisure lies in celebration" of nature, life, and
the divine in perfect calm and relaxation.[2]

During my two-year sojourn in the "island of June,"[3] I picked
up a copy of Bertrand Russell's celebrated book *In Praise of Idleness*. Russell, author of more than 60 books, was never idle—what
he really meant was leisure time to pursue one's own loves and
goals rather than working for someone else's objectives. In typical
contemptuous style, Russell lambasted the Western penchant for
hard labor: "The morality of work is the morality of slaves, and
the modern world has no need of slavery." Furthermore, "The
wise use of leisure . . . is a product of civilization and education. A
man who has worked long hours all his life will be bored if he
becomes suddenly idle. But without a considerable amount of
leisure a man is cut off from many of the best things. . . . We attach
too little importance to enjoyment and simple happiness." Russell
believed that ideally man should work only four hours and spend
the rest of the time engaged in playful activities, not passive activ-

107

ities like watching sports or television, but intellectual and scientific pursuits.[4]

Work Ethics: The East Versus the West

The Judeo-Christian West has always emphasized a strong work ethic, but what about the East? Lin Yutang, the celebrated Chinese libertarian philosopher, insisted that the American virtues of efficiency, punctuality, and goal-setting are actually "vices." "From the Chinese point of view," declared Lin, "the man who is wisely idle is the most cultured man. . . . Those who are wise won't be busy, and those who are too busy can't be wise." Referring to Western business practices, Lin ruminated, "Americans have now come to such a sad state that they are booked up not only for the following day, or the following week, but even for the following month. An appointment three weeks ahead of time is a thing unknown in China."[5]

Lin wrote his essay on loafing in 1937. Today Lin would be aghast at the degree in which the East has adopted the West's working patterns, and even surpassed them. Anyone who has been to Hong Kong, Japan, or Korea would laugh at any suggestion that Americans are overworked.

Is Overwork an Inherent Defect in Capitalism?

Yet that is precisely what Harvard economist Juliet Schor claims in her bestseller, *The Overworked American,* first written in the early 1990s. Critics of the market complain that the capitalist system inherently promotes overwork and discourages leisure. According to Schor, the constant demands of the consumer society and global competition are mandating more work hours and exploding consumer debt. Leisure time is on the decline, she says. Eight million Americans are holding two or more jobs, the highest figure since data were first collected 25 years ago. Schor writes that U.S. manufacturing employees work 320 more hours per year than their German or French counterparts. She proposes, among other things, a government-mandated three-week paid vacation for all U.S. employees.[6]

I question Schor's statistics. If Americans are working more and more, how does she explain the explosion in money spent on sports and recreational activities in the United States?

How Capitalism Liberates Man

The critics of capitalism misunderstand the role of the market. Only through capitalism can savings and surplus wealth—the foundation of leisure time—be achieved. Capitalism provides very powerful incentives to produce an abundance of material goods in less and less time (and thus at lower costs), hence freeing up time to pursue other interests. Greater leisure time is an inherent feature of an advancing capitalist system. What people do with their leisure time is another issue—some may choose to work another job, others may play. "In our opportunity economy," write W. Michael Cox and Richard Alm, "some professionals, managers and entrepreneurs are putting in killer hours. But that's the choice they make, in return for higher pay and faster career advancement than they might otherwise have. For the rank and file, the work week has continued to shrink in recent decades. Average weekly hours of production workers declined from 39.8 in 1950 to 34.5 in 2000."[7] The following graph demonstrates the gradual decline in average work hours.

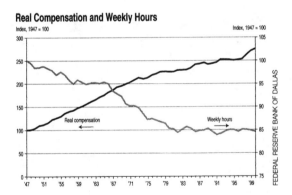

Real Compensation and Weekly Hours

Of course, America hasn't reach Bertrand Russell's goal of 20 work hours a week. In fact, average weekly hours have stagnated around 35 work hours over the past 20 years. Why? One reason ignored by Schor: Higher tax rates may be encouraging employees to work harder. A sharp cut in payroll taxes might reignite the downward trend in work hours. Schor should put that recommendation in her second edition.

1. Lin Yutang, *The Importance of Living* (New York: John Day, 1937), p. 148. Yutang's classic work on leisure has been reprinted in paperback by Quill.

2. Josef Pieper, *Leisure, The Basis of Culture* (Indianapolis: Liberty Fund, 1999 [1952]), pp. 28, 44–45.

3. See my essay "Easy Living: My Two Years in the Bahamas," originally published in *Liberty* magazine, December 1987, at www.mskousen.com.

4. Bertrand Russell, *In Praise of Idleness and Other Essays* (London: Unwin, 1976 [1935]), pp. 14, 22.

5. Lin Yutang, pp. 162–64.

6. Juliet B. Schor, *The Overworked American: The Unexpected Decline in Leisure* (New York: Basic Books, 1991).

7. W. Michael Cox and Richard Alm, "Have a Nice Day! The American Journey to Better Working Conditions," Federal Reserve Bank of Dallas, Annual Report 2000, p. 23. The Dallas Fed puts out the best annual reports (go to www.dallasfed.org).

Everything Is Cheap—and Getting Cheaper

"Capitalism is about turning luxuries into necessities."
—ANDREW CARNEGIE[1]

We all labor under the notion that the cost of living is high and rising every year. Yet, believe it or not, economic life is relatively inexpensive, and getting cheaper all the time.

This truth was reinforced recently when my friend and colleague Roger Clites told me about a little exercise he does regularly with his economics students. He first asks them whether college life is expensive or not. Most raise their hands. Then he asks the students to think of a good or service they regard as expensive. Last year one student responded, "Beer costs too much." Professor Clites assigned this student the task of making his own beer and bringing it to the next class. At the next meeting, the student confessed that it had cost him a great deal more to try to make a beer than to buy it in the store, and he still wasn't able to make it.

The point is simple but profound. Every day each of us profits handsomely from the specialization, knowledge, and abilities of millions of other individuals. Adam Smith called it the division of labor, which he regarded as the fundamental basis of capitalism. Without the work, expertise, and capital of others, our lifestyle would be profoundly barbaric. The opportunity cost of doing many tasks ourselves is so high that we must be grateful for the interactive market system we enjoy.

111

Economists often talk about negative externalities, such as air and water pollution caused by businesses that don't pay the full costs of production. Yet the number of positive externalities—benefits that we enjoy and that others create or pay for—are far more abundant.

Thus, compared to a situation in which each individual makes everything for himself, things are cheap. And that's not all.

The Real Standard of Living Is Rising . . .

Recently several studies have been published concluding that the real cost of living has been falling and the standard of living rising dramatically throughout the twentieth century in the United States. Even the poorer income classes have improved materially their economic condition under free enterprise.

I am a great fan of the work of Stanley Lebergott, professor emeritus of economics at Wesleyan University (see "The Rich Get Richer, And the Poor Get . . .," p. 100). His fascinating work *Pursuing Happiness: American Consumers in the Twentieth Century* (Princeton University Press, 1993) demonstrates that virtually all American consumers have been able to make an uncertain and often cruel world into a pleasanter and more convenient place to live and work. A typical homestead in 1900 had no central heating, electricity, refrigeration, flush toilets, or even running water. Today even a large majority of poor families benefit from these goods and services.[2]

. . . And the Real Cost of Living Is Declining

Now along come W. Michael Cox, an economist at the Federal Reserve Bank of Dallas, and Richard Alm, a business writer for the *Dallas Morning News,* who did an exhaustive study of the cost of basic goods and services in this century. They conclude that the real prices of housing, food, gasoline, electricity, telephone service, home appliances, clothing, and other everyday necessities have fallen significantly.

Examples: In 1919, it took two hours, 37 minutes of work to buy a three-pound chicken. Today, it's down to 14 minutes. In 1915, a three-minute long-distance telephone call from New York to San Francisco cost $20.70. Today, it's less than 50 cents, equal to two minutes of work at the average wage. In 1908, a Model T cost $850, equivalent to more than two years' wages for an average factory worker. Today, the average worker toils only about eight months to buy a Ford Taurus.

Many products have fallen dramatically in price (real, if not nominal) over the past 20 years, including computers, radios, stereos and color televisions, telephones, microwave ovens, gasoline, soft drinks, and most airline tickets. Cox and Alm do point to two exceptions: medical care and higher education. But even in these two cases, they argue that the medical care is better than it used to be, and that the higher costs of an education result in higher lifetime income.

Cox and Alm summarize, "As we enter the 21st century, Americans take for granted our ability to afford the trappings of the world's most envied middle-class lifestyle. It's the result of the decline of real prices in a dynamic economy, played out over and over."[3]

More and more Americans have benefited from an increase in the quantity, quality, and variety of goods and services because of the nature of the free-enterprise system: competition reduces costs, encourages new products and improved processes, and promotes quality improvements. In the labor market, increased productivity leads to higher wages, which allows workers to buy better, cheaper products.

Today the Poor Are Rich

Cox and Alm have also written a book with an intriguing title, *Myths of Rich and Poor*. Their research confirms the unorthodox view that the poor in America are catching up rapidly to the lifestyle of the rich. This perspective on the real cost of living goes counter to the conventional wisdom of most economists, who assert that the gap between rich and poor grew in the 1980s and 1990s. Perhaps it's time for economists to consider this new approach to measuring economic lifestyles.

With cheap financing, more and more poor people can afford a fully equipped home and automobile. They can have the best seat in the house for a ball game or concert through cable television.

They can travel to exotic lands or top vacation spots through discounted package fares. They can communicate with friends all over the world through cheap long-distance telephone service or e-mail. And they can find a wealth of information at their fingertips through the Internet.

The rich aren't so different after all.

---

1. Quoted in Paul Johnson, *A History of the American People* (New York: HarperCollins, 1997), p. 551. I highly recommend this new American history.

2. Also see Robert Rector, "America Has the World's Richest Poor People," *Wall Street Journal* (September 24, 1998).

3. Michael Cox and Richard G. Alm, "Buying Time," *Reason*, August/September 1998, p. 42. The full study is "Time Well Spent: The Declining Cost of Living in America, published in the 1997 Annual Report of the Federal Reserve Bank of Dallas.

In Defense of the Rich

"The substantial canons of the leisure-class scheme of life are
a conspicuous waste of time and substance and a withdrawal
from the industrial process."

—THORSTEIN VEBLEN[1]

E ver since Thorstein Veblen wrote *The Theory of the Leisure
Class* in 1899, wealthy Americans have been under assault.
Veblen had nothing good to say about the so-called idle rich and
robber barons—they were predatory, wasteful, and ostentatious.[2]
Politicians and Hollywood producers have followed up by por-
traying the rich as big spenders who use drugs, engage in
white-collar crime, avoid taxes, and dump their original mates in
favor of trophy wives.

But a study by Thomas J. Stanley, former professor of marketing at Georgia State University, shows that this pejorative image of
wealthy Americans is profoundly mistaken. According to his book
The Millionaire Mind millionaires are model citizens. Here are the
results of his survey of over 1,000 millionaires:

- They live far below their means and have little or no debt.
  Most pay off their credit cards every month; 40 percent have
  no home mortgage at all.
- They are frugal. They prepare shopping lists, resole their
  shoes, and save a lot of money. But they do not live Spartan
  lives.

- Ninety-seven percent are homeowners; they tend to live in fine homes in older neighborhoods. (Only 27 percent have ever built a custom home.)
- Ninety-two percent are married; only 2 percent are currently divorced. Millionaire couples have less than one-third the divorce rate of nonmillionaire couples. The typical couple in the millionaire group has been married for 28 years and has three children. Nearly 50 percent of the wives do not work outside the home.
- Most are one-generation millionaires who became wealthy as business owners or executives; they did not inherit wealth.
- Almost all are well educated: 90 percent are college graduates and 52 percent hold advanced degrees. However, few graduated top in their class; most were "B" students. They learned two lessons from college: discipline and tenacity.
- Most live balanced lives; they are not workaholics: 93 percent listed socializing with family members as their number-one activity; 45 percent play golf.
- Fifty-two percent attend church at least once a month, 37 percent consider themselves deeply religious.
- They share five basic ingredients to success: integrity, discipline, social skills, a supportive spouse, and hard work.
- Sixty-four percent contribute heavily to charity, church, and community activities.
- Their number one worry: taxes! Their average annual federal tax bill: $300,000. The top one-tenth of 1 percent of U.S. income earners pays 14.7 percent of all income taxes collected![3]
- "Not one millionaire had anything nice to say about gambling."[4] But 33 percent have played the lottery at least once during the year!

Thus we see how the upper-income families of this nation are not the ones contributing to crime, welfare, divorce, child abuse, and a spendthrift society. But they are paying a lot of taxes and making a lot of contributions to solve these social problems.

Low-Profile Living

Stanley is famous for his previous bestseller, *The Millionaire Next Door* (Pocket Books, 1998). His research revealed that most millionaires in America appear ordinary; they own modest homes and drive older cars. But they work hard, save a lot, and make their own investment decisions. In other words, the guy living next door may be a millionaire.

Although Stanley did not cover this issue, I've also seen studies indicating that higher-income individuals live, on average, five to ten years longer than the average American (76 years) and enjoy better health, fitness, and quality of life. They aren't the ones causing Medicare to go bankrupt.

The existence of a wealthy class provides numerous benefits to the entire economy:

• Wealthy people are the first to buy new consumer products. They are the only ones who can afford to buy automobiles, computers, cell phones, and other technological break-throughs when they are first introduced as high-priced prototypes. The profits from the wealthy consumers are used to expand operations and cut prices so that eventually everyone can afford them. As Andrew Carnegie said, "Capitalism is about turning luxuries into necessities." Inequality of income makes this possible.
• The wealthy class is the main source for investment capital. The rich provide the capital base for investing in new technologies, improved production processes, and job creation. Without the wealthy, there would be little surplus wealth for an expanding economy.
• The rich help finance higher education, libraries, churches, galleries, and charitable organizations.

Instead of bashing the rich, let's salute them. If indeed the wealthy are such good citizens, as Stanley's work suggests, we should aim not to impoverish the rich, but rather to enrich the poor.

1. Thorstein Veblen, *The Theory of the Leisure Class* (New York: Penguin Books, 1994 [1899]), p. 334.

2. For an excellent review of Veblen's philosophy, see John Patrick Diggins, *Thorstein Veblen: Theorist of the Leisure Class* (Princeton, N.J.: Princeton University Press, 1999 [1978]).

3. Thomas J. Stanley, *The Millionaire Mind* (Kansas City: Andrews McMeel, 2000), p. 375.

4. Ibid., p. 11.

Buddhist Economics and the Anti-Capitalistic Mentality

"In the excitement over the unfolding of his scientific and technical powers, modern man has built a system of production that ravishes nature and a type of society that mutilates man."

—E. F. SCHUMACHER[1]

In 1956, Ludwig von Mises countered myriad arguments against free enterprise in his insightful book *The Anti-Capitalistic Mentality.* "The great ideological conflict of our age," he wrote, "is, which of the two systems, capitalism or socialism, warrants a higher productivity of human efforts to improve people's standard of living."[2]

Unfortunately, Mises's counterattack has done little to stem the tide of anti-market sentiments. One that continues to be popular is E. F. Schumacher's 1973 book, *Small Is Beautiful,* which has been reprinted in an oversized text with commentaries by Paul Hawken and other admirers. Schumacher has a flourishing following, including Schumacher College (in Devon, England) and the Schumacher Society (in Great Barrington, Massachusetts). Hawken hails Schumacher as a visionary and author of "the most important book of [his] life."[3] Schumacher's message appeals to environmentalists, self-reliant communitarians, and advocates of "sustainable" growth (but not feminists—the old-fashioned Schumacher cited favorably the Buddhist view that "large-scale

119

employment of women in offices or factories would be a sign of economic failure"[4]).

From Austrian to Marxist to Buddhist

Oddly enough, Fritz Schumacher's background is tied to the Austrians. Schumacher was born in Germany in 1911 and took a class from Joseph Schumpeter in the late 1920s in Bonn. It was Schumpeter's course that convinced Schumacher to become an economist. While visiting England on a Rhodes scholarship in the early 1930s, Schumacher encountered F. A. Hayek at the London School of Economics and even wrote an article on "Inflation and the Structure of Production."[5] But his flirtation with Austrian economics ended when he discovered Keynes and Marx. He renounced his Christian heritage and became a "revolutionary socialist." The Nazi threat forced him to live in London, where he was "interned" as an "enemy alien" during World War II. After the war, he worked with Keynes and Sir William Beveridge and supported the nationalization of heavy industry in both Britain and Germany. But his real change of heart came during a visit to Burma in 1955, when he was converted to Buddhism. "The Burmese lived simply. They had few wants and they were happy," he commented. "It was wants that made a man poor and this made the role of the West very dangerous."[6]

Schumacher greatly admired Mahatma Gandhi and his saying, "Earth provides enough to satisfy every man's need, but not for every man's greed." Eventually he wrote a series of essays that became his classic, *Small Is Beautiful,* published in 1973. In the 1970s, he became passionate about trees and began a campaign against deforestation. After a successful book tour in the United States, including a visit with President Jimmy Carter, he died in 1977 of an apparent heart attack.

The Lure of Buddhist Economics

Schumacher's message is Malthusian in substance. *Small Is Beautiful* denounces big cities and big business, which "dehumanizes" the economy, strips the world of "nonrenewable" resources, and makes people too materialistic and overspecialized. According to Schumacher, individuals are better off working in smaller units and with less technology.

His most important chapter is "Buddhist Economics," with its emphasis on "right livelihood" and "the maximum of well-being with the minimum of consumption." Foreign trade does not fit into a Buddhist economy: "to satisfy human wants from faraway places rather than from sources nearby signifies failure rather than success."[7] In sum, traditional Buddhism rejects labor-saving machinery, assembly-line production, large-scale multinational corporations, foreign trade, and the consumer society.

There are two problems with Schumacher's glorification of Buddhist economics. First, it denies an individual's freedom to choose a capitalistic mode of production; it enslaves everyone in a life of "nonmaterialistic" values. And second, it clearly results in a primitive economy. Mises responded to both these issues: "What separates East and West is . . . the fact that the peoples of the East never conceived the idea of liberty. . . . The age of capitalism has abolished all vestiges of slavery and serfdom." And: "It may be true that there are among Buddhist mendicants, living on alms in dirt and penury, some who feel perfectly happy and do not envy any nabob. However, it is a fact that for the immense majority of people such a life would be unbearable."[8]

I have no objection to preaching the Buddhist value that sees "the essence of civilization not in a multiplication of wants but in the purification of human character." Nor do I disapprove of localized markets (see my favorable comments on the Grameen Bank, which makes small-scale loans to the poor, p. 61). But none of this idealism should be forced on any society. Ultimately we must let people choose their own patterns of work and enjoyment. Clearly, whenever Third World countries have been given their economic freedom, the vast majority have chosen capitalistic means of production and consumption. As a result, poor people have been given hope for the first time in their lives—a chance for their families to break away from the drudgery of hard labor, to become educated, see the world, and enjoy "right living."

Freedom is beautiful!

---

1. E. F. Schumacher, *Small Is Beautiful: Economics as if People Mattered: 25 Years Later with Commentary* (Point Roberts, Wash.: Hartley & Marks, 1999 [1973]), p. 248.

2. Ludwig von Mises, *The Anti-Capitalistic Mentality* (South Holland, Ill.: Libertarian Press, 1972 [1956]), p. 62.

3. Paul Hawken, Introduction to Schumacher, p. xiii.

4. Ibid., p. 40.

5. See *The Economics of Inflation*, ed. by H. P. Willis and J. M. Chapman (New York: Columbia University Press, 1935).

6. Quoted in Barbara Wood, E. F. *Schumacher: His Life and Thought* (New York: Harper & Row, 1984), p. 245.

7. Schumacher, p. 42.

8. Mises, p. 74.

Is Greed Good?

> "Unbridled avarice is not in the least the equivalent of capitalism, still less its 'spirit'."
>
> —Max Weber[1]

Greed has become a popular term of endearment. There was even briefly a TV game show by that name. In 1987, Oliver Stone released a popular movie called *Wall Street,* in which Gordon Gekko, the fictional dealmaker extraordinaire, declares, "Greed is good."

In the 1990s, as capitalism, technology, and the financial markets advanced, some free-market economists defended Gekko's speech, arguing that the pursuit of greed is beneficial and an integral feature of market capitalism. It motivates individuals to work harder, to create new and better products. As Bernard Mandeville wrote in *The Fable of the Bees* (1714), the private vices of greed, avarice, and luxury lead to abundant wealth.

On the other hand, critics of capitalism, from Thorstein Veblen to John Kenneth Galbraith, have long argued that capitalism unleashes greed, creating greater inequality, alienation, and deception in society. Capitalism is, in short, morally corrupting, both for the individual and business.

Which view is more accurate?

Part of the problem is in the definition of the word. If greed simply means enthusiastically pursuing one's self-interest, there is no harm in it and a great deal of good. Unfortunately, greed carries excessive baggage beyond honest initiative. Webster's Dictionary

123

defines greed as "excessive desire for acquiring or having." A greedy person "wants to eat and drink too much" or "desires more than one needs or deserves." This conjures up passages of conspicuous consumption from Veblen's *Theory of the Leisure Class*, or scenes of the miserly banker foreclosing on the poor in Frank Capra's film *It's a Wonderful Life*. Is that what capitalism leads to?

Greed is no virtue in the financial markets. Too many inexperienced, gullible investors get caught up in the latest hot market, only to buy in at the top. As J. Paul Getty warns, "The big profits go to the intelligent, careful and patient investor, not to the reckless and overeager speculator."[2]

Montesquieu to the Rescue

In researching my book *The Making of Modern Economics*, I uncovered several economic thinkers who make an important contribution to this issue. Charles de Montesquieu (1689–1755) was the first major figure during the Enlightenment to maintain that commercial activity restrains greed and other passions. In his classic work, *The Spirit of the Laws* (1748), Montesquieu expressed the novel view that the business of moneymaking serves as a countervailing bridle against the violent passions of war and abusive political power. "Commerce cures destructive prejudices," he declared. "It polishes and softens barbarous mores. . . . The natural effect of commerce is to lead to peace."[3] Commerce improves society: "The spirit of commerce brings with it the spirit of frugality, of economy, of moderation, of work, of wisdom, of tranquility, of order, and of regularity."[4]

Adam Smith (1723–90) held similar views. He wrote eloquently of the public benefits of pursuing one's private self-interest, but he was no apologist for unbridled greed. Smith disapproved of private gain if it meant defrauding or deceiving someone in business. To quote Smith: "But man has almost constant occasion for the help of his brethren. . . . He will be more likely to prevail if he can interest their self-love in his favour. . . . Give me that which I want, and you shall have this which you want, is the meaning of every such offer."[5] In other words, all legitimate exchanges must benefit both the buyer and the seller, not one at the expense of the other.

Smith's model of natural liberty reflects this essential attribute: "Every man, *as long as he does not violate the laws of justice,* is left perfectly free to pursue his own interest his own way, and to bring both his industry and capital into competition with those of any other man, or order of men."[6]

Smith favored enlightened self-interest and even self-restraint. Indeed, he firmly believed that a free commercial society moderated the passions and prevented a descent into a Hobbesian jungle, a theme echoing Montesquieu. He taught that commerce encourages people to defer gratification and to become educated, industrious, and self-disciplined. It is the fear of losing customers "which retrains his frauds and corrects his negligence."[7]

Finally, Smith supported social institutions—the competitive marketplace, religious communities, and the law—to foster self-control, self-discipline, and benevolence.[8]

In sum, no system can eliminate greed, fraud, or violence. Socialism and communitarian organizations promise paradise, but seldom deliver. Oddly enough, it may be a freely competitive capitalist economy that can best foster self-discipline and control of the passions.

---

1. Quoted in Jerry Z. Muller, *Adam Smith in His Time and Ours* (Princeton, N.J.: Princeton University Press, 1993), p. 194.

2. J. Paul Getty, *How to Be Rich* (New York: Jove Books, 1965), p. 154. This book is required reading for all investors.

3. Charles de Montesquieu, *The Spirit of the Laws* (Cambridge: Cambridge University Press, 1989), p. 338.

4. Quoted in Albert O. Hirschman, *The Passions and the Interests* (Princeton, N.J.: Princeton University Press, 1997), p. 71. I highly recommend this book on pre-Smithian views of capitalism.

5. Adam Smith, *The Wealth of Nations* (New York: Modern Library, 1965), p. 14.

6. Ibid., p. 651. Italics added.

7. Ibid., p. 129.

8. Muller, p. 2.

The Mother of All Myths

"Analysts watch consumer spending closely because it represents roughly two-thirds of all economic activity."

—*Associated Press*

In the early 1990s, in the depths of the recession, Range Rover, a British maker of sports-utility vehicles, ran an unusual ad in *USA Today*. It announced its formula for ending the downturn: "Buy Something." Of course, Range Rover wanted you to buy their car, but in any case, purchase something. "Buy a microwave, a basset hound, theater tickets, a Tootsie Roll, something." Anything to get the economy moving again.

In late 1991, Federal Reserve chairman Alan Greenspan suggested that the economic contraction was caused in part by retrenchment in consumer and business debt during the early 1990s. The implication is that the economy could be on its way to recovery if only consumers and business would start spending again, even if it meant spending beyond their means.

Finally, in 2001, President George W. Bush urged taxpayers to use their tax rebate to buy a car or other consumer good rather than put the money in a savings or investment account.

Falling Under the Keynesian Spell

For decades, members of the media, the financial community and the government have fallen under the Keynesian spell, emphasizing the importance of demand over supply, of deficits over sur-

126

pluses, of debt over equity, and of consumption over saving. For them, the key to prosperity is found in encouraging a high level of consumption, even if it means going deeply into debt. The establishment press is so enamored with consumption that it highlights monthly changes in consumer spending, consumer debt, consumer prices, and surveys of consumer confidence, looking for any encouraging signs. After all, doesn't consumer spending represent two thirds of total economic activity?

Pro-Consumption Mischief

Well, no, it doesn't. The idea that consumption is the largest sector of the economy is based on a grave misreading of Gross Domestic Product (GDP).

According to recent data, consumption expenditures represents 66.1 percent of GDP, or approximately two thirds. Government purchases are second at 18.3 percent, and investment, which includes residential housing, comes in third at 15.6 percent. Business fixed investment is only 11.5 percent of GDP. By making the standard assumption that GDP measures total economic activity, the unsophisticated journalist has concluded that consumer and government spending are by far the most important sectors of the economy, while investment rates a poor third.

Much mischief in government policy has arisen in consequence of this misinterpretation of national income statistics. Many lawmakers have passed legislation encouraging consumption at the expense of investment. At the same time, they see no reason to cut capital gains taxes or corporate income taxes, since the business investment sector appears to be relatively small and unimportant.

The Source of the Fallacy

What's gone awry? The source of the error is that GDP is *not* a measure of total economic activity. As anyone who has taken Econ 101 knows, GDP measures the purchase *of final* goods and services only. GDP deliberately leaves out spending by business in all the intermediate stages of production before the retail market. It does not include spending by natural resource companies, manufacturers, and wholesalers. Obviously, financial journalists need a refresher course in economics.

In sum, GDP does not measure total spending in the U.S. economy, only final retail purchases by consumers, business, and government.

Introducing a More Accurate Statistic

To determine total economic activity, we need to look at Gross Domestic Expenditures (GDE), a statistic I developed in my book *The Structure of Production* (New York University Press, 1990). It measures gross expenditures at all stages of production, from raw commodities to finished products. Based on the input-output data prepared by the U.S. Commerce Department, I estimate that consumption expenditures actually represent only about one-third of economic activity in the United States, not two-thirds as is commonly reported. Moreover, gross investment by business represents the majority (52 percent) of total spending in the economy if you add together gross intermediate expenditures, business fixed investment, and residential housing. Government purchases represent the remainder, or 11 percent.

This new statistic, GDE, provides a more complete indicator of total economic activity. As such, it suggests a far different interpretation of how the world works. In fact, we come to the opposite conclusion: Investment is far more important than consumption. The U.S. economy, like all economies, is investment-driven, not consumption-driven. Consumption is ultimately the effect, not the cause, of a nation's prosperity.

An individual becomes wealthy by producing and investing first, then increasing his consumption—not the other way around. To go on a spending spree using credit cards or other forms of debt may initially give the impression of a higher standard of living, but eventually the individual must pay the piper or face bankruptcy. The same principle applies to a nation as a whole.

"But," retort the big spenders, "if consumers stop buying, business will eventually stop producing." Granted, the whole purpose of production is eventual consumption. Per capita consumption is usually a reasonable measure of national well-being, and business must be responsive to consumer needs. But the real question is, how do we *improve* our standard of living? There is only one proven way, and that is by raising the amount of capital invested per worker. Economic progress is achieved when business increases its profits by providing customers with better products at cheaper prices. That requires a direct investment in capital. Those who postpone consumption now and invest their savings productively will be rewarded with higher consumption later.

Consumer Spending Not a Leading Indicator

If the U.S. economy is consumption-driven, why aren't retail sales a leading indicator of economic activity? Of the eleven components in the U.S. Department of Commerce's Index of Leading Indicators, only one, the Consumer Expectations Index, is directly linked to future retail sales. The other leading indicators are almost entirely related to capital investment and earlier stages of production, such as manufacturers' orders, sensitive materials' prices, contracts for plant and equipment, and stock prices.

Retail sales are in reality an unreliable indicator of where the economy and the stock market are headed. Industrial output is a much better forecaster. And, contrary to what the national media often reports, retail sales are relatively stable compared to industrial production, just as, consumer prices are nowhere near as volatile as commodity prices. Financial analysts seeking to pinpoint changes in the direction of the economy and the stock market will be disappointed if they rely entirely on retail sales as a guide.

The Crisis in Productivity and Investment

Stimulating consumer spending in the short run will undoubtedly encourage some lines of investment. If people go on a buying spree at a local grocery store or mall, merchants and their suppliers will see their profits go up. But the consumer spending binge will do little or nothing to construct a bridge, build a hospital, pay for a research program to cure cancer, or provide funds for a new invention or a new production process. Only a higher level of saving will do that. Thus, in nations following Keynesian pro-consumption policies, it is not surprising to see luxurious retail stores and malls along side dilapidated roads and infrastructure. Their consumption/investment ratio is systematically out of balance. Peter Drucker chastises the United States and other Keynesian industrial nations for a "crisis in productivity and capital formation" and "underinvesting on a massive scale."[1] The current administration has done little to reverse this trend.

Saving, investing, and capital formation are the principal ingredients of economic growth. Countries with the highest growth rates (most recently in Southeast Asia and Latin America) are those that encourage saving and investing, i.e., investing in new production processes, education, technology, and labor-saving devices. Such investing in turn results in better consumer products at lower prices. They do not seek to artificially promote consumption at the expense of saving. Stimulating the economy through excessive consumption or wasteful government programs may provide artificial recovery in the short run, but cannot lead to genuine prosperity in the long run.

Using our new statistic, GDE, we now see that cutting taxes on business and investments (interest, dividends, and capital gains) will have a dramatically favorable effect, far more than previously thought. When business investment represents 52 percent of the economy, not 15 percent, reducing investment taxes can have a multiplying impact on the nation's economy.

In sum, it is capital investment, not consumer spending, that ultimately drives the economy. As economist Ludwig von Mises declared 40 years ago, "Progressive capital accumulation results in perpetual economic betterment."[2]

---

1. Peter Drucker, *Toward the Next Economics and Other Essays* (New York: Harper & Row, 1981), p. 8.

2. Ludwig von Mises, "Capital Supply and American Prosperity," *Planning for Freedom*, 4th ed. (Spring Mills, Pa.: Libertarian Press, 1980), p. 197.

Say's Law Is Back

"Keynes . . . misunderstood and misrepresented Say's Law.
. . . This is Keynes's most enduring legacy and it is a legacy
which has disfigured economic theory to this day."
—STEVEN KATES[1]

I recently came across a remarkable book by Australian economist
Steven Kates, *Say's Law and the Keynesian Revolution*. According to Kates, John Maynard Keynes created a straw man in order to
produce a revolution in economics. The straw man was Jean-Baptiste Say and his famous law of markets. Steven Kates calls *The
General Theory* "a book-length attempt to refute Say's Law."

But to refute Say's Law, Keynes gravely distorted it. As Kates
states, "Keynes was wrong in his interpretation of Say's Law and,
more importantly, he was wrong about its economic implications."[2]

How Keynes Got It Wrong

In the introduction to the 1939 French edition of *The General
Theory*, Keynes focused on Say's Law as the central issue of
macroeconomics. "I believe that economics everywhere up to
recent times has been dominated . . . by the doctrines associated
with the name of J.-B. Say. It is true that his 'law of markets' has
long been abandoned by most economists; but they have not extricated themselves from his basic assumptions and particularly from

131

his fallacy that demand is created by supply. . . . Yet a theory so based is clearly incompetent to tackle the problems of unemployment and of the trade cycle."

Unfortunately, Keynes failed to understand Say's Law. By incorrectly stating it as "supply creates its own demand," he proposed, in effect, that Say meant that everything produced is automatically bought. Hence, Say's Law cannot explain the business cycle.[3]

Keynes went on to say that the classical model under Say's Law "assumes full employment." Other Keynesians have continued to make this point, but nothing could be further from the truth. Conditions of unemployment do not prohibit production and sales from taking place that form the basis of new income and new demand.

Moreover, Say's Law specifically formed the basis of a classical theory of the business cycle and unemployment. As Kates states, "The classical position was that involuntary unemployment was not only possible, but occurred often, and with serious consequences for the unemployed."[4]

Production and Consumption

Exactly what is Say's Law? Chapter 15 of Say's *A Treatise on Political Economy* describes his famous law of markets: "A product is no sooner created, than it, from that instant, affords a market for other products to the full extent of its own value."[5] When a seller produces and sells a product, the seller instantly becomes a buyer who has spendable income. To buy, one must first sell. In other words, production is the cause of consumption, and increased output leads to higher consumer spending.

In short, Say's Law is this: The supply (sale) of X creates the demand for (purchase of) Y.

Say illustrated his law with the case of a good harvest by a farmer. "The greater the crop, the larger are the purchases of the growers. A bad harvest, on the contrary, hurts the sale of commodities at large."[6]

Say has a point. According to business-cycle statistics, when a downturn starts, production is the first to decline, ahead of consumption. And when the economy begins to recover, it's because production starts up, followed by consumption. Economic growth begins with an increase in productivity, new products, and new markets. Hence, production spending is always ahead of consumption spending.

We can see why this is the case on an individual basis. The key to a higher standard of living is, first, an increase in your income, that is, your productivity, either by getting a raise, changing jobs, going back to school, or starting a money-making business. It would be foolish to achieve a higher standard of living by spending savings or going into debt to buy a bigger house or new automobile before you increase your productivity. You may be able to live high on the hog for a while, but eventually you will have to pay the piper . . . or the credit card bill.

According to Say, the same principle applies to nations. The creation of new and better products opens up new markets and increases consumption. Hence, "the encouragement of mere consumption is no benefit to commerce; for the difficulty lies in supplying the means, not in stimulating the desire of consumption; and we have seen that production alone, furnishes those means." Then Say added, "Thus, it is the aim of good government to stimulate production, of bad government to encourage consumption." [7]

The Cause of the Business Cycle

Say's Law states that recessions are not caused by failure of demand (Keynes's thesis), but by failure in the structure of supply and demand. Recession is precipitated by producers miscalculating what consumers wish to buy, thus causing unsold goods to pile up, production to be cut back, income to fall, and finally consumer spending to drop. As Kates elucidates, "Classical theory explained recessions by showing how errors in production might arise during cyclical upturns which would cause some goods to remain unsold at cost-covering prices." The classical model was a "high-sophisticated theory of recession and unemployment" that with one fell swoop by the illustrious Keynes was "obliterated." [8]

In his broad-based book, Kates highlights other classical economists, including David Ricardo, James Mill, Robert Torrens, Henry Clay, Frederick Lavington, and Wilhelm Röpke, who extended Say's Law. Many classical economists focused on how monetary inflation exacerbated the business cycle. They were precursors of the Austrians Ludwig von Mises and F.A. Hayek.

Free-market economists, such as W. H. Hutt and Thomas Sowell, have tried to rehabilitate Say's Law, but none carries the punch of Steven Kates.

1. Steven Kates, *Say's Law and the Keynesian Revolution* (Northampton, Mass.: Edward Elgar, 1998), p. 1.

2. Ibid., p. 212.

3. John Maynard Keynes, *The General Theory of Employment, Interest and Money* (London: Macmillan, 1936), pp. 25–26.

4. Kates, p. 18.

5. Jean-Baptiste Say, *A Treatise on Political Economy* (New York: Augustus M. Kelley, 1971 [1832]), p. 134.

6. Ibid., p. 135.

7. Ibid., p. 139.

8. Kates, pp. 18, 19, 20.

An Ignoble Prize
in Economics

"No sovereign government can be bankrupt as a result of debt in its own currency."
—ROBERT EISNER, *New York Times*, MARCH 19, 1994

Back in 1994 I nominated Robert Eisner, economics professor at Northwestern University and former president of the American Economic Association, for that year's Ignoble Prize in Economics. Eisner's article in the *Times*, aptly entitled "Off Balance," achieves a unique status in economic history. It contains more errors per column than any editorial ever published! I counted 15 mistakes, miscalculations, and misconceptions in the article, amounting to one error per column inch.

The subject is the federal deficit, Eisner's pet peeve. In his mind, and in the eyes of most of his colleagues, there is no deficit crisis. Never mind that the national debt has reached an astronomical $4.4 trillion, increasing at an average compounded growth rate of 7 percent over the past 40 years. Don't worry that the federal government has irresponsibly failed to balance its books since 1969. Don't concern yourself with the fact that interest payments account for nearly 20 percent of federal revenues, a percentage that will invariably increase as interest rates rise. According to Eisner & Co., the deficit is no economic time bomb, it's a false alarm.

135

The Federal Debt: Asset or Liability?

Some of Eisner's statements are fantastically naïve. For example: "The greater a person's debt, given his assets, the less his net worth; the greater the Government's debt, the greater the people's net worth."

Say again? Eisner ought to get out of his ivory tower and go down to the Chicago Board of Trade, where T-bonds trade. He would learn that his assertion is only true if the price of government securities stays constant or increases. Yet, as bondholders painfully discovered in 1994, prices of Treasury securities can fall sharply in the face of rising inflationary expectations. Indeed, excessive deficit spending can drive up interest rates and accelerate the collapse in bonds, as the inflationary 1970s demonstrated.

The Potential for National Bankruptcy

No sovereign government can be bankrupt as a result of debt in its own currency? Perhaps Eisner should stop by the history department at Northwestern and obtain a list of governments whose debt markets have collapsed over the centuries due to runaway inflation: Germany, Austria, France, Hungary, China, Brazil, and Peru, just to name a few.

Eisner will undoubtedly be surprised to learn that there is no bond market in *cruzeiros* in hyperinflating Brazil. Like many Latin American countries, Brazil can only finance its borrowing in U.S. dollars or other foreign currencies. Even then, many Third World governments defaulted on their dollar debts in the 1980s. Refinancing and moratoriums are technical terms for bankruptcy. Textbook writers Edwin G. Dolan and David E. Lindsey soberly declare the reality of the matter: "Creating new money to cover the government deficit is the source of runaway inflation, at rates of hundreds or even thousands of percent per year, that devastated such countries as Bolivia, Argentina, Brazil, and Israel in the early 1980s."[1]

Eisner's statement, "Government's debt is the liquid assets of the American people," is true today but may not be true tomorrow. Those "assets" can quickly lose value and become illiquid in a collapsing bond market. In fact, in the 1970s, Treasuries lost half their real value and occasionally faced "no bid" days. There are many scenarios which could bring about another round of "no bids" on T-bonds and even T-bills. A devastating recession, a collapsing dollar overseas, resurging inflation, a debilitating war, loss of tax base, etc. Washington has done a good marketing job in encouraging millions of Americans including conservatives who normally oppose deficit spending, to buy "savings" bonds and Treasury securities, but the Treasury market could face a treacherous future if U.S. finances get out of hand or the economy crumbles. Given the high level and short-term maturity of federal debt, trouble could arise unexpectedly.

I would agree with Eisner on one point. National bankruptcy is not imminent. As Adam Smith once said, "There is much ruin in a nation." We have a long way to go before the government runs out of its ability to dupe the American public into funding the deficit. The timetable in Harry Figgie's bestselling book, *Bankruptcy 1995* (Little, Brown, 1993), has been proven way off the mark. The federal deficit declined last year and is nowhere near the $730 billion level Figgie predicted for fiscal year 1994. Nor are the country's finances in such dire shape that a fiscal crisis can't be averted. A healthy tax cut, privatization, and a couple of years of budget surpluses would do wonders to the economy. Mexico was in far worse shape than the United States was in the 1980s, and it turned itself around. Today it is running a budget surplus.

Crowding Out and Economic Malaise

Right now the more serious effect of deficit spending is on economic growth. When billions of dollars in private savings are funneled each year into government coffers via the purchase of Treasury securities and U.S. savings bonds, economic growth suffers. Even Paul Samuelson, a fellow Keynesian, acknowledges this fact: "Perhaps the most serious consequence of a large public debt is that it displaces capital from the nation's stock of wealth. As a result, the pace of economic growth slows and future living standards will decline."[2]

Fiscal mismanagement is one major reason U.S. economic growth has been near the bottom of industrial nations since World

War II. Inflation and high taxes discourage saving, investment, and capital formation. By law, Social Security and other federal trust funds must invest solely in government securities. Imagine the favorable impact on Wall Street if $1 trillion in Social Security and other trust funds could be invested in U.S. stocks and bonds!

Crowding out is real. The Treasury market has grown so rapidly that it is now the world's largest financial market and as such systematically undermines the ability of private corporations to raise the capital necessary to produce new goods and services, adopt new technology and production processes, and create jobs. Today federal, state, and local governments consume 85 percent of all new debt issues, forcing major private corporations to issue so-called "junk" bonds and pay 300 to 400 basis points above Treasury rates to raise much needed capital. "Junk" bonds are an unfortunate label imposed on a form of financing that has been responsible for much job creation and economic growth.[3] The real junk bonds are the Treasury securities, which transfer massive amounts of capital from the productive profit centers of free enterprise to the unproductive, unprofitable centers of government waste.

Crowding Out or Crowding In?

Of course, Eisner, the last of the Old Keynesians, rejects the notion of crowding out. He believes in "crowding in," that "greater spending means increases in sales, profits, orders for production and hiring of workers." Those are the *visible* signs of government spending, but what are the *invisible* effects? As Frédéric Bastiat once said, "There is only one difference between a bad economist and a good one: the bad economist confines himself to the *visible* effect; the good economist takes into account both the effect that can be seen and those effects that must be foreseen." If the federal government is doing the spending, that means there are fewer funds available for free enterprise to buy, produce, and hire. And if the spending is monetized by the central bank, the result is inflation. There is no free lunch, Professor Eisner.

The Growing Threat

Hans Sennholz best sums up the ill-effects of deficit financing and the potential for serious harm: "At first, [federal debt] may consume only a small share of the individual savings coming to market, causing a slowdown in capital formation and economic development. In time, the share consumed by its apparatus of politics tends to grow until it depletes all savings and causes economic progress to grind to a halt. In a final frenzy of spending, it may actually consume capital accumulated by previous generations, and thus cause economic conditions to deteriorate."[4]

Let's hope we never reach the final stage Professor Sennholz describes. But if too many political leaders buy the arguments of Robert Eisner and become complacent about fiscal irresponsibility, it could become a reality.

---

1. Edwin G. Dolan and David E. Lindsey, *Economics,* 5th ed. (Hinsdale, Ill.: Dryden Press, 1988), p. 280. Dolan and Lindsey's textbook is one of the few textbooks which acknowledge the possibility of national bankruptcy.

2. Paul A. Samuelson and William D. Nordhaus, *Economics,* 14th ed. (New York: McGraw Hill, 1992), p. 633.

3. An dispassionate assessment of the high-yielding corporate bond market can be found in Glenn Yago, *Junk Bonds* (New York: Oxford University Press, 1991).

4. Hans F. Sennholz, *Debts and Deficits* (Spring Mills, Pa.: Libertarian Press, 1987), p. 76.

Are Financial Markets
Inherently Unstable?

"There is an urgent need to recognize that financial markets, far from trending towards equilibrium, are inherently unstable."

—GEORGE SOROS[1]

In the aftermath of the collapse of emerging economies in Asia, eastern Europe, and Latin America, many prominent economists and speculators, from Paul Krugman to George Soros, called for government intervention in financial markets. Recommended policies include monetary inflation and currency controls. The foundation of such state interference is the belief that free markets in general, and financial markets in particular, are inherently unstable and require strict government regulation.

The fathers of this thesis are the British economist John Maynard Keynes and his principal heir, Hyman P. Minsky, who devised a "financial instability hypothesis." Minsky, a Harvard-taught economist, wrote many books and articles during his academic career of nearly 50 years, most of which he spent at Washington University in St. Louis. He died in 1996.

According to Minsky, Keynes's general theory of the economy was really a financial theory of uncertainty and expectations. According to this thesis, the capitalist economy is primarily ruled by Wall Street, which is fundamentally fragile and destabilizing owing to excessive debt, lax government rules, and businessmen's "animal spirits" and "waves of irrational psychology." (Conservative economist Allan H. Meltzer of Carnegie Mellon University makes the same point.[2])

In the Keynes-Minsky model, full employment in an unregulated market economy is not a natural equilibrium point, but a transitory moment in a business cycle. Euphoric expectations lead to an overleveraged condition where the rate of credit expansion exceeds the rate of profit in the economy. Eventually, the boom turns into a debt deflation and depression.

Long-Run Damage by Government Intervention

To stabilize the business cycle, Keynesians favor big-government capitalism where central banks and the International Monetary Fund play major roles as lenders of last resort. Keynes advocated the "socialization of investment" and taxes on short-term trading.[3] However, Minsky rightly pointed out that interventionist policies validate the existing fragile financial structure and allow the problems to deepen. He warned that "Once borrowers and lenders recognize that the downside instability of profits has decreased there will be an increase in the willingness and ability of business and bankers to debt-finance."[4] Larger and more frequent interventions become necessary to fend off debt deflations and recessions.

Minsky correctly criticized neoclassical economics for largely minimizing the impact that financial markets can have on economies: "The neo-classical synthesis became the economics of capitalism without capitalists, capital assets, and financial markets."[5]

My only problem with Minsky is that he mistakenly blames the market itself for its instability.

Mises's Non-Neutrality Thesis

To understand the root cause of financial and economic instability, we need to go back to Ludwig von Mises's "non-neutrality" thesis in his breakthrough work, *The Theory of Money and Credit*. Mises pointed out that monetary intervention (easy money policies and artificial lowering of interest rates) is the principal source of uncertainty, false expectations, and excessive debt-leverage in the economy and on Wall Street. Under a stable monetary system, a laissez-faire economy would suffer occasional financial mishaps, bankruptcies, and down-days on Wall Street, but there would be no systematic "cluster of errors" that currently characterize today's global economy.[6] Fortunately, most economists now recognize that government's monetary and fiscal policies are the main source of economic and financial instability in the world today. In fact, more and more college textbooks teach up front that the economy is relatively stable at full employment; this is known as the "long-term growth model." The short-term Keynesian model is taught at the end of the textbooks, where government intervention is recognized as a destabilizing factor in the economy and the chief cause of the boom-bust cycle. See Roy Ruffin and Paul Gregory's *Principles of Economics* and N. Gregory Mankiw's *Economics*.

Maybe George Soros needs to take a refresher course from these textbooks.

1. George Soros, remarks before the House Banking Committee Hearing on International Economic Turmoil, September 15, 1998.

2. Allan H. Meltzer, *Keynes's Monetary Theory: A Different Interpretation* (Cambridge: Cambridge University Press, 1968).

3. John Maynard Keynes, *The General Theory of Employment, Money and Interest* (London: Macmillan, 1936), chapter 12, "The State of Long-Term Expectation." See also my article, "Keynes as a Speculator: A Critique of Keynesian Investment Theory," *Dissent on Keynes* (New York: Praeger, 1992), pp. 161–69.

4. Hyman P. Minsky, *Stabilizing an Unstable Economy* (New Haven: Yale University Press, 1986), p. 213.

5. Ibid., p. 120. For a favorable review of Minsky's work, see Robert Pollin, "The Relevance of Hyman Minsky," *Challenge* (March/April 1997), pp. 75–94.

6. Ludwig von Mises, *The Theory of Money and Credit* (Indianapolis: Liberty Classics, 1981 [1934]). See especially Murray Rothbard's excellent foreword in this edition.

The Mysteries of the Great Depression Finally Solved

"The depression . . . was endemic to the system: the economy
was not self-regulating and needed to be controlled."
—DAVID COLANDER AND HARRY LANDRETH[1]

The Great Depression of the 1930s may be a dim memory now,
but its impact is still being felt in policy and theory. The prolonged depression created an environment critical of laissez-faire
policies and favorable toward ubiquitous state interventionism
throughout the Western world. The depression led to the Welfare
State and boundless faith in Big Government. It caused most of the
Anglo-American economics profession to question classical free-
market economics and to search for radical anti-capitalist alterna-
tives, eventually converting to the new economics of Keynesianism
and demand-side economics.

Prior to the Great Depression, most Western economists
accepted the classical virtues of thrift, limited government, balanced budgets, the gold standard, and Say's Law. While most
economists continued to defend free enterprise and free trade on a
microeconomic scale, they rejected traditional views on a macroeconomic level in the postwar period, advocating consumption
over saving, fiat money over the gold standard, deficit spending
over a balanced budget, and active state interventionism over limited government. They bought the Keynesian argument that a free

market was inherently unstable and could result in high levels of unemployed labor and resources for indefinite periods. They blamed the Great Depression on laissez-faire capitalism and contended that only massive government spending during World War II saved the capitalist system from defeat. In short, the depression opened the door to widespread collectivism in the United States and around the world.

Fortunately, free-market economists have gradually punctured holes in these arguments and the pendulum has slowly shifted toward a re-establishment of classical free-market economics. Three questions needed to be addressed: What caused the Great Depression? Why did it last so long? Did World War II restore prosperity? Economic historian Robert Higgs had dubbed these three arenas of debate the Great Contraction, the Great Duration, and the Great Escape.

The Cause of the Great Contraction

Many free-market economists had attempted to answer the first question, including Benjamin M. Anderson and Murray N. Rothbard,[2] but none had the impact equal to Milton Friedman's empirical studies on money in the early 1960s. His was the first effective effort to destroy the argument that the Great Depression was the handiwork of an inherently unstable capitalistic system. Friedman (and his co-author, Anna J. Schwartz) demonstrated forcefully that it was not free enterprise, but rather government—specifically the Federal Reserve System—that caused the Great Depression. In a single sentence underlined by all who read it, Friedman and Schwartz indicted the Fed: "From the cyclical peak in August 1929 to a cyclical trough in March 1933, the stock of money fell by over a third."[3] (This statement was all the more shocking because until Friedman's work, the Fed didn't publish money supply figures, such as M1 and M2!)

Friedman and Schwartz also proved that the gold standard did not cause the depression, as some Keynesian economists have alleged. During the early 1930s, the U.S. gold stock rose even as the Fed perversely raised the discount rate and allowed the money supply to shrink and banks to collapse.[4]

The Prolonged Slump

Economic activity and employment stagnated throughout the 1930s, causing a paradigm shift from classical economics to Keynesianism. Friedrich Hayek, the Austrian economist who challenged Keynes in the thirties, was so disheartened about the state of the free-world economy that he abandoned the study of economics in favor of political philosophy.

Why did the depression last so long? Many free-market economists have picked up where Murray Rothbard's *America's Great Depression* left off, at the time Franklin Delano Roosevelt took office in 1933. Gene Smiley (Marquette University) attempted an Austrian perspective on the perverse role of fiscal policy in the 1930s. I summarized the causes of stagnation and persistent unemployment, such as the Smoot-Hawley Tariff, tax increases, government regulation and controls, and pro-labor legislation.[5]

More recently, Robert Higgs of the Independent Institute has made an in-depth study of the 1930s' malaise and focused on the lack of private investment during this period. According to Higgs, private investment was greatly hampered by New Deal initiatives that destroyed investor and business confidence, the key to recovery.[6] In short, the New Deal prolonged the depression.

What Got Us Out?

In another brilliant study, Higgs attacked the commonly held view that World War II saved us from the depression and restored the economy to full employment. The war gave only the appearance of recovery, when in reality private consumption and investment declined while Americans fought and died for their country. A return to genuine prosperity—the true Great Escape—did not occur until after the war ended, when most of the wartime controls were abolished and most of the resources used in the military were returned to civilian production.[7] Only after the war did private investment, business confidence, and consumer spending return to form.

In sum, it has been a long and hard-fought war to restore the case for free-market capitalism. Finally, through the pathbreaking work of Friedman, Rothbard, Smiley, Higgs, and other scholars, we can now say the battle has been won.

---

1. David C. Colander and Harry Landreth, eds. *The Coming of Keynesianism to America* (Northampton, Mass.: Edward Elgar, 1996), p. 16.

2. Benjamin M. Anderson, *Economics and the Public Welfare* (Indianapolis: Liberty Press, 1979 [1949]) and Murray N. Rothbard, *America's Great Depression* (Princeton, N.J.: D. Van Nostrand, 1963).

3. Milton Friedman and Anna J. Schwartz. *A Monetary History of the United States, 1867–1960* (Princeton, N.J.: Princeton University Press, 1963), p. 299.

4. Friedman and Schwartz, *Monetary History*, pp. 360–361. See also "Did the Gold Standard Cause the Great Depression?," page 151.

5. Gene Smiley, "Some Austrian Perspectives on Keynesian Fiscal Policy and the Recovery of the Thirties," *Review of Austrian Economics* (1987), 1:146–79, and Mark Skousen, "The Great Depression," in Peter Boettke, ed., *The Elgar Companion to Austrian Economics* (Northampton, Mass.: Edward Elgar, 1994), pp. 431–439.

6. Robert Higgs, "Regime Uncertainty: Why the Great Depression Lasted So Long and Why Prosperity Resumed After the War," *The Independent Review* (Spring 1997), 1:4, pp. 561–590.

7. Robert Higgs, "Wartime Prosperity? A Reassessment of the U.S. Economy in the 1940s," *Journal of Economic History* 52 (March 1992), pp. 41–60. See also Richard K. Vedder and Lowell Gallaway, "The Great Depression of 1946," *Review of Austrian Economics* 5:2 (1991), pp. 3–31.

What's Missing from
The Picture?

"Gold is just another commodity."
—WALL STREET BROKER

The *New York Times,* that bastion of conventional wisdom, is missing a key element in its digest of financial markets. It leaves out the single most significant asset that each day reflects accurately the level of economic, political, and military stability around the world.

The commodity? Gold!

Instead, The *Times* uses oil, a crude and misleading substitute commodity, to measure inflation. Apparently the Midas metal doesn't "fit" the *Times'* definition of headline news.

The *New York Times* isn't the only establishment publication to fundamentally misread how the world works. The *Wall Street Journal's* front-page summary of the markets highlights stocks, bonds, currencies, and commodities, including oil. There's plenty of room to list the yellow metal, yet gold is omitted—deliberately.

The reason is simple: The establishment prefers fiat money over the gold standard. It wants government rather than the market to maintain authority over money. It doesn't want to legitimatize a "non-performing" asset that might be warning of trouble down the road. The establishment is quite happy that the "barbarous relic" has been relegated to the commodity trading pits. "Gold is just another commodity," they say.

Oil—A Misleading Substitute

The majority view is that gold is an impractical monetary metal unrelated to real economic activity. Oil is a much better choice, they say, because energy is a critical determinant of the ups and downs of the economy. After all, didn't the energy shocks precipitate the recessions of 1973–75, 1979–82, and 1991–92?

Well, not exactly. All major industrial nations suffered sharp economic downturns in 1973–75, the time of the first energy crisis, but since then the relationship between the price of oil and economic performance has been cloudy. For example, Japan, which imports virtually all its oil, avoided the 1979–82 recession even though crude prices more than doubled. Germany, also a heavy oil importer, escaped relatively unscathed, while the United Kingdom, a net oil exporter, suffered the worst recession among industrial nations in 1979–82.

In 1986, crude prices fell by half, from $28 a barrel to $14. According to the establishment view, lower oil prices should have boosted economic growth. "If energy were an important ingredient in business cycles, you should have had a worldwide boom," declares energy economist Douglas Bohi. "There wasn't one." (*Forbes*, January 31, 1994, p. 66)

Bohi, director of the energy and natural resource division of Resources for the Future in Washington, D.C., is one of the few economists who have studied carefully the impact of energy costs on economic growth. After examining the evidence in the United States, Japan, Germany, and the UK, he concludes that oil prices did not have the impact on economic activity that most economists believed.[1] Bohi discovered that energy accounts for only 3–4 percent of the total cost of producing goods and services in the United States. Oil itself accounts for only 2 percent. The cost of energy is simply too small to have a significant impact on economic growth. Also if the oil price goes from $18 a barrel to $14 a barrel, that's a 22 percent drop for oil—but the reduction in costs for the economy as a whole is less than one-half of 1 percent. By the same token, Bohi does not expect the current increase in oil prices to reduce economic growth.

The Tie Between Money and Gold

If oil isn't the driving force behind economic boom and bust, what is? Bohi is convinced that monetary policy has a much broader influence on economic activity. Higher energy prices often reflect a general inflation, forcing most central banks to tighten money and bring about a recession. But not always. In 1979–82, when most world economies were suffering a recession, Japan did not impose a tight money policy and therefore escaped recession.

What better monitor of monetary inflation exists than the price of gold? There has been a strong correlation over the years between monetary policy and the price of gold. When central banks adopt easy-money policies, gold tends to rise. When they impose tight money, gold tends to decline.

The Midas metal is an ideal compass for monetary policy. Gold has certain unique features that make it the most sensitive measure of inflationary fears. It is not just another commodity. Unlike oil, soybeans, or pork bellies, gold is indestructible and is never consumed. Thus annual production is only a tiny fraction of the world's total stock. Annual production seldom exceeds 2 percent of the outstanding gold supplies. The fiat money supply may rise rapidly or fall sharply, depending on the whims of central bankers (usually more the former than the latter). But gold supplies never decline and seldom increase significantly. Even during the gold rushes in California, Alaska, Australia, and South Africa, world gold supplies never increased by more than 5 percent per year.[2]

In his exhaustive historical and statistical study of the purchasing power of gold, Berkeley economist Roy W. Jastram concludes, "Gold does maintain its purchasing power over long periods of time. . . . Its purchasing power in the middle of the twentieth century was very nearly the same as in the midst of the seventh century."[3] A $20 St. Gaudens gold coin would buy a tailor-made suit in the 1920s. That same coin, worth over $500 today, can still buy a tailor-made suit.

In short, gold is as steady as a rock, a standard bearer by which all currencies can be accurately measured. If the price of gold is volatile, it is not because gold itself is volatile, but because government policy is reckless and unstable.

Sharply rising gold prices are a sign of trouble ahead, whether it be inflation, war, or some other man-made crisis. Lower prices mean a return to normalcy and the avoidance of chaos or war. Stable gold prices suggest genuine prosperity and stability. Skyrocketing gold prices in the 1970s reflected a high level of inflation and financial crisis. The decline in gold in the 1980s suggested a disinflationary environment. The recent rise of gold implies a growing fear of more inflation. It is not surprising that Alan Greenspan and other central bankers are using the price of gold as an important gauge of inflationary expectations. Take heed, Wall Street!

---

1. Douglas R. Bohi, "On the macroeconomic effects of energy price shocks," *Resources and Energy* 13 (1991), pp. 146–62.

2. See chapter 11, "The Gold Standard," in my book, *Economics on Trial* (Irwin Professional Publishing, 1991, 1993), pp. 128–44. In this chapter, I outline all the arguments for and against the gold standard, and expose several common myths about the yellow metal.

3. Roy W. Jastram, *The Golden Constant: The English and American Experience, 1560–1976* (John Wiley & Sons, 1977), p. 189.

Did the Gold Standard Cause the Great Depression?

> "Far from being synonymous with stability, the gold standard itself was the principal threat to financial stability and economic prosperity between the wars."
>
> —BARRY EICHENGREEN[1]

Berkeley Professor Barry Eichengreen has fueled the flames of anti-gold in his recent historical work, *Golden Fetters: The Gold Standard and the Great Depression, 1919–1939* (Oxford University Press, 1992). Essentially, the author argues that (1) the international gold standard caused the Great Depression and (2) only after abandoning gold did the world economy recover. The book has been praised by colleagues, further dampening enthusiasm for the precious metal as an ideal monetary system.

It should be noted at the outset that Eichengreen, a Keynesian, is extremely biased against gold. In 1985, while teaching at Harvard, he edited a collection of essays entitled *The Gold Standard in Theory and History* (New York: Methuen, 1985), which pretends to offer a "complete picture" of how an international gold standard would operate, with pro's and con's. Yet he failed to include a single article by a gold supporter! His last chapter, "Further reading," makes no reference to Mises, Hayek, Röpke, Rothbard, Sennholz, Laffer, and other noted defenders of gold. So much for objectivity and what MIT professor Peter Temin calls "the best collection of readings on the gold standard available today."

Despite his extensive research and history, Eichengreen cannot crucify mankind upon a cross of gold. In reality, the blame for the Great Depression must be laid at the feet of Western leaders who blundered repeatedly in re-establishing an international monetary system following the First World War. Their mistake was establishing a fatally flawed mixture of gold, fiat money, and central banking, known as the "gold exchange standard," instead of returning to the "classical gold standard" that existed prior to the Great War.

Eichengreen rightly points out that the mischief began during the First World War, when the European nations went off the gold standard and resorted to massive inflation to pay for the war. Following the Armistice, European nations desired to return to gold-convertible currencies, but they created a weak monetary system known as the "gold exchange standard," where currencies were pegged primarily to the British pound and the American dollar rather than to gold itself. The gold exchange standard created a pyramid of paper claims upon other paper claims, with gold playing a far lesser role.

Austrian economists, such as Ludwig von Mises and F. A. Hayek, and the American sound-money school, led by Benjamin M. Anderson and H. Parker Willis, recognized that the fractional-reserve, fixed-exchange gold standard was a recipe for disaster. They predicted an eventual economic crisis under the gold exchange standard.

Monetary troubles worsened when, in 1925, Britain made the fateful error of pegging the pound at the exchange rate that prevailed before World War I at $4.86, clearly an artificially high rate. As a result, Britain suffered a deflationary depression for the rest of the 1920s. Moreover, to help Britain return to gold at the prewar exchange level, the Federal Reserve pushed down interest rates in 1924 and 1927, igniting a fateful inflationary boom in the U.S.

Eichengreen blames the gold standard, but the real fault lies in Britain's nationalistic zeal to return to gold at an artificially high rate. A more sensible solution would have been for all European nations, including Britain, to return to gold at a redefined rate that recognized the increased supply of money and price levels following the war. In Britain's case, this would have meant a new exchange rate of approximately $3.50.

Eichengreen also blames the gold standard for the monetary crises of the 1920s and 1930s, but it was really a gradual movement away from a genuine gold standard that caused the economic debacle of the 1930s.

Eichengreen even admits that the prewar classical gold standard worked well. He writes, "For more than a quarter of a century before World War I . . . the gold standard had been a remarkably efficient mechanism for organizing financial affairs" (p. 3). Eichengreen attributes exchange-rate stability and prosperity to international cooperation, but the underlying reason was that industrial nations largely avoided inflation and strictly linked their monetary policy to gold flows during this period.

The classical gold standard required issuers of money to hold sufficient gold reserves to handle the demands of anyone who wished to redeem their currencies into lawful money. National banknotes and bank reserves were redeemable in gold coins or bullion at any time. For example, each gold certificate issued by the U.S. Treasury contained the following declaration: "This certifies that there has been deposited in the Treasury of the United States of America TWENTY DOLLARS IN GOLD COIN payable to the bearer on demand." Although the U.S Treasury did not maintain 100 percent specie reserves for all its legal obligations under the classical gold standard, it did hold more than 100 percent reserves to cover its gold certificates.

Auburn University economist Leland Yeager explains the virtues of a fully-backed commodity standard: "Under a 100 percent hard-money international gold standard . . . the government and its agencies would not have to worry about any drain on their reserves. . . . There would be no danger of gold deserting some countries and piling up excessively in others . . ."[2] Because of monetary stability under the prewar gold standard, Milton Friedman and Anna J. Schwartz conclude, "The blind, undesigned, and quasi-automatic working of the gold standard turned out to produce a greater measure of predictability and regularity—perhaps because its discipline was impersonal and inescapable—than did deliberate and conscious control exercised within institutional arrangements intended to promote monetary stability."[3]

Was the Depression Inevitable Under Gold?

Eichengreen and other gold critics have pointed out that in a crucial time period, 1931–33, the Federal Reserve raised the discount rate for fear of a run on its gold deposits. If only the U.S. had not been on a gold standard, the critics say, the Fed could have avoided this reckless credit squeeze that pushed the country into depression and a banking crisis. However, Friedman and Schwartz demur, pointing out that the U.S. gold stock rose during the first two years of the contraction. But the Fed reacted ineptly. "We did not permit the inflow of gold to expand the U.S. money stock. We not only sterilized it, we went much further. Our money stock moved perversely, going down as the gold stock went up."[4]

In short, even under the defective gold exchange standard, there may have been room to avoid a devastating worldwide depression and monetary crisis.

How should we solve our continuing monetary problems? After recounting the chaotic events between the world wars, Eichengreen opposes the strict discipline of gold. Amazingly, he calls for more international cooperation between central banks, which even he admits is "weak soup for dinner at the end of a bitter cold day" (p. 398). A much better solution would be to return to the classical gold standard.

---

1. Barry Eichengreen, *Golden Fetters: The Gold Standard and the Great Depression, 1919–1939* (New York: Oxford University Press, 1992), p. 4.

2. Leland Yeager, "An Evaluation of Freely Fluctuating Exchange Rates," quoted in Mark Skousen, *Economics of a Pure Gold Standard*, 2nd ed. (Auburn, Ala.: Mises Institute, 1988), pp. 81–82.

3. Milton Friedman and Anna J. Schwartz, *A Monetary History of the United States, 1867–1960* (Princeton: Princeton University Press, 1963), p. 10.

4. Ibid., pp. 360–61.

The Battle for
Diamond Head: A Case of
Market Failure?

"Hawaii's great and beloved landmark . . . is too precious an
asset to be sacrificed."
                                    —*Honolulu Advertiser* EDITORIAL (1967)

Should government protect a local landmark from commercial
development? Are zoning laws and other building restrictions
necessary in a free society to stop "greedy" speculators and "fast
buck" promoters from creating "urban sprawl" and unsightly
commerce?

Whenever I visit Hawaii and walk along famed Waikiki Beach,
I can't help noticing how a string of high-rise apartments and
hotels halted abruptly along the Diamond Head shoreline.

The Story of Diamond Head

Why the sudden abatement? In the late 1960s Diamond Head
was the center of a fierce debate between the developers and the
conservationists. Following statehood in 1959, tourists flocked to
this paradise of the Pacific, and Waikiki Beach, sandwiched
between downtown Honolulu and Diamond Head, became the
hottest real estate market for resort hotels and condominiums.
Honolulu newspapers ran photos of a rapidly disappearing view

of Diamond Head, and local citizens became alarmed. A grass-roots organization, Save Diamond Head Association, was formed in 1967 and demanded a halt to building any more skyscrapers along the shoreline.

Why save Diamond Head? In the nineteenth century, British sailors found crystalline rocks on its slopes and mistook them for diamonds. Conservationists argue that Diamond Head is a symbol of paradise, the mid-Pacific's most famous beacon. One visitor wrote during the debate, "I found Diamond Head, which has been declared a state monument, in imminent danger of turning into a monument for the fast buck, its craggy profile threatened with disappearance behind a palisade of tall concrete buildings."[1]

Here's the conflict: Hawaii's natural beauty and delightful climate attracted millions of new tourists in the 1960s. The tourist boom in turn created a rush in real estate development. But the high-rise buildings—along with enormous billboards—were blocking out the natural beauty that attracted tourists in the first place. What to do?

The fight between the developers and environmentalists came to a head in December 1967. After a packed four-hour public hearing, five members of the nine-member city council voted against further commercial development. The other four members abstained. In 1968, Diamond Head was designated an official national landmark.

Is There a Market Solution?

Could the market properly plan for a growing Hawaii without destroying its natural beauty and aloha spirit, or must government intervene?

Sometimes the market faces a difficult choice between two conflicting goals. In the case of Diamond Head, it was the battle between development and a landmark symbol. Unfortunately, it's events like these that give capitalism a bad name. Could private developers have done better? Could it have been in their own self-interest to limit the height of hotels and condos and preserve Oahu's historic skyline while still making a profit? Can progress and profit go together?

What do free-market economists have to say about zoning and building codes? In *The Constitution of Liberty*, F.A Hayek notes that local governments have often done a poor job of city planning, sometimes amounting to "administrative despotism."[2] He cites rent controls, zoning regulations, and excessive taxation as examples. Nevertheless, he does support "some regulation of buildings permitted in cities," including minimum building codes.[3]

Economists have often been critical of zoning laws as an infringement of property rights. In a book on the subject, Tom Bethell asserts that zoning laws hurt the poor, cause urban sprawl, and invite political corruption. He points to Houston as an example of a dynamic city which has grown without zoning regulations.[4]

If conservationists really wanted to save Diamond Head, why didn't they buy the shoreline property and keep developers out? Instead of running to the City of Honolulu, Save Diamond Head Association should have raised the capital to stave off builders. Since 1953, Nature Conservancy, a nonprofit environmental organization with 900,000 members, has been buying and preserving land and habitats (now totaling over 10 million acres in the United

States). Of course, such a plan would have been costly, with Waikiki property prices around $1 million an acre in 1967–68.

Property rights should include the right to be left alone from noise and air pollution. Should these rights also include the right of original owners to view Diamond Head?

---

1. Kenneth Lamott, *Holiday Magazine*, July 14, 1967, quoted in Helen Geracimos Chapin, *Shaping History: The Role of Newspapers in Hawaii* (Honolulu: University of Hawaii Press, 1996), p. 268. Chapter 26 of Chapin's book, "Above Ground: The Battle for Diamond Head," summarizes the history of this conflict through the eyes of two local newspapers, the *Star Bulletin* and the *Advertiser*.

2. F. A. Hayek, *The Constitution of Liberty* (Chicago: University of Chicago Press, 1960), p. 355. Hayek devotes an entire chapter to "Housing and Town Planning," an area often ignored by economists.

3. Ibid., pp. 354–57.

4. Tom Bethell, *The Noblest Triumph: Property and Prosperity Through the Ages* (New York: St. Martin's Press, 1998), pp. 297–99.

Classical Economists—
Good or Bad?

"The classical and the Austrian schools and their allies have developed virtually all of the great positive truths of economic science."

—George Reisman[1]

"Adam Smith . . . shunted economics on to a false path. . . . Under Ricardo, this unfortunate shift in focus was intensified and systematized."

—Murray N. Rothbard[2]

Until the Keynesian revolution in the 1930s, most economists taught the sound principles of classical economics: free trade, balanced budgets, the gold standard, and laissez faire. Adam Smith (1723–1790), the founder of classical economics, has been lionized as the foremost exponent of these principles. David Ricardo, Thomas Malthus, and John Stuart Mill, among others, have played supporting roles.

Many free-market economists congratulate Adam Smith for his profundity and wisdom in *The Wealth of Nations*, published in 1776. His work almost singlehandedly destroyed the mercantilist arguments for protectionism and other forms of government intervention. George Stigler concludes, "It's all in Adam Smith."

In his monumental book *Capitalism*, George Reisman carries on this tradition of extolling the virtues of Adam Smith and David

159

Ricardo (1772–1823). In his judgment, there are four great economists, whom he ranks in the following order: Ludwig von Mises, Adam Smith, David Ricardo, and Eugen Böhm-Bawerk. Although he does not ignore their weaknesses, Reisman considers Smith and Ricardo great economists who have been much maligned.

Rothbard's Challenge

But consider Murray Rothbard's critique of classical economists in his two-volume work *Economic Thought Before Adam Smith* and *Classical Economics,* published at the time of his death in January 1995. He lambastes Smith, Ricardo, and Mill, among others, arguing that the classical economists moved away from the sound doctrines and theories previously developed by pre-Adamites such as Richard Cantillon, Anne Robert Turgot, and the Scholastics. According to Rothbard, Adam Smith's contributions were "dubious," that "he originated nothing that was true, and that whatever he originated was wrong," and *The Wealth of Nations* is "rife with vagueness, ambiguity and deep inner contradictions."[3] He has little better to say of Ricardo and Mill.

How can free-market economists see things so differently? Having read both Reisman and Rothbard, as well as the major works of Smith and Ricardo, I have an answer: Smith and Ricardo were largely right on policy, but often wrong on theory.

A Critique of Classical Economics

If you look at the theories developed by the classical economists, you can easily find fault. Smith advanced an exploitation theory of labor, referred to the work of ministers, physicians, musicians, orators, actors, and other producers of services as "unproductive, frivolous" occupations, and made a distinction between "production for profit" and "production for use." All of these Smithian concepts gave ammunition to Karl Marx and other socialists.

Ricardo furthered the Marxist cause by implying that profits could only increase at the expense of workers' wages, which tended toward the subsistence level. As rents earned by idle landlords increased, profits would decline, he predicted. He also invented what economists call the "Ricardian Vice," whereby theorists build models based on false and misleading assumptions that lead inexorably to the desired results. Ricardo used this device to "prove" his labor theory of value. As a result, some commentators have identified Ricardo as the source of today's highly abstract, mathematical, and ahistorical theoretical model-building.[4]

Positive Contributions

Despite these theoretical blunders, Smith and Ricardo were consistent defenders of laissez-faire capitalism. Smith ably defended the right to immigrate. He opposed minimum-wage laws, and argued for lower taxes and a simpler tax code. War was bad for the economy, according to Smith. He pleaded for balanced budgets. He spoke favorably about saving and capital investment. His "invisible hand" doctrine declared that the voluntary self-interest of millions of individuals creates a stable, prosperous society (what Smith called "natural harmony") without the need for central direction by the state. Smith viewed free-market capitalism overall as socially humanizing and prosperous, while Marx saw capitalism as dehumanizing and alienating. Smith eloquently promoted the principle of "natural liberty," the freedom to do what you wish without interference from the state. His words literally changed the course of politics, dismantling the old mercantilist doctrines of protectionism and human bondage. *The Wealth of Nations* was the ideal document to accompany the Industrial Revolution.

Despite his pessimism about the future, David Ricardo favored a strict 100 percent gold standard, was opposed to public welfare and the corn laws, and was a firm believer in free trade.

In short, the classical economists had much to offer the world. Their theories weren't always on target, but they usually proposed the right solution.

---

1. George Reisman, *Capitalism* (Ottawa, Ill.: Jameson Books, 1996), p. 2.

2. Murray N. Rothbard, *Classical Economics: An Austrian Perspective on the History of Economic Thought* (London: Edward Elgar, 1995), p. xi.

3. Rothbard, "The Celebrated Adam Smith," *Economic Thought Before Adam Smith* (London: Edward Elgar, 1995), pp. 435–6.

4. For critiques of Ricardo, see Graeme Donald Snooks, *Economics Without Time* (Ann Arbor, Mich.: University of Michigan Press, 1993) and Elton Mayo, *The Social Problems of an Industrial Civilization* (Cambridge, Mass.: Harvard University, 1945).

Neither Left nor Right

"Those who control the adjectives win."
—LARRY ABRAHAM

The use of the political labels "left" and "right" may be popular in today's media, but there are several reasons why the dichotomy is a false and misleading guide to political and economic philosophy. It implies that "left" is equally as extreme as "right," while the "middle of the road" position appears the more moderate and balanced position.

I call this system the pendulum approach, where each individual is categorized along a political spectrum from "extreme left" to "extreme right." Recently I encountered an example in an economics textbook.

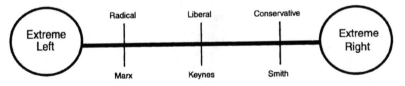

Source: Mark Maier and Steve White, *The First Chapter*, 3rd ed. (New York: McGraw-Hill, 1998), p. 42.

The problem with the pendulum approach is that Adam Smith is characterized as "extreme" as Karl Marx. By implication, neither economist is sensible. Yet the evidence is overwhelming that Adam Smith's system of natural liberty has advanced civilization far more than Karl Marx's inexorable system of alienation and exploitation.

Moreover, in the pendulum approach, the middle-of-the-road position held by John Maynard Keynes appears to be the moderate ideal. A pendulum that experiences friction will eventually come to rest in the middle, between both extremes. But is that the best way to go?

A New Alternative: The Totem-Pole Approach

I prefer a fresh approach, which I call the top-down or "totem pole" way. Instead of left to right, I use top to bottom. In Indian folklore, the most-favored chiefs are placed at the top of the totem pole, followed by less important chiefs below. Look at the next page for my rendition of the same three economists according to the totem-pole method.

In this system, I rank Adam Smith first, Keynes second, and Marx third. Of the three, Adam Smith advocated the highest degree of economic freedom. Nations that have adopted Smith's

vision of laissez-faire capitalism have fared the best. Next is Keynes. He usually favored maximum freedom in the microeconomic sphere, but frequently endorsed heavy intervention (inflation and deficit spending) in the macro sphere. His big-government formula has resulted in slower economic growth in many industrial nations. The low man on the totem pole is Marx, who advocated a command economy at both the micro and macro level. Historically, centrally planned Marxist nations have vastly underperformed the market economies.

Political and economic positions should not be divided by left and right. They are either right or wrong. As Milton Friedman has said many times, "There's only good economics and bad economics."

Avoid Being Close-Minded

A second reason why I avoid the left-right labels is that it puts people and ideas into boxes. When someone's theories are labeled and compartmentalized, thinking stops and name-calling begins. There has been far too much bad blood spilt over the years between camps that spend more time shouting epithets than engaging in legitimate dialogue.

This criticism applies equally to the worn-out adjectives "liberal" and "conservative." If John Kenneth Galbraith is a "liberal," why should conservatives listen to him? If Milton Friedman is a "conservative," why should liberals read his books? I try not to prejudice myself. To me, both are economists who have ideas worth examining.

The media will continue to use the hackneyed political lexicon of yesteryear and engage in character assassination. But I will resist the outdated and misleading left-wing/right-wing/liberal-conservative battle lines, and treat every scholar, candidate, and philosopher on his own merits, and not according to some arbitrary label.

Breakthroughs in Economics

Warren Buffett vs.
A Monkey: Can You
Beat the Market?

"A blindfolded monkey throwing darts at a newspaper's financial pages could select a portfolio that would do just as well as one carefully selected by the experts."

—BURTON MALKIEL[1]

If there's any group who should hate economists the most, it should be the Wall Street stock analyst, a man who is paid a six-figure income to pick the right stocks. Now some ivory-tower academic professor comes along and announces to the world that stock analysts are useless, even worse than useless, they may well underperform the S & P 500 index! Some economists even go so far as to say that a monkey can do a better job. . . .

The academic economist who started this monkey business is Harry M. Markowitz, the father of modern portfolio theory. Born in Chicago, Markowitz was a 25-year-old whiz-kid graduate student at the University of Chicago when he wrote a 14-page paper, "Portfolio Selection," for the March 1952 issue of the *Journal of Finance*. It was this article that won him the Nobel Prize in economics in 1990, which he shared with two colleagues, Merton Miller and William Sharpe.

Modern Portfolio Theory

Why did he win the Nobel Prize? Prior to Markowitz and modern portfolio theory, investors had no scientific method for measuring risk. Markowitz's primary contribution was to quantify risk and develop ways to reduce risk while increasing investment return. Modern portfolio theory is highly mathematical, but essentially Markowitz and other founders of the theory (Merton Miller, William Sharpe, Franco Modigliani, Myron Scholes, Paul Samuelson, James Tobin, Fischer Black, Eugene Fama, and Burton Malkiel, among others) made three general recommendations for investors:

1. Diversify as much as possible. Diversification reduces risk and increases return. Financial economists usually recommend a broad-based index fund, such as the S&P 500 Index Fund.

2. If you seek high returns, expect to take high risks. This concept is known as the "efficient frontier." If you invest in low-risk Treasury bills or money-market funds, you won't lose your principal, but you won't make much money either. You can double or triple your money in aggressive growth stocks (such as technology stocks or gold shares), but you can also lose half your investment, maybe more.

3. Don't try to beat the market. Only a handful of investors can consistently outperform the overall market, such as the S&P 500. This is known as the "efficient market theory," which I will discuss shortly. It argues that "high return/low risk" situations are hard to find and when they occur they disappear quickly due to competition in the financial marketplace.

A Random Walk Down Wall Street

The thesis that you cannot beat the market is known as the "efficient market hypothesis." The efficient-market theory was first raised by academic economists in the 1960s. Burton G. Malkiel, professor of economics at Princeton University, wrote a book on the subject in 1973 called *A Random Walk Down Wall Street*, which has gone through eight editions. Malkiel sums up the efficient market theory as follows:

"It means that short-run changes in stock prices cannot be predicted. Investment advisory services, earnings predictions, and complicated chart patterns are useless. . . . Taken to its logical extreme, it means that a blind-folded monkey throwing darts at a newspaper's financial pages could select a portfolio that would do just as well as one carefully selected by the experts."[2]

The efficient market proponents were labeled "random walkers" because of their belief that short-term movements in the stock market appear unpredictable and random, like a drunken sailor meandering down Wall Street.

Taking a cue from Malkiel's book, editors of the *Wall Street Journal* engage in a contest every six months between the editors, who pick stocks by throwing darts at the stock listings, and professional analysts who pick their favorite stocks. (So far the professionals have won most of the contests, but not all.)

What do random walkers propose? They argue that fund managers trading stocks are not likely to beat the market. In addition to increasing the likelihood of losing money, traders face transaction costs (commissions, bid-ask spreads, and taxes) when they trade. Their strategy is simple: be a passive investor. Buy a large number of individual stocks, or a stock index fund, and hold for the long term, taking dips and bear markets in stride. As simplistic as it may seem, such a strategy has been highly profitable during the 1980s and the 1990s, with the S&P 500 index funds returning 15 percent per annum over a 20-year period.

The random-walk theories of academia created a furor on Wall Street. Highly paid securities analysts and fund managers felt that their careers were threatened by evidence that they underperformed the market averages. Nevertheless, it was hard to contradict the evidence. Few professional investors have been able to top the returns of the S&P 500 since 1980. See the figure on the next page.

As a result, Wall Street has joined the ivory-tower professors of finance, and stock market index funds have become very popular since the 1980s. The Vanguard group of mutual funds, based in Valley Forge, Pennsylvania, was the first to offer an index fund, and the Vanguard Index Trust 500 Portfolio remains the largest index fund today, with more than $70 billion in assets under management. Now there are hundreds of index funds, including international index funds.

INDEX FUNDS TEND TO OUTPERFORM MONEY MANAGERS

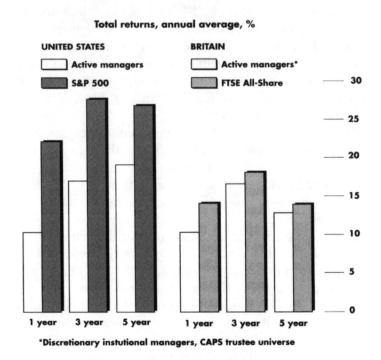

Total returns, annual average, %

Figure 13.5.
Source: The Economist, (29 May, 1999).

Who Can Beat the Averages?

Meanwhile, active fund managers still try to beat the indexes, and some of them have been successful, including Warren Buffett, Peter Lynch, Michael Price, and Value Line. Warren Buffett's closed-end fund, Berkshire Hathaway, is without question the most successful fund to outperform the indexes over the long run. (The fund traded for $20 a share in the early 1970s and recently was selling for $70,000.) The Omaha billionaire has been a sharp critic of the efficient-market theory. Berkshire Hathaway, as well as earlier partnerships Buffett was involved in with his mentor, Benjamin Graham, the father of fundamental analysis, consistently beat the averages. The problem with the efficient-market hypothesis is that it always assumes efficiency. Warren Buffett responds, "Observing correctly that the market was frequently efficient, they [the academic random walkers] went on to conclude incorrectly that it was always efficient. The difference between these propositions is night and day."[3]

A few commodity traders have vastly outperformed the averages as well, but again, it is a small minority of traders.

One of the most interesting new funds seeking to the beat market averages is the Marketocracy Masters 100 Fund (symbol MOFQX). Ken Kam, the fund manager, seeks to identify superior money managers and invest in stocks based on their decisions. Marketocracy.com offers traders the opportunity to create their own virtual million dollar mutual fund. So far over 55,000 traders have tried their hand at running a mutual fund. Kam identifies the best-performing 100 investors and buys and sells stocks based on their recommendations. The fund is relatively new but has so far outperformed the S&P 500 by a considerable margin. There is a market incentive to do well: Masters 100 investors are compensated based on the market capitalization of the fund. (For more information, go to www.marketocracy.com)In sum, competition and entrepreneurship are in a constant battle in the financial markets. Entrepreneurs seek to outperform other investors and managers, but competition and imitation are so strong in this highly efficient field that it is difficult, though not impossible, to beat the averages.

A Vienna Waltz Down Wall Street

The financial markets are neither perfectly efficient nor totally irrational. The truth lies somewhere in between, what we might label "imperfectly efficient." Undervalued and overvalued conditions exist in the marketplace, but if you don't take advantage quickly, the opportunities will disappear.

Similarly, our knowledge of the financial markets and the future is not perfect, but neither it is broken. Economic events and investment prices are not always predictable, but sometimes they are quite forecastable. Markets are not completely efficient, but neither are they completely inefficient. The middle-ground position is similar to F. A. Hayek's view of money in the economy. Hayek asked the question, "What is the relationship between changes in the money supply and economic activity?" He concluded that the relationship was neither a "tight joint" (close relationship) nor a "broken joint" (unpredictable relationship), but a "loose joint" (loose relationship). By the same token, our knowledge of future stock prices is neither perfect nor unknowable, but somewhere in between—"imperfect."[4]

Which means there's plenty of room to make money.

---

1. Burton G. Malkiel, *A Random Walk Down Wall Street*, 5th ed. (New York: Norton, 1990), p. 24.

2. Ibid.

3. Warren Buffett, 1998 *Annual Report to Shareholders*, Berkshire Hathaway.

4. Friedrich A. Hayek, *The Pure Theory of Capital* (University of Chicago Press, 1941), p. 408. The idea of a "loose joint" in economics in more fully developed in Roger Garrison, "Time and Money: The Universals of Macroeconomic Thinking," *Journal of Macroeconomics* (Spring 1984), and Mark Skousen, "The Economist as Investment Advisor," *Economics on Trial* (Homewood, Ill.: Irwin, 1991), pp. 261–63.

Beyond GDP: A Breakthrough in National Income Accounting

"It is apparent that a large part of a country's total production serves for the production of capital goods and not for the production of consumer goods, and that the production of capital goods must itself become a specialized branch of manufacturing."

—WILHELM RÖPKE[1]

Good news! The U.S. Department of Commerce, which compiles Gross Domestic Product (GDP), has added a new national income statistic, Gross Output (GO), as a measure of total spending in the economy. I have been making the case for this new statistic for over ten years. Now it is a reality.

In *The Structure of Production* (1990) and *Economics on Trial* (1993), I was critical of GDP for two reasons:

First, GDP is a Keynesian concept that measures only the output of final goods and services and excludes intermediate production. Second, government spending is included in GDP data, an autonomous addition to national output.[2]

Both peculiarities of GDP have led to much mischief. In the first case, by focusing solely on final output, many economists and commentators in the media have concluded that consumer spending is more important than capital investment in an economy, based on the fact that consumption expenditures usually represent about two-thirds of GDP. In the second case, including government spending in GDP has led many pundits to believe that an increase in that spending—even if accomplished through deficit spending—will automatically increase economic growth (or conversely, a cut in government spending will inevitably lead to a recession). Both conclusions are false.

Most students of economics are unaware of the fact that GDP was created by Simon Kuznets during World War II to quantify final aggregate demand according to the new economics of Keynes. As such, GDP ignores all intermediate spending in the economy, based on the tenuous argument that earlier stages of production constitute double counting.

However, the goods-in-process sector of the economy—the natural resource, manufacturing, and wholesale stages—are important for several reasons. Austrian economist Eugen von Böhm-Bawerk and German economist Wilhelm Röpke, among others, demonstrated that interest rates and technology greatly influence the structure of production and that changes in the early stages are especially important in the business cycle.

In an effort to measure intermediate production, *The Structure of Production* introduced a new national income statistic, Gross Domestic Expenditure (GDE)—a more complete measure of spending at all stages of production—as an "Austrian" alternative to the Keynesian GDP. It counts spending (sales or revenues) of firms at all stages of production, not just at the retail level.

GO: A New National Statistic

For a decade I thought my criticisms of GDP had fallen on deaf ears and no one was interested in using a new national income statistic like GDE that accurately included total spending in the economy, not just final output. However, I am happy to report that the Commerce Department's Bureau of Economic Analysis has just begun to publish a series called "Gross Output," an annual measure of total spending at all stages. GO is defined as Intermediate Input (II) plus GDP (final output).[3]

Intermediate Input (II) represents the sale of all products in the natural resource, manufacturing, and wholesale markets. GDP represents the final retail market.

I am currently working on a professional paper analyzing GO and II statistics and how they increase our understanding of the economy. Since this paper will not be published for some time, let me give you a few of my preliminary conclusions. Overall, much of the data appears to confirm several Austrian themes.

First, the data support the Austrian theory that the structure of production lengthens as an economy grows. Indeed, from 1987 until 1998 real GDP rose from $6.1 trillion to $8.8 trillion, or 39 percent (using 1996 as a base year). But real Intermediate Input (II) increased from $4.3 trillion to $6.5 trillion, or 53 percent, much faster than GDP. In other words, the producer/capital goods market grew more rapidly than the consumer/retail good market. This suggests that the number of stages of production increased.

Second, the data seem to confirm the Austrian view that production in the intermediate processes tends to be more volatile than final output and thus more sensitive to the business cycle. For example, during the 1990–91 recession, real GDP fell $31.5 billion, while real II fell $74.6 billion—more than twice retail sales. Since then, intermediate production has grown substantially faster (41 percent) than consumer spending (27 percent) from 1991 to 1998. I would like to test these statistics during previous boom-bust cycles (such as 1973–75 and 1980–82), but unfortunately, the data for II and GO are incomplete prior to 1987.

Third, GO data support the Austrian argument that business investment—not consumer spending—is the driving force behind economic growth. The Keynesian argument that consumer spending is the largest sector of the economy is specious and is based on a misunderstanding of GDP statistics. It is true that personal consumption expenditures typically represent 67 percent of GDP, but GDP is not total spending in the economy. On measuring total spending (GO), one sees that the capital/producer goods industry is substantially larger than the final consumer/retail goods industry. Using 1998 data, we find that personal consumption expenditures amount to $5.8 trillion, only 38 percent of GO, and gross business investment (which includes all intermediate production, plus gross fixed investment) amounts to $7.9 trillion, 52 percent of total spending.

In sum, intermediate production does matter, and GO is a better indicator of what is happening in the entire economy, not just the retail sector. Hopefully, the next step will be for the Commerce Department to release up-to-date quarterly data for GO and II as they currently do for GDP. We could learn a lot more about the direction of the economy with these new Austrian national income statistics.

---

1. William Röpke, *Economics of a Free Society* (Chicago: Henry Regnery & Co., 1963), p. 43.

2. See *The Structure of Production* (New York: New York University Press, 1990), chapter 6, and *Economics on Trial* (Homewood, Ill.: Irwin, 1993), chapter 4.

3. See "Improved Estimates of Gross Product by Industry for 1947–98," *Survey of Current Business* 80:6 (June 2000), pp. 24–63. Table 8 measures Gross Output 1987–98, and table 9 measures Intermediate Input 1987–98.

Imperial Scientists Score
Another Win

"Until a business returns a profit that is greater than its cost of capital, it operates at a loss."

—PETER F. DRUCKER

The English essayist (and economist) Walter Bagehot once remarked, "No real Englishman in his secret soul was ever sorry for the death of an economist."

Quite a few security analysts and fund managers on American shores probably feel that way about the economists who came up with the efficient market hypothesis and proved that 95 percent of professionals can't beat a blindfolded monkey in picking stocks. Highly paid Wall Street analysts don't like being compared to sightless apes. Yet after decades of heated exchange between Wall Street and academia, the eggheads are winning the argument. Today index funds—the professors' favorite investment vehicle—are the fastest-growing sector on Wall Street.

The latest group to sympathize with the words of Walter Bagehot are the accountants. Over the past decade, ivory-tower economists (mainly professors teaching modern finance theory at MBA schools) have taken on the accounting departments, damning them for not taking into account the full opportunity cost of capital.

179

Are Accounting Profits for Real?

For years, economists have complained that conventional accounting distorts the true economics of the firm by not including a charge for common equity in its earnings reports and balance sheets. Generally accepted accounting principles treat equity as if it were free. Thus, publicly traded corporations release quarterly reports showing substantial earnings that in fact are losses. "True profits don't begin until corporations have covered a normal return on investment," declares Al Ehrbar, senior vice president of consultants Stern Stewart & Co., specialists in EVA—a new performance technique for business.[1]

What is EVA? It stands for "economic value added" (also called economic profit or residual income). Essentially, EVA is a precise measurement of the opportunity cost of capital. For years, opportunity cost was a nebulous concept known only to professors. The term, coined by Austrian economist Friedrich Wieser in the early twentieth century, refers to the universal principle that all human action involves giving up other opportunities. When you invest in a stock, lend money, or create a new product, you give up the chance to invest elsewhere. If you invest in a high-flying computer stock, you can't buy T-bills. If you build a new office building, your money is tied up for years in concrete and can't be invested in AT&T.

EVA is a practical application of classical economics and modern finance theory. The Austrians elucidated the concept of opportunity cost, and Nobel laureates Merton H. Miller and Franco Modigliani used it in their model of the firm to determine its true value. In the 1980s, G. Bennett Stewart III created EVA as a financial yardstick to measure opportunity costs in business.

EVA is fairly simple to determine: it is after-tax operating profits minus the appropriate capital charge for both debt and equity. If a company issues debt, the opportunity cost is linked to the Treasury rate (currently 5–6 percent), plus the credit risk of the issuer. If the company issues stock, the opportunity cost is measured by the long-term annualized return on the stock market, approximately 12 percent. In short, EVA recognizes that investors must earn enough to compensate for risk of their investment capital.

If a firm earns more than these opportunity costs, it has "added value" to its shareholders and created wealth in the world economy. Hence, the phrase "economic value added." If EVA is positive, shareholders and the economy are making real contributions to the bottom line. Otherwise, the business should shut down and invest shareholders' funds in Treasuries or an index fund. As British economist John Kay declares, "In the long run, firms that fail to add value in a competitive market will not survive, nor do they deserve to."[2]

Okay, so what good is EVA to corporate managers? EVA analysis helps identify potential acquisitions, expansion plans, and nonperforming assets and assists in eliminating low-profit-margin operations that are clearly unprofitable when full costs are taken into account. EVA is also being used as an incentive system for managers and employees. Bonuses are linked to economic earnings, not just accounting earnings, and EVA has proven effective in boosting productivity.

EVA makes a lot of sense and has made significant inroads into the financial world. Already over 300 major corporations, including Coca-Cola, Eli Lilly, and Sprint, use EVA as a capital accountability tool to reinforce the idea that profits don't begin until corporations have covered their normal return. Wall Street analysts at Goldman Sachs and First Boston, among others, use EVA to evaluate stocks. According to Ehrbar, EVA explains stock performance and market value better than any other accounting measure, including return on equity, cash flow, earnings per share, or sales. EVA makes company officers focus more clearly on creating shareholder value and a higher stock price. Stern Stewart issues an annual EVA report on the top 1,000 U.S. corporations. For several years now, Intel has had the highest EVA ranking and GM the lowest.

EVA Wins the Battle

Accountants still have a dominant grip on the way corporate financial statements are submitted, but the popularity of EVA has forced them to take notice. All five accounting firms offer an EVA-type statistic to their clients. Most accounting textbooks now include a significant section on economic value added, economic profit, or residual income. Previous editions did not mention EVA or opportunity cost.

Want more? Check out Al Ehrbar's highly readable *EVA* or John Kay's brilliant *Why Firms Succeed.* See also www.eva.com.

I like EVA. Companies adopting it appear to perform better in creating wealth and shareholder value. But it may have potential drawbacks. EVA puts enormous pressure on managers to over-achieve and to create constant above-average profit centers. Imagine not earning a true profit unless your company or division beats last year's Dow Jones Industrial Average. It could be depressing. Wonder what your company's EVA will look like in the next recession? Heads could roll.

Some managers may want to join Wall Street analysts and accountants in shooting those dismal scientists.

---

1. Al Ehrbar, *EVA: The Real Key to Creating Wealth* (New York: John Wiley & Sons, 1998), p. viii.

2. John Kay, *Why Firms Succeed* (New York: Oxford University Press, 1995), p. 19.

What Is the Best Measure of Inflation?

"The Consumer Price Index overstates increases in the cost of living by about 1.1 percentage point a year."
— MICHAEL BOSKIN, STANFORD UNIVERSITY[1]

According to recent surveys, most professional economists believe that the Consumer Price Index (CPI) consistently overstates the cost of living in the United States by one percentage point or more. Even pro-market economists such as Michael Boskin and Milton Friedman assert that the CPI, which is prepared monthly by the Bureau of Labor Statistics, exaggerates changes in the living expenses.

As a result of these studies, the government hopes to establish a more accurate CPI and thus save Washington billions of dollars. The CPI is used to index federal taxes and Social Security payments. A lower CPI could increase tax revenues by $70 billion and reduce Social Security checks by $75 billion over a five-year period. It could substantially reduce the federal deficit.

The CPI is determined each month by a survey of prices of 364 items that compose a typical bundle purchased by urban consumers during the base period, 1982–84. Items include food, consumer goods and services, rent, and property taxes. Each month several hundred survey workers visit approximately 21,000 stores in urban areas and collect prices on these items. The CPI is a market basket index of these items, valued according to a weighted average.

What's Missing in the CPI?

Unfortunately, the price-index methodology is defective in two ways. First, the current CPI fails to take into account quality improvements, new products, substitutes, and sale prices. As a result of these omissions, many economists argue that the CPI tends to *overestimate* the cost of living in the United States.

Second, the CPI does not include all items determining an individual's cost of living, and this fact may cause the CPI to consistently *underestimate* the cost of living. How many people buy a fixed market basket of goods and services that match in any way the government's survey for an urban family of four?

For example, at various times, I have had one or more children in college. According to government surveys, college tuition and related expenses have risen at double-digit rates over the past decade or two. But the CPI doesn't cover college expenses.

My family and I also travel frequently outside the United States. Overseas the dollar has lost much of its purchasing power over the past 20 years. How does the CPI reflect the dollar's decline? It doesn't.

Crime has been a problem in our community, so we bought an expensive security protection plan for our home. The CPI doesn't include such an expenditure in its fixed basket of services.

What if interest rates rise? The CPI does not directly account for the costs of borrowed money or mortgage payments.

The Biggest Omission

But probably the most serious defect of the CPI is that it does not register the largest item in everyone's household budget—taxes. The CPI covers property taxes, but not sales taxes or income taxes. Today, government expenditures (the most accurate measure of total taxation) represent 32.2 percent of the economy (GDP). If the CPI is supposed to represent the *cost of living,* doesn't it make sense that it should include taxation, the cost of government?

Taxes and government spending have been rising rapidly throughout the twentieth century, as the following graph shows:

The Growth of Government Expenditures, 1929–1995
(as a percent of GDP)

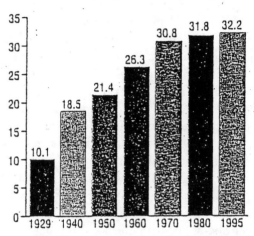

Source: Economic Report of the President

Since 1982–84, the base period for the current CPI, total government expenditures have increased from $1.1 trillion to $2.5 trillion, a 127 percent increase. During this same period, the CPI has risen only 60 percent. Clearly, if taxes were included in the CPI, it would be rising at a much higher rate.

In short, you have two major deficiencies in the CPI, one that overestimates inflation and another that underestimates inflation. Which force is stronger? I don't know, but it would be national folly to include the former and ignore the latter.

Mises to the Rescue

In determining the best measure of inflation, we should remember the words of Ludwig von Mises. Mises refers to the level of prices as inappropriate and untenable because changes in the purchasing power of money must necessarily affect the prices of different commodities and services at different times and to different extents. He goes on to say, "The pretentious solemnity which statisticians and statistical bureaus display in computing indexes of purchasing power and cost of living is out of place. These index numbers are at best crude and inaccurate illustrations of changes which have occurred."[2]

According to Mises, inflation (deflation) is defined as increases (decreases) in the supply of fiat paper money by government, not changes in the prices of individual goods and services. According to this definition, the cost of living and declining purchasing power of the dollar have been extraordinarily and unnecessarily high in modern times. If we use the monetary base (funds on deposit by the Federal Reserve) as a measure of fiat money, the money supply has increased 141 percent since the 1982–84 base period. If we use a broader definition, M2 (coins, currency, checking accounts, and money market funds), the money supply has increased 75 percent. Either way, monetary inflation has been significantly higher than the CPI's 60 percent. Perhaps increases in the money supply should be used as a better gauge of inflation. But it wouldn't make Washington happy—it would mean less tax revenue and higher Social Security checks.

---

1. *Wall Street Journal*, February 25, 1997, p. A24. Professor Boskin headed a government panel investigating the CPI.

2. Ludwig von Mises, *Human Action*, 3ʳᵈ ed. (Chicago: Regnery, 1966), p. 222.

A Golden Comeback, Part I

"A more timeless measure is needed; gold fits the bill perfectly."

—MARK MOBIUS

When speaking of the Midas metal, I'm reminded of Mark
Twain's refrain, "The reports of my death are greatly exag-
gerated." After years of central-bank selling and a bear market in
precious metals, the *Financial Times* recently declared the "Death
of Gold." But is it dead?

Following the Asian financial crisis in late 1997, Mark Mobius,
the famed Templeton manager of emerging markets, advocated
the creation of a new regional currency, the *asian,* convertible to
gold, including the issuance of Asian gold coins. "All their M1
money supply and foreign reserves would be converted into asians
at the current price of gold. Henceforth asians would be issued
only upon deposits of gold or foreign-currency equivalents of
gold."[1] Mobius castigated the central banks of Southeast Asia for
recklessly depreciating their currencies. As a result, "many businesses and banks throughout the region have become bankrupt,
billions of dollars have been lost, and economic development has
been threatened." Why gold? "Because gold has always been a
store of value in Asia and is respected as the last resort in times of
crisis. Asia's history is strewn with fallen currencies. . . . The
beauty of gold is that it limits a country's ability to spend to the
amount it can earn in addition to its gold holdings."

Not Just Another Commodity

Recent studies give support to Mobius's new monetary proposal. According to these studies, gold has three unique features: First, gold provides a stable numeraire for the world's monetary system, one that closely matches the "monetarist rule." Second, gold has had an amazing capacity to maintain its purchasing power throughout history, what the late Roy Jastram called "The Golden Constant." And, third, the yellow metal has a curious ability to predict future inflation and interest rates.

Let's start with gold as a stable monetary system. With most commodities, such as wheat or oil, the "carryover" stocks vary significantly with annual production. Not so with gold. Historical data confirm that the aggregate gold stockpile held by individuals and central banks always increases and never declines.[2] Moreover, the annual increase in the world gold stock typically varies between 1.5 and 3 percent, and seldom exceeds 3 percent. In short, the gradual increase in the stock of gold closely resembles the "monetary rule" cherished by Milton Friedman and the monetarists, where the money stock rises at a steady rate (see Chart I).

Compare the stability of the gold supply with the annual changes in the paper money supply held by central banks. As

Chart I

**The World Stock of Gold and the Share
Held by Central Banks, 1913-96**

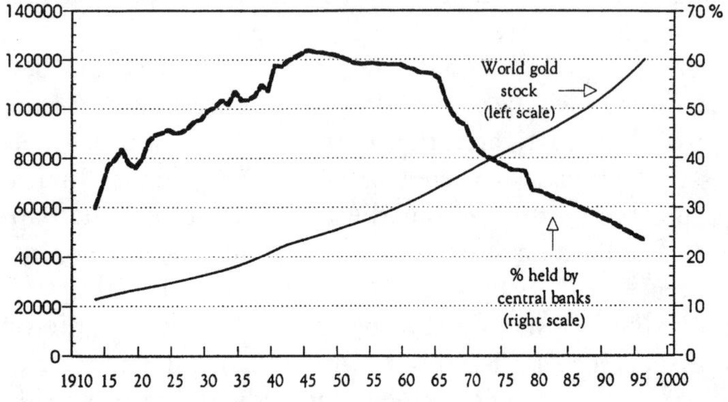

Source: H.C. Wainwright & Co.

Chart II indicates, the G-7 money-supply index rose as much as 17 percent in the early 1970s and as little as 3 percent in the 1990s. (Why has monetary growth slowed, even under a fiat money standard? The financial markets, especially the bondholders, have demanded fiscal restraint of their governments.) Moreover, the central banks' monetary policies were far more volatile than the gold supply. On a worldwide basis, gold proved to be more stable and less inflationary than a fiat money system.

Critics agree that gold is inherently a "hard" currency, but complain that new gold production can't keep up with economic growth. In other words, gold is too much of a hard currency. As noted, the world gold stock rises at a miserly annual growth rate of less than 3 percent and oftentimes under 2 percent, while GDP growth usually exceeds 3 or 4 percent and sometimes 7 or 8 percent in developing nations. The result? Price deflation is inevitable under a pure gold standard. My response: Critics are right that gold-supply growth is not likely to keep up with real GDP growth. Only during major gold discoveries, such as in California and Australia in the 1850s or South Africa in the 1890s, did world gold supplies grow faster than 4 percent a year.[3]

Chart II

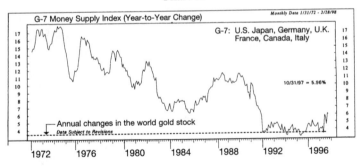

Courtesy: Dick Davis Digest

Prices Must Be Flexible

Consequently, an economy working under a pure gold standard will suffer gradual deflation; the price level will probably decline 1 to 3 percent a year, depending on gold production and economic growth. But price deflation isn't such a bad thing as long as it is gradual and not excessive. There have been periods of strong economic growth accompanying a general price deflation, such as the 1890s, 1920s, and 1950s. But price and wage flexibility is essential to make it work.

Next chapter: Update on Jastram's study *The Golden Constant,* and gold's amazing ability to maintain its purchasing power over the past 400 years.

---

1. Mark Mobius, "Asia Needs a Single Currency," *Wall Street Journal,* February 19, 1998, p. A22.

2. See the chart on page 84 of my *Economics of a Pure Gold Standard,* 3rd ed. (1997), available from FEE. Note how the world monetary stock of gold never has declined between 1810 and 1933.

3. Ibid., p. 86.

A Golden Comeback, Part II

"Gold maintains its purchasing power over long periods of
time, for example, half-century intervals."
—Roy Jastram, *The Golden Constant*[1]

In the previous essay, I focused on gold's inherent stability as a
monetary numeraire. Historically, the monetary base under gold
has neither declined nor increased too rapidly. In short, it has
operated very closely to a monetarist rule.

What about gold as an inflation hedge? In this essay, I discuss
the work of Roy Jastram and others who have demonstrated the
relative stability of gold in terms of its purchasing power—its ability to maintain value and purchasing power over goods and services over the long run. But the emphasis must be placed on the
"long run." In the short run, gold's value depends a great deal on
the rate of inflation and therefore often fails to live up to its reputation as an inflation hedge.

The classic study on the purchasing power of gold is *The
Golden Constant: The English and American Experience,
1560–1976*, by Roy W. Jastram, late professor of business at the
University of California, Berkeley. The book, now out of print,
examines gold as an inflation and deflation hedge over a span of
400 years.

Two Amazing Graphs

The accompanying two charts are from Jastram's book and updated through 1997 by the American Institute for Economic Research in Great Barrington, Massachusetts. They tell a powerful story:

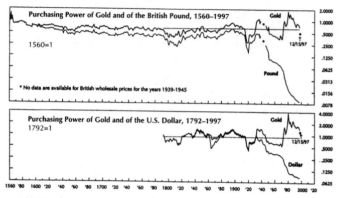

Courtesy the American Institute for Economic Research

FIGURE 1–1

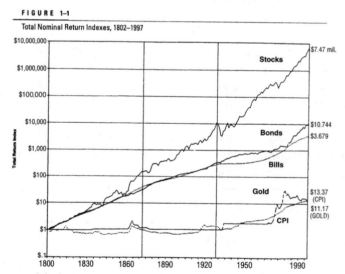

First, gold always returns to its full purchasing power, although it may take a long time to do so; and

Second, the price of gold became more volatile as the world moved to a fiat money standard beginning in the 1930s. Note how gold has moved up and down sharply as the pound and the dollar have lost purchasing power since going off the gold standard.

In my economics classes and at investment conferences, I have demonstrated the long-term value of gold by holding up a $20 St. Gaudens double-eagle gold coin. Prior to 1933, Americans carried this coin in their pockets as money. Back then, they could buy a tailor-made suit for one double eagle, or $20. Today this same coin—which is worth between $400 and $600, depending on its rarity and condition—could buy the same tailor-made suit. Of course, the double-eagle coin has numismatic, or rarity, value. A one-ounce gold-bullion coin, without numismatic value, is worth only around $300 today. Gold has risen substantially in dollar terms but has not done as well as numismatic U.S. coins.

Gold as an Inflation Hedge

The price of gold bullion was over $800 an ounce in 1980 and has steadily declined in value for nearly two decades. Does that mean it's not a good inflation hedge? Indeed, the record shows that when the inflation rate is steady or declining, gold has been a poor hedge. The yellow metal (and mining shares) typically responds best to accelerating inflation. Over the long run, the Midas metal has held its own, but should not be deemed an ideal or perfect hedge. In fact, U.S. stocks have proven to be much profitable than gold as an investment.

The work of Jeremy Siegel, professor of finance at the Wharton School of the University of Pennsylvania, has demonstrated that U.S. stocks have far outperformed gold over the past two centuries. Like Jastram, Siegel confirms gold's long-term stability. Yet gold can't hold a candle to the stock market's performance. As the chart, taken from his book, *Stocks for the Long Term*, shows, stocks have far outperformed bonds, T-bills, and gold. Why? Because stocks represent higher economic growth and productivity over the long run. Stocks have risen sharply in the twentieth century because of a dramatic rise in the standard of living and America's free-enterprise system.

One final note: Stocks tend to do poorly and gold shines when price inflation accelerates. As Siegel states, "Stocks turn out to be great long-term hedges against inflation even though they are often poor short-term hedges."[2] Price inflation is the key indicator: When the rate of inflation moves back up, watch out. Stocks could flounder and gold will come back to life. In the next chapter, I'll discuss the ability of gold to predict inflation and interest rates.

1. Roy W. Jastram, *The Golden Constant: The English and American Experience, 1560–1976* (New York: Wiley & Sons, 1977), p. 132.

2. Jeremy J. Siegel, *Stocks for the Long Run: A Guide to Selecting Markets for Long-Term Growth* (Burr Ridge, Ill.: Irwin, 1994), pp. 11–12.

A Golden Comeback, Part III

"A free gold market . . . reflects and measures the extent of the lack of confidence in the domestic currency."
—LUDWIG VON MISES

In the previous two chapters, I've highlighted the uses and misuses of gold. Despite occasional calls for a return to a gold standard, the Midas metal has largely lost out to hard currencies as a preferred monetary unit and monetary reserve. Most central banks are selling gold.

Gold has also done poorly as a crisis hedge lately. It has not rallied much during recent wars and international incidents. U.S. Treasury securities and hard currencies such as the Swiss franc have become the investments of choice in a flight to safety.

Nor has gold functioned well as an inflation hedge over the past two decades. The cost of living continues to increase around the world, yet the price of gold has fallen from $800 an ounce in 1980 to under $400 today.

What's left for the yellow metal? I see two essential functions for gold: first, a profitable investment when general prices accelerate and, second, an important barometer of future price inflation and interest rates.

Gold as a Profitable Investment

Since the United States went off the gold standard in 1971, gold bullion and gold mining shares have become well-known cyclical investments. The first graph demonstrates the volatile nature of gold and mining stocks, with mining shares tending to fluctuate more than gold itself. The gold industry can provide superior profits during an uptrend, and heavy losses during a downtrend.

One of the reasons for the high volatility of mining shares is their distance from final consumption. Mining represents the earliest stage of production and is extremely capital intensive and responsive to changes in interest rates.[1]

Gold as a Forecaster

Gold also has the amazingly accurate ability to forecast the direction of the general price level and interest rates. Recently, I ran an econometric model with the assistance of John List, economist at the University of Central Florida. We tested three commodity indexes (Dow Jones Commodity Spot Index, crude oil, and gold) to determine which one best anticipated changes in the Consumer Price Index (CPI) since 1970. It turned out that gold proved to be the best indicator of future inflation as measured by the CPI. The lag period is about one year. That is, gold does a good job of predicting the direction of the CPI a year in advance. (All three indexes did a poor job of predicting changes in the CPI on a monthly basis.)

Richard M. Salsman, economist at H. C. Wainwright & Co. in Boston, has also done some important work linking the price of gold with interest rates. As the second graph demonstrates, the price of gold often anticipates changes in interest rates in the United States. As Salsman states, "A rising gold price presages higher bond yields; a falling price signals lower yields. . . . Gold predicts yields well precisely because it's a top-down measure. It is bought and sold based purely on inflation-deflation expectations; thus it's the purest barometer of changes in the value of the dollar generally."[2]

In sum, if you want to know the future of inflation and interest rates, watch the gold traders at the New York Merc. If gold enters a sustained rise, watch out: higher inflation and interest rates may be on the way.

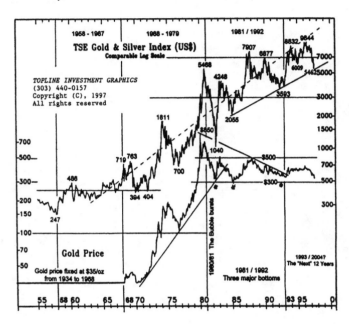

Figure Two

Gold Price and Treasury Bond Yields
1967 - present

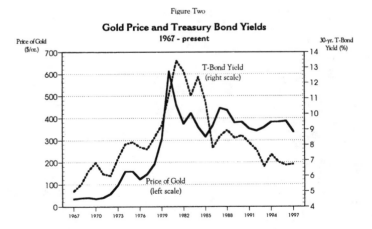

1. For further discussion regarding the inherent volatility of the mining industry, see my work *The Structure of Production* (New York: New York University Press, 1990), pp. 290–94.

2. Richard M. Salsman, "Looking for Inflation in All the Wrong Places," *The Capitalist Perspective* (Boston: H. C. Wainwright & Co. Economics), October 15, 1997.

Amazing Graph

"Both liberal and strict religious groups are more dynamic
when they have to compete for members on a level playing
field."

—GARY BECKER[1]

In the first essay of this book, "The Imperial Science," I argue
that the economics profession, like an invading army, is overrunning the whole of social science. I use examples in law, finance,
politics, history, and sports, concluding that it was high time to
replace the phrase "the dismal science" with the "imperial science."

Religion is another area where economic research has recently
made its mark. Lawrence Iannoccone (Santa Clara University) is
one of a handful of economists who specialize in religion and economics.[2] In the late 1980s Iannoccone tested Adam Smith's
hypothesis that freedom of religion would lead to a higher level of
attendance in church services. Smith believed that competition
benefits religious groups because they're forced to learn to satisfy
the needs of their members.[3] In testing this theory, Iannoccone
compared attendance at church and the degree of religious
monopoly in various Protestant and Catholic countries between
1968 and 1976. His test produced a striking result: church attendance varied inversely with church concentration in Protestant
nations. Church attendance among Protestants was high in freely

199

competitive nations, such as the United States, and low in countries monopolized by a single Protestant denomination, such as Finland. In short, the more religious freedom a nation enjoys, the more religious people are (as measured by church attendance).[4]

Soon after Iannoccone's study was completed, two sociologists applied market principles to the history of American religion and came to the same conclusion: religion thrives in a free-market environment. Roger Finke (Purdue) and Rodney Stark (University of Washington) found the United States to be almost a perfect experiment in what they termed an "unregulated, free market, religious economy." By the start of the American revolution, religious persecution had largely ended and tolerance gradually gave way to religious freedom. The largest denominations sought a tax-supported state religion, and even formed cartels aimed at preventing competition, but all efforts failed. Most states followed Virginia's lead in opposing any state church.

Finke and Stark came to the following remarkable findings using their explicit market model in studying religion in America:

First, fierce competition and the constant evolution of new religions in America resulted in a steady rise in church participation over the past two centuries. Amazingly, "America shifted from a nation in which most people took no part in organized religion to a nation in which nearly two thirds of American adults do."[5] (See the figure on the next page.)

The Impossible Dream of One Faith

The sociologists found, second, that it is impossible for one faith to dominate the nation in an environment of relentless competition. In colonial times, the Congregationalists and Episcopalians dominated. But they could not cope with the fierce competition from the Methodists, Catholics, and Baptists during the frequent revival periods of American history. Just as no corporate monopoly lasts forever, so also does it seem impossible for a mainstream religion to stay on top for long. Finke and Stark conclude that no religion, no matter how successful in the short run, can convert the whole world. Christians just don't seem to be content with one church, just as consumers can't agree on one car model or one type of tennis shoes. Over time, all markets—whether for automobiles, shoes, or religions—tend to show an increase in

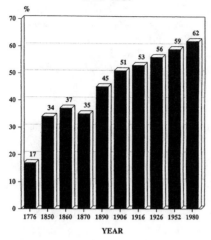

**Rates of Religious Adherence,
1776–1980**

Source: Finke and Stark, *The Churching of America*, p. 16.

quantity, quality, and variety. As Finke and Stark demonstrate, despite the constant call for all Christian groups to be "as one," unification efforts have repeatedly failed. The conventional wisdom that "all churches are alike" is inaccurate. Diversity is the lifeblood of religious life in America.

Third, Finke and Stark discovered that mainstream churches which compromised their principles and eliminated their "strong doctrines" invariably experienced widespread defection and ultimate failure, while churches that maintained high doctrinal standards, such as the Catholic Church, prospered. In other words, the market rewards the quality of religious worship. "We argue repeatedly that religious organizations can thrive only to the extent that they have a theology that can comfort souls and motivate sacrifice."[6]

Fourth, the scholars refuted the popular belief that urban communities are less religious than country life. Debunking the preachers' myth that city life is "wicked and secular," Finke and Stark provide evidence that church attendance rates are higher in cities than in rural areas.

In sum, we can see that the principles of economics are universal. Incentives, competition, quality, and choice apply not only to the material world, but to the spiritual realm as well.

1. Gary S. Becker and Guity Nashat Becker, *The Economics of Life* (New York: McGraw Hill, 1997), p. 16.

2. Another is Robert H. Nelson, author of two excellent books, *Reaching for Heaven on Earth: The Theological Meaning of Economics* (Savage, Md.: Rowman & Littlefield, 1991) and *Economics as Religion: From Samuelson to Chicago and Beyond* (University Park, Pa.: Penn State Press, 2001).

3. See Adam Smith, *The Wealth of Nations* (New York: Modern Library, 1965 [1776]), pp. 744–48. I discuss Adam Smith's views on religion in more detail in my book *The Making of Modern Economics* (New York: M.E. Sharpe, 2001), p. 27.

4. Lawrence Iannaccone, "The Consequences of Religious Market Structure," *Rationality and Society* (April 1991), pp. 156–77. See also "Adam Smith's Hypothesis on Religion," chapter 10 in Edwin G. West, *Adam Smith and Modern Economics* (Hants, England: Edward Elgar, 1990).

5. Roger Finke and Rodney Stark, *The Churching of America, 1776–1990: Winners and Losers in Our Religious Economy* (New Brunswick, N.J.: Rutgers University Press, 1992), p. 1.

6. Ibid., p. 5.

Ain't Misbehavin':
The New Science of
Behavorial Economics

"The human mind is charming in its unreasonableness, its
inveterate prejudices, and its waywardness and unpredictabil-
ity."

—Lin Yutang[1]

"Behavioral" finance is the hot new field in the rapidly growing "imperial" science of economics. Consider the titles of
recent books on the subject: *Irrational Exuberance* by Robert
Shiller of Yale University, who correctly warned investors in the
year 2000 that the bull market on Wall Street was not sustainable,
and *Why Smart People Make Big Money Mistakes* by Gary Belsky
and Thomas Gilovich.

Essentially, these writers take issue with a fundamental principle of economics—the concept of "rational" predictable behavior.
They argue that investors, consumers, and business people don't
always act according to the "rational economic man" standard,
but instead suffer from overconfidence, overreaction, fear, greed,
herding instincts, and other "animal spirits," to use John Maynard
Keynes's term.[2]

Their basic thesis is that people make mistakes all the time. Too
many individuals overspend and get into trouble with credit; they
don't save enough for retirement; they buy stocks at the top and

sell at the bottom; they fail to prepare a will. Economic failure, stupidity, and incompetence are common to human nature. As Ludwig von Mises notes, "To make mistakes in pursuing one's ends is a widespread human weakness."[3]

Fortunately, the market has a built-in mechanism to minimize mistakes and entrepreneurial error. The market penalizes mistakes and rewards correct behavior (witness how well business responded to the Y2K threat in the late 1990s). As Israel Kirzner states, "Pure profit opportunities exist whenever error occurs."[4]

But the new behavioral economists go beyond the standard market approach. They argue that new institutional measures can be introduced to minimize error and misjudgments, without involving the government.

At the American Economic Association meetings in Atlanta in January 2002, Richard Thaler of the University of Chicago presented a paper on his "SMART" savings plan, which is being tested by five corporations in the Chicago area. Thaler, author of *The Winner's Curse* and a pioneer in behavioral economics, has developed a new institutional method to increase workers' savings rates. Thaler noted that the average workers' savings rates are painfully low. I blame the low rate on high withholding taxes, but Thaler suggested that part of the problem is the way retirement programs are administered. He convinced these corporations to adopt his plan to have their employees enroll in an "automatic" investment 401(k) plan. Most corporations treat 401(k) plans as a voluntary program and, as a result, only half choose to sign up. In Thaler's plan, employees are automatically invested in 401(k) plans unless they choose to opt out.

Result? Instead of 49 percent signing up (as they do in a typical corporate investment plan), 86 percent participate.

Raises Invested

In addition, Thaler has participating employees automatically invest most of any pay increase in higher contributions to their 401(k) plans, so they never see their paychecks decline, even though their 401(k) plans are increasing. Consequently, employees under this SMART plan have seen their average savings rate increase from 3 to 11 percent.

Robert Shiller was a discussant at the session and rightly called Thaler's plan "brilliant." I agree. Having authored several investment books advocating "automatic investing" and dollar-cost-averaging plans,[5] I applaud Professor Thaler for taking the concept of automatic investing to a new level. If companies everywhere adopt his plan, it could indeed revolutionize the world and lead not only to a much more secure retirement for workers but to a higher saving and investment rate. The result could be a higher economic growth and standard of living throughout the world.

Most important, Thaler's plan is a private-sector initiative and does not require government intervention. In short, through innovative management techniques and education, individuals can solve their own financial and business problems without the help of the state.

---

1. Lin Yutang, *The Importance of Living* (New York: John Day Company, 1937), p. 57.

2. References to "animal spirits" and "waves of irrational psychology" can be found in John Maynard Keynes, *The General Theory of Employment, Interest, and Money* (New York: Macmillan, 1973 [1936]), pp. 161–62.

3. Ludwig von Mises, *Theory and History* (New Haven: Yale University Press, 1957), p. 268. However, Mises refuses to call bad decisions "irrational." He states, "Error, inefficiency, and failure must not be confused with irrationality. He who shoots wants, as a rule, to hit the mark. If he misses it, he is not 'irrational' he is a poor marksman."

4. Israel M. Kirzner, "Economics and Error" in *Perception, Opportunity, and Profit* (Chicago: University of Chicago Press, 1979), p. 135.

5. Mark and Jo Ann Skousen, *High Finance on a Low Budget* (Chicago: Dearborn, 1993) and *Mark Skousen's 30-Day Plan for Financial Independence* (Washington, D.C.: Regnery, 1995).

Who Is Henry Spearman?

> "So if there is a real model for Spearman, his identity remains
> a mystery, at least to me."
> — Herbert Stein, foreword,
> *Murder at the Margin*

Recently I took a break from writing and decided to read three murder mystery novels, all authored by Marshall Jevons, a penname for William Breit and Kenneth G. Elzinga, professors of economics at Trinity University (now retired) in San Antonio and the University of Virginia, respectively.

Elementary Economics, My Dear Watson

What makes these mysteries fascinating is the ingenious way the writers incorporate basic principles of economics to solve the murders. Marginal utility, the law of demand, consumer surplus, opportunity cost, profit maximization, game theory, and Adam Smith's invisible hand all play a part in advancing the stories and ultimately catching the culprits. As Henry Spearman, the detective-hero, says to the local police investigator in *Murder at the Margin,* "Elementary, my dear Vincent. Elementary economics, that is!"

Let me give you an example from each novel, without revealing the entire plot. In *Murder at the Margin* (Princeton University Press, 1978; paperback, 1993), Spearman is able to dismiss Mrs. Forte as a suspect in the killing of her husband because "a woman usually would be financially far better off by divorcing her husband than by killing him." Mrs. Forte's alimony payments over her expected lifetime would far exceed the death benefits from an insurance policy. Clearly, someone else must have killed Mr. Forte.

In the second novel, *Fatal Equilibrium* (MIT Press, 1985; Ballantine Books paperback, 1986), Spearman uncovers a fraud in the research of a fellow Harvard professor. In reviewing the professor's book on prices of various commodities in a remote island, Spearman discovers a statistic that violates the law of utility maximization. The sleuth quickly concludes that his colleague made up the figures . . . and therefore engaged in murder to hide his fictitious research.

In the third novel, *A Deadly Indifference* (Carroll & Graf, 1995), Spearman is led to suspect an individual who purchases an automobile even though another car in better condition is available at the same price. Obviously, Spearman reasons, the suspect values something in the first car to justify the monetary difference. That something leads to the murderer.

Defending the Free Market

Another likeable feature is the free-market bias running through the mystery series. Henry Spearman consistently defends economic liberty and attacks socialist thinking. He supports free trade, economic inequality, imperfect competition, and private property rights. The economist takes on collectivists of all shades—anthropologists, sociologists, environmentalists, social democrats, Keynesians, and Marxoids.

Who Is This Free-Market Economist?

Who is Henry Spearman, this remarkable proponent of free markets? Spearman is described as a short, balding, stubborn, frowsy professor, former president of the American Economic Association, and a "child of impecunious Jewish immigrants." Breit and Elzinga admit that they originally had Milton Friedman in mind, except that instead of the University of Chicago, Spearman comes from Harvard. "There is no such thing as a free lunch," Spearman declares in *Murder at the Margin* (p. 90). And like Friedman, Spearman is old-fashioned, using a pencil and paper, rather than a computer, to solve problems. Yet the focus of the amateur sleuth is decidedly microeconomic in nature, not monetary policy or macro-theorizing.

Austrian economists will be happy to find a great deal of Ludwig von Mises in Henry Spearman as well. (I thank Roger Garrison for this observation.) The detective-economist defends Say's Law, the financial markets, advertising, competition, commodity money, even methodological dualism. "Economics is different from chemistry," Spearman declares. "The methods are different. What goes on in one place doesn't necessarily go in another" (*Fatal Equilibrium*, p. 111). In *A Deadly Indifference*, the august professor delivers an unpopular speech before the Cambridge faculty in the mid-1960s, forecasting the collapse of Communism because it "is inconsistent with all that we know about the motivations of human action" (p. 36). Like Mises, who predicted the impossibility of socialist economic calculation, Spearman is ridiculed for his extreme position.

More Like Becker?

However, having read all three novels, my feeling is that Henry Spearman is more like Gary Becker than anyone else. Becker, Chicago professor and Nobel laureate, applies economics to marriage, crime, and other non-traditional areas. (See, for example, his book, *The Economic Approach to Human Behavior*, University of Chicago Press, 1976.) So does Spearman, "pushing his economics into criminology." He declares, "Love, hate, benevolence, malevolence or any emotion which involves others can be subject to economic analysis" (*Murder at the Margin*, p. 61).

Spearman, like Becker, also favors Marshall's definition of economics as the "study of man in the ordinary business of life." "Spearman took this definition seriously even though it was considered a bit old-fashioned to some of his younger colleagues who saw economics as a solving of abstract puzzles unrelated to real events" (*Murder at the Margin*, p. 113). The authors write that Spearman is trained in statistics and corroborates his "high logical standards" with "empirical evidence" (*Fatal Equilibrium*, p. 103).

Gary Becker's faithful application of microeconomic principles to solving problems is consistent with Henry Spearman's *modus operandi*. He may not look like Spearman, but he acts like him.

Breit and Elzinga are to be congratulated for developing a creative, clever way to expound the principles of free-market economics. The response has been gratifying. Many professors make *Murder at the Margin* and the other novels required reading in their classes. I recommend you put them on your summer reading list.

Changing People's Lives

Paul Samuelson's Last Hurrah

"Ours is the 'ruthless economy.'"
—PAUL A. SAMUELSON, "Valediction," *Economics* (1998)

Paul A. Samuelson, the MIT professor and Nobel laureate who introduced Keynesian economics to millions, published the 50th anniversary edition of *Economics* in 1998 (Irwin/McGraw-Hill, 16th edition). It is the most popular textbook of any kind ever written: it has sold over four million copies and has been translated into 46 languages. The latest edition may be his last.

Back to the Future: From Keynes to Adam Smith

In my writings, I have documented the dramatic changes in Samuelson's thinking over the past few years.[1] Along with the rest of the economics mainstream, he has shifted gradually from standard Keynesian analysis to the Classical model of Adam Smith. In the new edition, Samuelson replaces the old anti-saving doctrine known as the "paradox of thrift" with a major section bemoaning the low saving rate in the United States. Deficit spending, a perennial policy recommendation in earlier editions, is now anathema. Today monetary policy dominates fiscal policy. "The growing orientation toward the market," writes Samuelson, "has accompanied widespread desire for smaller government, less regulation, and lower taxes" (p. 735).

The 16th edition is remarkable in many ways. Samuelson and his coauthor, Yale professor William D. Nordhaus, cite free-mar-

213

ket economists Gary Becker and Julian Simon. They include a major biographical sketch of Joseph A. Schumpeter, an Austrian-born economist who later became one of Samuelson's valued professors at Harvard. (Schumpeter is best known for his emphasis of the role of the entrepreneur, criticism of the welfare state, and defense of big business.) And Samuelson finally admits that lighthouses were originally privately owned in Great Britain, after long maintaining that they were public goods that the free market could not provide.

Not Enough Friedman

However, his conversion to Classical free-market economics has often been grudging and incomplete. Take his treatment of Milton Friedman, the most influential free-market economist of the twentieth century. While Samuelson's new edition contains biographies of Adam Smith, John Maynard Keynes, Karl Marx, and even his colleague Robert Solow, there's none of Milton Friedman. Friedman cannot be ignored, of course, and he is cited briefly for his contributions to monetarism, the Phillips Curve debate, the natural rate of unemployment hypothesis, and the negative income tax. But nowhere does Samuelson credit him for his most important contribution, for which he won the Nobel Prize: his monumental work (co-authored with Anna J. Schwartz), *A Monetary History of the United States, 1867–1960* (Princeton University Press, 1963). In particular, Friedman demonstrated that government (the Federal Reserve), not free enterprise, caused the Great Depression by permitting the money supply to decline by one-third from 1929 to 1933.

Why did Samuelson deliberately omit Friedman's vital contribution? Because the old Keynesian cannot break with his mentor, Keynes, whom he proclaims as "this century's greatest economist" (p. 734). Samuelson still clings to the old-fashioned Keynesian view that blames the Great Depression on unbridled laissez-faire capitalism. His newest edition gives only the Keynesian interpretation of the 1930s. In his introductory remarks, "A Golden Birthday," he asserts: "The Great Depression of 1929–1935 had finally been licked by forceful programs that threw out the window the old orthodoxies of do-nothing monetary and fiscal policies" (p.

xxiv). I'd hardly call tight-money deflation of the Fed, massive tax increases, and Smoot-Hawley tariffs as "do-nothing" policies!

Friedman and other economic historians have demonstrated quite powerfully that inane government policies, not the free workings of the marketplace, are the cause of the debacle of the 1930s.

Classical vs. Keynesian Models: Which Comes First?

Samuelson and Nordhaus have also kept the Keynesian model first and foremost ahead of the Classical model. The Keynesian short-term model of business cycles (aggregate supply and demand or AS-AD) is introduced in Part 5 of *Economics,* and the Classical long-term model of economic growth is in Part 6. I have pointed out that long-term growth is more important than short-term business cycles, but Samuelson and Nordhaus are determined to stick with this traditional approach. Gregory Mankiw's popular textbook, *Economics* (Dryden Press, 1997) does just the opposite—it puts the Classical model first as the "general" theory, and the Keynesian model last as the "special" case. By making this counterrevolutionary change, Mankiw, who considers himself a New Keynesian, has essentially betrayed Keynes.[2] But Samuelson and Nordhaus refuse to do so.

Samuelson ends his 50th anniversary edition on a sour note. He senses that his view of economics has gradually lost out to the new dynamic forces of the global marketplace. He lashes out at the "ruthless" economy characterized by the "relentless pursuit of profits." He complains of the "growing" inequality of incomes and the "harsh" competitive environment where "old-fashioned loyalty to firm or community counts for little." I guess he's never read David Packard's *The HP Way* or noticed the growing number of firms offering profit-sharing and 401(k) plans. He admits there's a "silver lining behind this ruthlessness"—millions of new jobs in the dynamic U.S. economy versus rising unemployment in welfare-statist Europe. But does this new competitiveness generate "good jobs, adequate income, and a safe environment"? He doubts it.

Throughout his career, Samuelson has always praised the glories of the "mixed economy," free-market capitalism with a heavy dose of government interventionism. Now he must be content with what he unenthusiastically labels the "*limited* mixed economy."

---

1. See my columns in *The Freeman: Ideas on Liberty,* March 1994; October 1995; February 1996; September 1997. See also my article "The Perseverance of Paul Samuelson's *Economics,*" *The Journal of Economic Perspectives* (Spring 1997).

2. See my article, "Keynesianism Defeated," *Wall Street Journal,* editorial page, October 9, 1997.

Milton Friedman, Ex-Keynesian

> "I had completely forgotten how thoroughly Keynesian I then was."
>
> —Milton Friedman[1]

What?! The world's most famous free-market economist a former Keynesian?

Yes, it's true. One of the more remarkable revelations in Milton and Rose Friedman's autobiography, *Two Lucky People,* is Milton Friedman's flirtation with Keynesian economics in the early 1940s. During his stint with the Treasury Department, Friedman was asked to give testimony on ways to fight inflation during World War II. His reply, couched in Keynesian ideology, mentioned several options: cutting government spending, raising taxes, and imposing price controls. Amazingly, nowhere did he mention monetary policy or controlling the money supply, the things Friedman is famous for today.

During the 1930s, Friedman had also favored Keynesian-style deficit spending as a way out of the Great Depression. His mentor was not Keynes himself but Friedman's teachers at the University of Chicago. Friedman recounts, "Keynes had nothing to offer those of us who had sat at the feet of [Henry] Simons, [Lloyd W.] Mints, [Frank] Knight, and [Jacob] Viner."[2] In short, Chicago economists were Keynesian before Keynes.

In his autobiography, Friedman says he was "cured" of Keynesian thinking "shortly after the end of the war," but doesn't elaborate. In correspondence, he denies ever being a thorough Keynesian. "I was never a Keynesian in the sense of being persuaded of the virtues of government intervention as opposed to free markets." It should also be pointed out that Friedman's teachers at Chicago blamed the Great Depression on "misguided government policy." Friedman indicates he was "hostile" to the Keynesian idea that the Depression was a market phenomenon.[3]

Despite these statements, many free-market economists have long accused Friedman of being a quasi-Keynesian.

On December 31, 1965, *Time* magazine put John Maynard Keynes on the cover and quoted Friedman as saying, "We are all Keynesians now." Later, Friedman said he was quoted out of context. "In one sense, we are all Keynesians now; in another, no one is a Keynesian any longer. We all use the Keynesian language and apparatus; none of us any longer accepts the initial Keynesian conclusions."[4]

In an article published in 1986, Friedman glorified Keynes as a "brilliant scholar" and "one of the great economists of all time." He described *The General Theory* as a "great book," although he considers his *Tract on Monetary Reform* as his best work. Moreover, he declared, "I believe that Keynes's theory is the right kind of theory in its simplicity, its concentration on a few key magnitudes, its potential fruitfulness."[5]

Many conservatives wonder how Milton Friedman, defender of free markets, could speak so highly of a man considered the intellectual architect of the postwar inflation and the modern welfare state.

Friedman is known as the leader of the Monetarist opposition to the Keynesian revolution. According to Friedman, monetary policy (manipulation of the money supply and interest rates) influences economic activity far more than fiscal policy (taxes and government spending). Yet it must be remembered that monetary and fiscal policies are both forms of state intervention in the economy. Accordingly, some free-market advocates see Keynes and Friedman as partners in crime.

Granted, Friedman, as opposed to the Keynesians, favors a strict limit on monetary growth. Yet even Friedman occasionally succumbs to interventionist fever. In late 1997, he endorsed this remedy for Japan's sluggish economy: print more money. Apparently Friedman felt that the easy-money policy in effect in Japan since 1994 (recent M1 was growing at 9.9 percent, M2 at 4.3 percent) was insufficient. "The surest road to a healthy economic recovery," he wrote, "is to increase the rate of monetary growth." What about tax relief, deregulation, and open markets? Friedman failed to list any of these options.[6] Undoubtedly he favors these remedies, but the article rekindled the old accusation that "only money matters" to Friedman.

Friedman the Anti-Keynesian

I have to admit that, like many free-market economists, I am surprised by these findings and the favorable comments Friedman has made about Keynes. I've always viewed the leader of the Chicago school as strongly anti-Keynesian. His *Monetary History of the United States* clearly contradicts Keynes's contention that the capitalist system is inherently unstable.[7] The book shows that the Fed's inept policies, not free enterprise, caused the Great Depression. Friedman's permanent-income hypothesis modifies Keynes's consumption function and undermines the case for progressive taxation. His natural-rate-of-unemployment doctrine denies any long-run tradeoff between inflation and unemployment (the Phillips curve). In *Capitalism and Freedom*, Friedman challenges the effectiveness of the Keynesian multiplier and declares that the federal budget is the "most unstable component of national income in the postwar period."[8] And, as early as 1963, he labeled as "erroneous" the Keynesian proposition that the free-market economy an be stuck indefinitely at less than full employment.[9]

So where does that leave us? In one of the more controversial contributions to my edited volume *Dissent on Keynes*, Roger Garrison of Auburn University asks, "Is Milton Friedman a Keynesian?" Garrison contends he can argue it either way. Indeed. Yet, in the final verdict, I can't help but think that Friedman, as an open-minded scholar, is willing to investigate and test all theories, no matter their source, and this methodology has gradually led him to discard most of Keynesianism. As he himself has written, "I have been led to reject it . . . because I believe that it has been contradicted by experience."[10]

1. Milton Friedman and Rose Friedman, *Two Lucky People* (Chicago: University of Chicago Press, 1998), p. 113.

2. Milton Friedman, "Comments on the Critics," in Robert J. Gordon, ed., *Milton Friedman's Monetary Framework* (Chicago: University of Chicago Press, 1974), p. 163.

3. "Comments on Critics," pp. 48–49.

4. Milton Friedman, "Why Economists Disagree," *Dollars and Deficits* (New York: Prentice-Hall, 1968), p. 15.

5. Milton Friedman, "Keynes's Political Legacy," in John Burton, ed., *Keynes's General Theory: Fifty Years On* (London: Institute of Economic Affairs, 1986), pp. 47–48, 52.

6. Milton Friedman, "Rx for Japan: Back to the Future," *Wall Street Journal*, p. A22, December 17, 1997.

7. With Anna J. Schwartz (Princeton: N.J.: Princeton University Press, 1963).

8. Milton Friedman, *Capitalism and Freedom* (Chicago: University of Chicago Press, 1962), p. 76.

9. Milton Friedman and David Meiselman, "The Relative Stability of Monetary Velocity and the Investment Multiplier in the United States, 1897–1958," in E. Cary Brown, et al., ed., *Stabilization Policies* (New York: Prentice-Hall, 1963), p. 167. See also Friedman's recently published article, "John Maynard Keynes," *Economic Quarterly*, Federal Reserve Bank of Richmond, 83/2, Spring 1997.

10. "Keynes's Political Legacy," p. 48.

Great Turnabouts in Economics: Stigler, Heilbroner, Robbins

> "There is no harm in being sometimes wrong—especially if one is promptly found out."
>
> —John Maynard Keynes

The gradual transformation of Paul Samuelson from Keynesian to classical economics is a major chapter in famous cases of economists changing their minds.

Nobody likes to admit he's wrong. You can probably count on your fingers the number of times scholars have renounced their theories and switched positions. Most academics have a tendency to cling to old dogmas, especially if they have built a reputation on a particular doctrine. We can only admire the scholar who is willing to change when he is convinced by the facts or a new theory. It takes a strong dose of courage and honesty to go against one's vested interest, especially after publishing books and articles on the subject.

Three prominent economists have admitted error and changed their thinking, and we can learn much from their experience.

George Stigler and Antitrust

George Stigler, the towering Chicago professor and Nobel Laureate, was a firm defender of antitrust laws in the 1940s and 1950s. He was influenced by Henry Simons, a leading spokesman for the Chicago School. Simons taught that big business posed a serious problem in the United States and advocated the nationalization of railroads, utilities, and all other "uncompetitive" industries—all in a book ironically entitled *Economic Policy for a Free Society* (University of Chicago, 1948). Stigler moved in a different direction, advocating the breakup of "concentrated" big businesses and punishment of companies engaged in collusion. He appeared before Congress in 1950 and proposed that U.S. Steel Corporation be broken up.

By the early 1970s, however, Stigler had changed his mind. Influenced by the work of Aaron Director and Joseph Schumpeter and a new theory of oligopoly, he found himself shifting his views. "What is still more embarrassing is that I no longer believe the economics I was preaching," he declared.[1] Concluding that concentration did not necessarily lead to monopolistic pricing, Stigler switched positions and actively opposed most antitrust legislation.

Robert Heilbroner and Socialist Planning

For most of his life, Robert Heilbroner, author of *The Worldly Philosophers,* a best-selling history of economics, was a socialist. Under the influence of Adolph Lowe and the New School of Social Research, he became enamored with Marxism. When the Polish economist Oskar Lange assailed Ludwig von Mises's attack on socialist central planning in the 1930s, Heilbroner joined the rest of the profession and concluded that Mises was wrong and socialism could work.

By the end of the 1980s, however, Heilbroner dramatically altered his views. In a stunning series of articles in *The New Yorker,* he wrote that the long-standing debate between capitalism and socialism was over, and "capitalism has won."[2] In a follow-up article after the demise of the Eastern Bloc, he was even more explicit: "Socialism has been a great tragedy this century. . . . But collapse! No one expected collapse. . . . There is no doubt that the collapse marks its end as a model of economic clarity."[3] Furthermore, the debate between Lange and Mises had to be re-examined in light of contemporary events. "It turns out, of course, that Mises was right," declared Heilbroner. Needless to say, Heilbroner's change of heart did little to endear him to socialists.

Lionel Robbins and Austrian Economics

Not every event is positive for free-market economics. The most notorious example of switching sides occurred when Lionel Robbins, a major proponent of the Austrian school of free-market economics, converted to Keynesianism. In the United States, several prominent classical economists had already changed views, especially Harvard's Alvin Hansen. But Robbins's conversion was infamous because, as chairman of the economics department at the London School of Economics, he had brought F. A. Hayek from Austria to England, and had been instrumental in translating and publishing Hayek's and Mises's works. He also wrote extensively about Austrian economics, including the illuminating *The Great Depression* (Macmillan, 1934).

However, he fell under the trance of John Maynard Keynes during World War II. In his autobiography, he repudiated the Austrian connection: "I shall always regard this aspect of my dispute with Keynes as the greatest mistake of my professional career, and the book, *The Great Depression,* which I subsequently wrote, partly in justification of this attitude, as something which I would willingly see forgotten."[4]

I should hope that if Lionel Robbins were alive today he would reconsider his views and see the Keynesian episode more of a "diversion" from sound classical economics (to use a term created by Leland Yeager) than as a "general" economic theory.

---

1. George J. Stigler, *Memoirs of an Unregulated Economist* (New York: Basic Books, 1988), p. 99.

2. Robert Heilbroner, "The Triumph of Capitalism," *The New Yorker,* January 23, 1989, p. 98. Note he wrote this article before the collapse of the Berlin Wall and the Soviet Union.

3. Heilbroner, "Reflections After Communism," *The New Yorker,* September 10, 1990, pp. 91–2.

4. Lionel Robbins, *Autobiography of an Economist* (New York: Macmillan, 1971), p. 154.

Great Turnabouts in
Economics: Mark Blaug

"I used to love hedgehogs but those were 'my salad days when
I was green in judgement'. Now I prefer foxes—Smith over
Ricardo, Mill over Senior, Marshall over Walras."
                                            —MARK BLAUG[1]

In the last essay, I reported on three economists who coura-
geously reversed their published views. Now, I'd like to add a
fourth: Mark Blaug. He is a prolific and intense writer, and most
famous for his arduous textbook, *Economic Theory in Retrospect*
(Cambridge University Press, 1997). Blaug is primarily a historian
of economic ideas and as such, he is, to borrow from Peter
Drucker, a "bystander," an unbiased reporter and critic of economic ideas. And my, does Mark Blaug write with profundity and
wit. His book, *Not Only an Economist: Recent Essays by Mark
Blaug*, is one of the most delightful books I've read in a long time.
I found myself making notes and exclamation points on practically
every page.

As perhaps the most profound keeper of economic thought
since Joseph Schumpeter, Blaug has made remarkable progress.
His unrelenting search for truth has led him along the intellectual
road from Karl Marx to Adam Smith, and even now shows
increasing sympathy with Joseph Schumpeter, F. A. Hayek, and
the Austrian school.

Blaug's intellectual odyssey is curiously broad: like Whittaker

Chambers, he started out a Marxist and a card-carrying member of the American Communist Party, then became disillusioned and betrayed. He flirted with Freud, but now recognizes Freudian psychology to be a "tissue of mumbo-jumbo." Regarding religion, Blaug "was brought up an orthodox Jew, achieved pantheism by the age of 12, agnosticism by the age of 15, and militant atheism by the age of 17."[2] He has shifted ground as frequently as he has transferred allegiance: born in the Netherlands, educated in the United States, and now a resident of Great Britain.

The Perversity of Ricardo, Marx, and Sraffa

Blaug's sojourn in economics is equally diverse. Leaving Marx, he became a convert to the British economist David Ricardo, wrote his Ph.D. dissertation on Ricardian economics, and even named his first son after him. But eventually he concluded that Ricardian economics is flawed and too formalistic. Blaug is especially disturbed by the development of a perverse version of Ricardian economics known as Sraffian economics. Sraffian economics is named after Piero Sraffa, author of the obscure theoretical work *Production of Commodities by Means of Commodities* (Cambridge University Press, 1960), which has highly influenced Marxists and post-Keynesians. Essentially, Sraffa uses a Ricardian model to claim that national output is completely independent of wages, prices, or consumer demand. Accordingly, governments can pursue their grandest redistributive schemes without damaging economic growth in the least.

In a scathing critique of *The New Palgrave Dictionary of Economics,* Blaug lambastes Sraffian economics as mathematically obtuse and irrelevant to the real world, and assails the editors for citing Marx and Sraffa "more frequently, indeed, much more frequently, than Adam Smith, Alfred Marshall, Léon Walras, Maynard Keynes, Kenneth Arrow, Milton Friedman, Paul Samuelson or whomever you care to name."[3]

Recently, Blaug has criticized modern economics for the "noxious influence" of Swiss economist Léon Walras in creating the "perfectly competitive general equilibrium model," or GE for short. Most of the textbook writers, including Paul Samuelson, are enamored with GE, because of its mathematical precision. For example, the perfect competition model focuses on the final end-state of competition, rather than the competitive process itself. Blaug labels perfect competition a "grossly misleading concept" that ignores the role of the entrepreneur. He urges economists to "rewrite the textbooks" and replace the current Walrasian GE model with the dynamic Austrian view of the competitive process.[4]

Blaug on Austrian Economics

Joseph Schumpeter, F.A. Hayek, and Israel Kirzner have been in the forefront of developing the Austrian view of competition. Blaug writes favorably about them all. Although belittling Mises's methodology ("cranky and idiosyncratic") and his business-cycle theory ("empty"), he grants Mises and Hayek "the better case" in the socialist calculation debate. He rates Schumpeter's *The Theory of Economic Development* (1911) one of the three most important books ever written by an economist. Ultimately he prefers Hayek: "In short, it is Hayek, not Mises, who deserves to be patron saint of Austrian economics."[5]

Incomplete Conversion

Blaug's conversion toward free-market capitalism is on the right track. He has gradually shifted toward Adam Smith and Hayek, though he is still enamored with John Maynard Keynes, who he says caused a "permanent revolution." Keynes divides the time line between Blaug's two biographical works, *Great Economists Before Keynes* and *Great Economists Since Keynes*. His current attitude is summed up as "capitalism tempered by Keynesian demand management and quasi-socialist welfarism."[6] Hopefully, that's not the final word on his economic philosophy.

One last note. Regarding Blaug's intolerance of religion, I'm reminded of G.K. Chesterton's response to H.G. Wells's atheism: "H.G. suffers from the disadvantage that if he's right he'll never know. He'll only know if he's wrong."[7] And the last thing that Mark Blaug wants to find out is that he is wrong.

1. Mark Blaug, *Economic Theory in Retrospect,* 5th ed. (Cambridge: Cambridge University Press, 1997), preface. According to the Greek poet Archilochus (c. 680 B.C.), "The fox knows many things, but the hedgehog knows one great thing."

2. Mark Blaug, *Not Only an Economist: Recent Essays by Mark Blaug* (London: Edward Elgar, 1997), preface.

3. Mark Blaug, *Economics Through the Looking Glass: The Distorted Perspective of The New Palgrave Dictionary of Economics* (London: Institute of Economic Affairs, 1988), p. 15.

4. Mark Blaug, "Competition as an end-state and a process," *Not Only an Economist,* pp. 78–81.

5. Ibid., pp. 90–91.

6. Ibid., p. 9.

7. Quoted in Joseph Pearce, *Wisdom and Innocence: A Life of G. K. Chesterton* (Washington, D.C.: Ignatius Press, 1996), p. 133.

A One-Armed
Economist, Please:
Sen vs. Bauer

"[W]hile purity is an uncomplicated virtue for olive oil, sea
air, and heroines of folk tales, it is not so for systems of collective choice."

—AMARTYA SEN[1]

President Harry Truman hated what he termed two-armed economists, those who would advise him first "on the one hand"
and then "on the other hand." Give me a one-armed economist, he
demanded, an adviser who wouldn't waffle.

I was reminded of this story when I read some of the writings of
the Indian economist Amartya Sen, the winner of the 1998 Nobel
Prize in economics. He won the prestigious award (worth nearly
$1 million) for his work on poverty, famine, inequality, growth
theory, human rights, and ethics, all those wide-ranging debate
topics common to development economics.

Writing on these topics is commendable; I just wish I knew what
he was saying. Sen is one of those economists that Truman complained about. He represents everything that is wrong-headed
about modern economics, which Peter Drucker has rightly
described as "clever, brilliant, and bankrupt economics."[2]

Too Much Sen

Sen has all the establishment credentials. He's taught at Harvard and Cambridge and was president of the American Economic

Association in 1994. His mentors are Joan Robinson, Kenneth Arrow, and philosopher John Rawls. A prolific scholar, Sen has written and read everything imaginable on his favorite subjects. He cites dozens and dozens of authors. He engages in heavy mathematical modeling and game theory. He weighs the pros and cons of every nuance of high theory. And yet, when it comes to his own view, he never seems to come to a simple conclusion. For Sen, everything is complex and indeterminate.

For example, in 1985 he gave a series of lectures at Cambridge University, subsequently published as *The Standard of Living* (Cambridge University Press, 1987). Is it possible to measure and compare living standards between individuals or nations? Sen is never sure. In his works on inequality, he rejects utility-based comparisons of income and even distinguishes between "well-being" and "standard of living." When you're through reading Sen, you feel like joining the pure subjectivists-relativists. In an often-cited article, "Rational Fools," Sen offers a critique of utilitarianism and self-interest, saying at one point, "this approach presumes both too little and too much."[3] Only in Sen's world would that be possible.

The only case I know where Sen establishes a clear position is on famines, an area he knows firsthand. Liberal democracies, he says, avoid famines. "In the terrible history of famines round the world, no substantial famine has ever occurred in a democracy."[4]

In trying to be ultra-scholarly, Sen obfuscates more than he elucidates. As Sylvia Nasar wrote in the *New York Times* (October 15, 1998), Sen is "highly influential, but wide-ranging, diffuse, lacking a single killer theorem." The Chinese philosopher Lin Yutang put it best, "If one is too well-read, then one does not know right is right and wrong is wrong."[5]

"One-Armed" Bauer

Give me a one-armed economist! In development theory, that candidate would have been the late Lord Bauer. Whether you agreed with him or not, you had no doubt where he stood. He was an ardent polemicist in defense of democratic capitalism (including private property, free trade, and limited government) in developing countries.

P. T. Bauer was a long-time dissenter in development economics who was finally vindicated. In that sense, he followed in the footsteps of other free-market economists—including Milton Friedman, who was ultimately proven right about the efficacy of monetary policy, and Ludwig von Mises and F. A. Hayek, who accurately predicted that socialist central planning could never work.

In the postwar period, Bauer waged a lonely battle against foreign aid, comprehensive central planning, nationalization, and other anti-market schemes. He denied the then-current orthodoxy, such as the vicious cycle of poverty and W. W. Rostow's stages of economic growth. Today even Rostow admits, "there are, evidently, serious and correct insights in the Bauer position; for example, the shrewd and quick responsiveness of farmers to incentives and disincentives, the superiority of competitive private over public trading systems."[6]

Like Sen, Bauer had extensive experience in the developing world, having spent years in Asia and Africa as a writer and consultant. He warned the Indian government repeatedly that its five-year plans would never achieve their lofty goals. (The only Indian economist he respected was B.R. Shenoy, a lone dissenter.)

The IMF could learn a lot from reading Bauer's classic textbook, *The Economics of Under-Developed Countries,* co-authored by B.S. Yamey (Cambridge University Press, 1957). And one of the best short essays ever written is "The Lesson of Hong Kong."[7] Other essays can be found in *Dissent on Development* (Harvard University Press, 1976) and *The Development Frontier* (Harvester, 1991). The Cato Institute has also published a book, *The Revolution in Development Economics,* edited by James A. Dorn, Steve H. Hanke, and Alan S. Walters, that was dedicated to Lord Bauer and includes many of his articles. Nothing could be better, short of a Nobel Prize.

---

1. Amartya K. Sen, *Collective Choice and Social Welfare* (San Francisco: Holden-Day, 1970), p. 200.

2. Peter F. Drucker, *The Unseen Revolution* (New York: Harper & Row, 1976), pp. 114–15.

3. Amartya K. Sen, "Rational Fools: A Critique of the Behavioral Foundations of Economic Theory," cited in H. Harris, ed., *Scientific Models and Men* (New York: Oxford University Press, 1978), pp. 317–44.

4. Amartya Sen, *Prospect*, October 1995, cited in Chris Patten, *East and West* (New York: Macmillan, 1998), p. 198.

5. Lin Yutang, *The Importance of Living* (New York: John Day Company, 1937), p. viii. Yutang's profound book has been reprinted by William Morrow. I highly recommend it.

6. W. W. Rostow, *Theorists of Economic Growth from David Hume to the Present* (New York: Oxford University Press, 1990), p. 386.

7. P. T. Bauer, "The Lesson of Hong Kong," *Equality, the Third World and Economic Delusion* (Cambridge, Mass.: Harvard University Press, 1981). P. T. Bauer died in the spring of 2002, shortly after he was named winner of the Milton Friedman Prize for Advancing Liberty by the Cato Institute.

What It Takes to Be an
Objective Scholar

"It was the facts that changed my mind."
—JULIAN SIMON[1]

During the 1990s, we watched the Dow Jones Industrial Average increase fourfold and Nasdaq stocks tenfold. Yet there were well-known investment advisers—some of them my friends—who were bearish during the entire period, missing out on the greatest bull market in history.[2]

By the same token, the early 2000s witnessed a dramatic bear market that many bullish advisers failed to predict.

How is this possible? What kind of prejudices would keep an intelligent analyst from missing an overwhelming trend? In the financial business the key to success is a willingness to change your mind when you're wrong. Stubbornness can be financially ruinous. When a market goes against you, you should always ask, "What am I missing?"

Over the years, I've encountered three kinds of investment analysts: those who are always bullish; those who are always bearish; and those whose outlook depends on market conditions. I've found that the third type, the most flexible, are the most successful on Wall Street.

Confessions of a Gold-Bug Technician

A good friend of mine is a technical analyst who searches the movement of prices, volume, and other technical indicators to determine the direction of stocks and commodities. Most financial technicians are free of prejudices and will invest their money wherever they see a positive upward trend, and avoid (or sell short) markets that are seen in a downward trend. But my friend is a gold bug and no matter what the charts show, he somehow interprets them to suggest that gold is ready to reverse its downward trend and head back up. Equally, he always seems to think the stock market has peaked and is headed south. As a result, throughout the entire 1990s, he missed out on the great bull market on Wall Street and lost his shirt chasing gold stocks.

I also see this type of prejudice in the academic world. Some analysts are anti-market no matter what. Take, for example, Lester Brown, president of the Worldwatch Institute in Washington, D.C., who puts out the annual *State of the World* and other alarmist surveys and data. He gathers together all kinds of statistics and graphs showing a decline in our standard of living and the growing threat of population growth, environmental degradation, the spread of the AIDS virus, and so on. For example, despite clear evidence of sharply lower fertility rates in most nations, Brown concludes, "stabilizing population may be the most difficult challenge of all."[3]

Too bad Julian Simon, the late professor of economics at the University of Maryland, is no longer around to dispute Brown and the environmental doomsdayers. Simon was as optimistic about the world as Brown is pessimistic. Simon's last survey of world economic conditions, *The State of Humanity,* was published in 1995. That book, along with his *The Ultimate Resource* (and its second edition), came to the exact opposite of Brown's conclusions. "Our species is better off in just about every measurable material way."[4]

Yet Julian Simon was not simply a Pollyanna optimist. He let the facts affect his thinking. In the 1960s, Simon was deeply worried about population and nuclear war, just like Lester Brown, Paul Ehrlich, and their colleagues. But Simon changed his mind after investigating and discovering that "the available empirical data did not support that theory."[5]

Scholars Who See the Light

The best scholars are those willing to change their minds after looking at the data or discovering a new principle. They admit their mistakes when they have been proven wrong. You don't see it happen often, though. Once a scholar has built a reputation around a certain point of view and has published books and articles on his pet theory, it's almost impossible to recant. This propensity applies to scholars across the political spectrum.

We admire those rare intellectuals who are honest enough to admit that their past views were wrong. For example, when New York historian Richard Gid Powers began his history of the anticommunist movement, his attitude was pejorative. He had previously written a highly negative book on J. Edgar Hoover, *Secrecy and Power*. Yet after several years of painstaking research, he changed his mind: "Writing this book radically altered my view of American anticommunism. I began with the idea that anticommunism displayed America at its worst, but I came to see in anticommunism America at its best."[6] That's my kind of scholar.

---

1. Julian L. Simon, *The Ultimate Resource 2* (Princeton, N.J.: Princeton University Press, 1996), preface.

2. See the revealing article, "Down and Out on Wall Street," *New York Times,* Money & Business Section, Sunday, December 26, 1999.

3. Lester R. Brown, Gary Gardner, and Brian Halweil, *Beyond Malthus* (New York: Norton, 1999), p. 30.

4. Julian L. Simon, *The State of Humanity* (Cambridge, Mass.: Blackwell, 1995), p. 1.

5. Simon, *The Ultimate Resource 2*, preface.

6. Richard Gid Powers, *Not Without Honor: The History of American Anticommunism* (New York: Free Press, 1996), p. 503.

Today's Most
Influential Economist?

"But half a century later, it is Keynes who has been toppled
and [_____], the fierce advocate of free markets, who is
preeminent."

—DANIEL YERGIN AND JOSEPH STANISLAW,
The Commanding Heights[1]

Fill in the blank. Who is the mysterious economist named
above? Most of my colleagues named Milton Friedman, but in
Daniel Yergin and Joseph Stanislaw's bestseller, the Chicago
economist runs a close second to. . . . F.A. Hayek, the Austrian
economist!

Why Hayek? Because, according to Yergin and Stanislaw,
Hayek has done more than any other economist to debunk socialism in its many forms—Marxism, communism, and industrial
planning—and to promote free markets as an alternative system.
Hayek's influence perfectly illustrates John Maynard Keynes's
remark that politicians, "madmen in authority," are the "slaves of
some defunct economist."[2]

Indeed, Hayek's influence has been ubiquitous. As Yergin and
Stanislaw point out, *The Road to Serfdom* greatly affected Margaret Thatcher in reforming Great Britain and raised doubts about
industrial planning. Hayek's criticisms of Keynesianism (*A Tiger
by the Tail*) called into question deficit spending and the ability of

235

the state to fine-tune the economy. His theory of decentralized knowledge and competition as a discovery process has had an impact on microeconomic theory and experimental economics. His work on the trade cycle and the denationalization of currencies has influenced monetary policy. His co-founding of the Mont Pelerin Society spread the gospel of free markets, property rights, and libertarian thought throughout the globe.[3]

A Surprising Victory

Yergin and Stanislaw's revelation in *The Commanding Heights: The Battle Between Government and the Marketplace That Is Remaking the World* is a monumental victory for Austrian economics. It is all the more remarkable given Yergin's background as an establishment journalist and author of *The Prize,* a Pulitzer Prize-winning book about big oil.

At the beginning of this decade, I argued in *Economics on Trial* that the "next economics" would be the Austrian model, with its focus on entrepreneurship, microeconomics, deregulation, savings, free enterprise, and sound money.[4] But even I am surprised how rapidly Hayek and the Austrian school have achieved recognition.

The next step is to see how quickly the economics profession absorbs Austrian economics in its theories and textbooks. A quick review of the current top-ten textbooks reveals only two with significant entries on Hayek and the Austrians: Roy Ruffin and Paul Gregory's sixth edition of *Principles of Economics,* and James Gwartney and Richard Stroup's eighth edition of *Economics: Private and Public Choice.* Ruffin and Gregory give credit to Hayek (and Mises) for the fall of socialism, one of Ruffin and Gregory's "defining moments in economics." Curious note: Ruffin and Gregory's fifth edition had no references to Hayek or Mises; clearly Ruffin and Gregory are quick to recognize a paradigm shift.

Other textbook writers are not so prescient. Samuelson's 16th (50th anniversary) edition highlights only Joseph A. Schumpeter. Textbooks by David Collander, John Taylor, and Joseph Stiglitz cite Hayek only once, while top sellers by Roger LeRoy Miller; Michael Parkin; William Baumol and Alan Blinder; Campbell

McConnell and Stanley Brue; and Paul Heyne make no references to Hayek and the Austrians.

A Tale of Two Cities

Yergin and Stanislaw rightly point to two schools of free-market economics responsible for the shift from government to private enterprise as the solution to world economic problems. "And the eventual victory of this viewpoint was really a tale of two cities— Vienna and Chicago," declare the authors.[5]

In the judgment of many economists, Milton Friedman and the Chicago school have had even a greater influence than Hayek and the Austrians. Yergin acknowledges Friedman as "the world's best-known economist," noting that "the Chicago School loomed very large" in its sway on monetarism at the Federal Reserve and economic policy (under Ronald Reagan). And, of course, all top-ten textbooks in economics have significant sections on Friedman and his theories (monetarism, natural rate of unemployment, welfare reform, privatization). Friedman and the Chicago school have mounted an effective counter-revolution to Keynesianism.

The Great U-Turn

But Keynes's principal rival in the 1930s was Hayek. Teaching at the London School of Economics, Hayek defended the classical model of thrift, balanced budgets, the gold standard, and free markets, while Keynes (Cambridge University) promoted the "new economics" of consumption, deficit spending, easy money, and big government. Keynes won the first battle for the hearts of economists, and his brand of "mixed economy" swept the profession. Hayek fell out of favor and went on to write about law and political science. The task of dethroning Keynes fell to Friedman; he has accomplished it masterfully.

Since winning the Nobel Prize in economics in 1974, Hayek and the Austrians have had a rebirth. Equally, Friedman and the Chicago school have come out of obscurity into prominence. Fifty years ago the Keynesian-collectivist consensus expressed the sentiment, "The state is wise and the market is stupid." Today, the

growing consensus is just the opposite: "The market is wise and the state is stupid."
Break out the champagne. It's time to celebrate.

---

1. Daniel Yergin and Joseph Stanislaw, *The Commanding Heights: The Battle Between Government and the Marketplace That Is Remaking the Modern World* (New York: Simon & Schuster, 1998), p. 15.

2. John Maynard Keynes *The General Theory of Employment, Interest and Money* (London: Macmillan, 1936), p. 383.

3. For a good overview of Hayek's works, see *The Essence of Hayek*, ed. Chiaka Nishiyama and Kurt R. Leube (Stanford, Calif.: Hoover Institution, 1984). For a partial autobiography, see *Hayek on Hayek* (Chicago: University of Chicago Press, 1994). For a full-scale intellectual biography of Hayek, see Alan Ebenstein, *Hayek: Philosopher of Libertarianism* (Chicago: University of Chicago Press, 2001).

4. Mark Skousen, "The Next Economics," *Economics on Trial* (Baldwinsville, N.Y.: Irwin, 1991), pp. 274–90.

5. Yergin and Stanislaw, p. 141. See my column "Vienna and Chicago: A Tale of Two Schools," *The Freeman: Ideas on Liberty*, February 1998.

Who Deserved the
Nobel Prize?

"Prizes shall be awarded to those persons who during the previous year have rendered the greatest service to mankind."
—ALFRED NOBEL'S LAST WILL (1895)

Since 1969, the Nobel Memorial Prize in Economic Science has
been awarded to dozens of eminent economists, including Paul
Samuelson, Friedrich Hayek, Milton Friedman, James Tobin, and
Robert Solow. In 1995 the winner was Robert Lucas, the Chicago
economist who developed the rational expectations theory.

Lucas's winning the Nobel Prize reflected the growing dominance of free-market economics in the profession. In fact, economists from the University of Chicago received the award in five of
the six years from 1990 to 1995. The prize, established by the
Bank of Sweden, is awarded by a six-man committee, headed by
Assar Lindbeck, who has gradually grown more conservative over
time. In a *Business Week* article, economist Robert Kuttner
bemoaned the fact that several prominent Keynesians were
ignored by the Nobel committee during their lifetimes: Joan
Robinson, Nicholas Kaldor, and Sir Roy Harrod.

Are there any free-market economists who failed to receive the
Nobel Prize? I asked several colleagues to name their favorite
deceased economist who was still alive in 1969, why that economist deserved the award, and what major works should be cited.
Their choices were as follows.

239

Ludwig von Mises

Ludwig von Mises (1881–1973), the pre-eminent Austrian economist, was everyone's first choice. Of his many original contributions, three stand out: the theory of the business cycle, the socialist calculation debate, and methodology. Most important works: *Theory of Money and Credit* (1912), *Socialism* (1922), and *Human Action* (1949, 1966).

Murray N. Rothbard

Murray N. Rothbard (1926–1995), the libertarian iconoclast who popularized Misesian economics in America, was nearly everyone's second choice. He made original contributions in welfare economics and monopoly and tax theory, but was best known for his remarkable ability to write clearly and profoundly about money, business cycles, and government policy. Major works: *Man, Economy, and State* (1962), *America's Great Depression* (1963), and *Power and Market* (1970). His booklet *What Has the Government Done to Our Money?* has probably had the greatest influence of all. Several colleagues also mentioned his last great work, a two-volume history, *Economic Thought Before Adam Smith* and *Classical Economics* (Edward Elgar, 1995).

W. H. Hutt

William H. Hutt (1899–1988), a classical economist who for half a century taught at the University of Cape Town, was frequently mentioned as a third candidate. Hutt's major contribution was in labor economics, wherein he argued that persistent unemployment was due to above-market wage rates imposed by government regulations. He was a long-time critic of Keynesian economics and apartheid in South Africa. Major works: *The Theory of Idle Resources* (1939), *Keynesianism: Retrospect and Prospect* (1963), and *Economics of the Colour Bar* (1964).

My fellow economists also recommended several other names: Oskar Morgenstern for his *Theory of Games and Economic Behavior* (1944, co-authored by John von Neumann) and *On the*

Accuracy of Economic Observations (1950); Gottfried Haberler for his *Prosperity and Depression* (1937) and his exposition of the Austrian theory of the trade cycle; Frank Knight for his *Risk, Uncertainty and Profit* (1921); Jacob Viner for his history of economic thought and the development of cost theory in *The Long View and the Short* (1958); and Henry Hazlitt for his *Failure of the "New Economics"* (1959).

Surprisingly, several free-market economists felt that Joan Robinson (1903–1983) merited the Nobel Prize, not for her politics, but for her scientific contributions, such as *The Economics of Imperfect Competition* (1933). In 1975, she was widely expected to win the Nobel Prize, but was ultimately denied it because of her extreme political views and her admiration of Mao's China and Kim Il Sung's North Korea.

What Nobel Really Wanted

In reviewing the winners of the Nobel Prize, I wonder how well the Nobel committee has matched Alfred Nobel's original desires. His last will and testament created five prizes (physics, chemistry, physiology or medicine, literature, and peace), all for actions that were to benefit mankind in a very practical sense, much like his invention of dynamite. Dynamite is not used solely as a tool of war; it plays a valuable role in mining, construction, and transportation. Nobel's last will is filled with words such as "discovery," "invention," "improvement," "ideal," "brotherhood," and "peace." In sum, scientists, authors, and activists who have improved the lot of mankind deserve the Nobel Prize.

In the past, the Swedish academies have given prizes to outstanding citizens who have rendered the "greatest services to mankind": Roentgen for discovering x-rays, Marconi for developing the wireless telegraph, Banting for isolating insulin, and Fleming for discovering penicillin. Yet, at the same time, the Swedish Royal Academy has awarded many obscure and sometimes minimal contributors while ignoring many noteworthy individuals. In literature, for example, Mark Twain and Leo Tolstoy never received Nobel honors.

In science, the following were overlooked: Thomas Edison for the electric light bulb; August and Louis Lumière for motion pictures; Willis Haviland Carrier for air-conditioning; Orville and Wilbur Wright for the airplane; Henry Ford for mass production; George Washington Carver for agricultural techniques; Vladimir Zworykin and Isaac Shoenberg for television; Robert Watson-Watt for radar; Frank Whittle and Hans Pabst von Ohain for the jet engine; Chester Carlson for xerography; Howard Aiken, John P. Eckert, Jr., and John W. Mauchly for the digital computer; Jonas Salk for the polio vaccine; and Ted Hoff for the microprocessor. (I thank Michael H. Hart, author of *The One Hundred: A Ranking of the Most Influential Persons in History* [Citadel, 1992], for providing this wish list of potential Nobel winners.) Surely these men have made a significant difference in our way of life and standard of living.

A Nobel for W.E. Deming?

In keeping with the spirit of Nobel, the Nobel Memorial Prize in Economic Science ought to expand its universe from high theory to applied science. If the Nobel Prize can go to finance theorists such as Harry Markowitz, perhaps it could be extended to management theorists, statisticians, and entrepreneurs. For example, surely W. Edwards Deming (1900–1993) deserved the Nobel Prize in economics. Although not a trained economist, his dynamic "quality-control/consumer research" approach developed in postwar Japan revolutionized the world of production, consumption, and job creation as much as any Friedman or Samuelson.

What's Left of Marxism?

"The world described by Marx and Engels in 1848 in passages of dark, laconic eloquence, is recognizably the world we live in 150 years later."

—ERIC HOBSBAWM[1]

Communism as a political movement may be dead, but Marxism as an intellectual movement lives on. The year 1998 marked the 150th anniversary of the publication of Karl Marx and Frederick Engel's profound polemic, *Manifesto of the Communist Party*. The date may have been missed by devotees of the free market, but the 1848 pamphlet was reviewed and celebrated by radical intellectuals everywhere. A dressed-up "modern" edition was published, with an introduction by historian Eric Hobsbawm, who presumably would like to reignite the dying flames of Marxist dogma.

Gary North has his "fat book" theory: all revolutionary works are tomes of biblical proportion. Adam Smith's *The Wealth of Nations*, Ludwig von Mises's *Human Action*, and Ayn Rand's *Atlas Shrugged* come to mind. Marx wrote a three-volume work, *Das Kapital*. But there are also a handful of declarations, pamphlets, and small books that have changed the world. Thomas Jefferson's "Declaration of Independence," Tom Paine's *Common Sense*, and the Four Gospels of the New Testament are good examples.

The Communist Manifesto fits into the second category. In rereading it, I couldn't help feeling the passionate power, the pun-

243

gent style, and the astonishing simplicity of Marx and Engels's words. I can easily see how a young revolutionary could be swayed by these unforgettable lines: "A specter is haunting Europe—the specter of Communism. . . . The history of all hitherto existing society is the history of class struggles. . . . Let the ruling classes tremble at a communistic revolution. The proletarians have nothing to lose but their chains. They have a world to win. WORKING MEN OF ALL COUNTRIES, UNITE!"

I can remember feeling similar emotions when I read Murray N. Rothbard's *What Has Government Done to Our Money?*, first published in 1963 (Mises Institute, 1990). It will change forever your view on money and economics. And his penetrating essay, "The Great Society: A Libertarian Critique," will forever change your outlook on government.[2] Rothbard is the free market's answer to Marx.

Market vs. Government Failure

But the attraction of *The Communist Manifesto* is ideological as well as emotional. How can anyone not be moved—favorably or unfavorably—by this critical appraisal of "bourgeois" capitalism: "The bourgeoisie . . . has left remaining no other nexus between man and man than naked self-interest, than callous 'cash payment.' It has drowned the most heavenly ecstasies of religious fervour, of chivalrous enthusiasm, of philistine sentimentalism, in the icy water of egotistical calculation. It has resolved personal worth into exchange value, and in place of the numberless indefeasible chartered freedoms, has set up that single, unconscionable freedom—free trade. In one word, for exploitation, veiled by religious and political illusions, it has substituted naked, shameless, direct, brutal exploitation."[3]

Marxist rulers may no longer control the political and economic lives of millions, but their ideology of exploitation, alienation, and class struggle still haunts the academic world of law schools, sociology departments, and literary-theory classes. According to Hobsbawm, Marx's insights on capitalism are relevant today. Hobsbawm envisions capitalism as "a world system capable of marshalling production on a global scale; its devastating impact on all aspects of human existence, work, the family and the distribution of wealth; and the understanding that, far from being a stable, immutable system, it is, on the contrary, susceptible to enormous convulsions and crisis, and contains the seeds of its own destruction."[4] And I thought Austrians were doomsdayers!

The Marxists of yesteryear are the social democrats of today. M.E. Sharpe, publisher of *Challenge* magazine, recognizes the mistakes of Marx and Engels, such as failing to consider the vast improvement in the living standards and real wages of "the working class" during the twentieth century, but still grants Marx's main theme, "the celebrated characterization of mid-century capitalism as an enormously expansive but unstable system of production."[5]

But modern-day followers of Marx focus too much on the alleged failures of the market. Today the best and the brightest of economists are investigating the problems of society in terms of "government failure"—public education, corporate welfarism, monetary manipulation, price controls, and state interventionism.

The Declining Marx

Fortunately, Marxist influence among academic economists appears to be on the wane. It was in its heyday in the turbulent 1970s, when Paul Samuelson remarked in the tenth edition of his celebrated economics textbook (1976) that "at least a tenth of U. S. economists" fell into the "radical" category.[6] E.K. Hunt's radical textbook, *Economics: An Introduction to Traditional and Radical Views,* was last published in 1990 and is out of print. Today's hotbeds of Marxism may still exist in a few universities in Massachusetts and California—and strangely enough Utah—but in the main, Marxism has lost its mystique. The Union of Radical Political Economists still gathers the faithful at the annual meetings of the American Economic Association, but attendance is low.

Marx's Critics

There have been some excellent criticisms of Marx. Austrian economist Eugen Böhm-Bawerk was the first to offer a devastating attack on Marxist's theory of exploitation and surplus value, from which the Marxists have never fully recovered. Böhm-Bawerk demonstrated that entrepreneur-capitalists take greater risks than wage-earners, which justifies the disparity in income levels. Oddly enough, Böhm's book, *Karl Marx and the Close of His System* (Orion Editions, 1984), is published by Marxists, with rebuttals by Rudolf Hilferding and Paul M. Sweezy. More recently, David Conway's *A Farewell to Marx* (Penguin Books, 1987) has received high praise for his deft criticisms. The best biography of the father of communism remains by far Robert Payne's *Marx* (Simon & Schuster, 1968). Given the renewed interest in *The Communist Manifesto*, perhaps it's time to bring Payne's book back in print.[7]

---

1. Eric Hobsbawm, "Introduction," *The Communist Manifesto: A Modern Edition*, by Karl Marx and Frederick Engels (London: Verso, 1998), p. 16.

2. It is reprinted in Richard Romano and Melvin Leiman, eds., *Views on Capitalism* (Glencoe, Ill.: Glencoe Press, 1970), pp. 86–94.

3. Marx and Engels, pp. 37–38.

4. Hobsbawm, dustjacket, Marx and Engels.

5. M. E. Sharpe, "Review of *The Communist Manifesto*," *Challenge*, May-June 1998, p. 114.

6. Paul A. Samuelson, *Economics*, 10th ed. (New York: McGraw-Hill, 1976), p. 849. The 9th edition (1973) contained a nine-page appendix on Marxian economics. Today's 16th edition (1998) contains only one page on Marx, and Samuelson is generally critical of Marxian economics.

7. A fascinating update on Marx's life is found in Gary North, "The Marx Nobody Knows" in *Requiem for Marx*, ed. Yuri N. Maltsev (Auburn, Ala.: Mises Institute, 1993). This book contains some excellent material on Marxism written by Austrian economists.

Changing the
Course of History

One Graph Says It All*

"But the free market is not primarily a device to procure
growth. It is a device to secure the most efficient use of
resources."

—HENRY C. WALLICH[1]

In celebrating 50 years of service by the Foundation for Economic Education, we observe one overriding lesson of history:
Freedom is, on balance, a great blessing to all mankind.

Now, this may seem to be obvious; today we all nod our heads
in agreement with this conclusion. But not everyone concurred
during the postwar era. In fact, for much of the past 50 years, sup-
porters of economic liberty were on the defensive. After World
War II, laissez faire was an unwelcome phrase in the halls of government and on college campuses. Governments both here and
abroad nationalized industry after industry, raised taxes, inflated
the money supply, imposed price and exchange controls, created
the welfare state, and engaged in all kinds of interventionist mischief. In academia, Keynesianism and Marxism became all the
rage, and many free-market economists had a hard time obtaining
full-time positions on college campuses.

The big-government economy was viewed by the establishment
as an automatic stabilizer and growth stimulator. Many top economists argued that central planning, the welfare state, and industrial policy lead to higher growth rates. Incredibly, as late as 1985,
Paul Samuelson (MIT) and William D. Nordhaus (Yale) still

---

*Written as tribute to FEE's 50th anniversary in 1996.

249

declared, "The planned Soviet economy since 1928 . . . has out-paced the long-term growth of the major market economies."[2] Mancur Olson, a University of Maryland economist, also stated, "In the 1950s, there was, if anything, a faint tendency for the countries with larger welfare states to grow faster."[3]

Henry C. Wallich, a Yale economics professor and former member of the Federal Reserve Board, wrote a whole book arguing that freedom means lower economic growth, greater income inequality, and less competition. In *The Cost of Freedom*, he concluded, "The ultimate value of a free economy is not production, but freedom, and freedom comes not at a profit, but at a cost."[4] And he was considered a conservative economist!

The New Enlightenment

Fortunately, the attitudes of the establishment have gradually changed for the better. In recent years the defenders of the free market have gained ground and, since the collapse of the Berlin Wall and Soviet central planning, have claimed victory over the dark forces of Marxism and socialism. Today, governments around the world are denationalizing, privatizing, cutting taxes, controlling inflation, and engaging in all kinds of market reforms. And free-market economists can now be found in most economics departments. In fact, almost all of the most recent Nobel Prize winners in economics have been pro-free market.

Furthermore, new evidence demonstrates forcefully that economic freedom comes as a benefit, not a cost. Looking at the data of the 1980s, Mancur Olson concluded, "it appears that the countries with larger public sectors have tended to grow more slowly than those with smaller public sectors."[5] Contrast that with his statement about the 1950s.

Now comes the *coup de grâce* from an exhaustive study by James Gwartney, economics professor at Florida State University, and two other researchers. They painstakingly constructed an index measuring the degree of economic freedom for more than 100 countries and then compared the level of economic freedom with their growth rates between 1975 and 1995. Their conclusion is documented in the following remarkable graph:

If ever a picture was worth a thousand words, this graph is it:

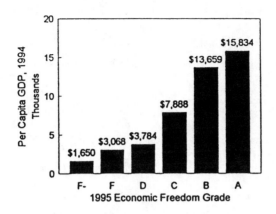

Clearly, the greater the degree of freedom, the higher the standard of living (as measured by per capita real GDP growth). Nations with the highest level of freedom (e.g., United States, New Zealand, Hong Kong) grew faster than nations with moderate degrees of freedom (e.g., United Kingdom, Canada, Germany) and even more rapidly than nations with little economic freedom (e.g., Venezuela, Iran, Congo). The authors conclude, "No country with a persistently high economic freedom rating during the two decades failed to achieve a high level of income."

What about those countries whose policies changed during the past twenty years? The authors state: "All 17 of the countries in the most improved category experienced positive growth rates. . . . In contrast, the growth rates of the countries where economic freedom declined during 1975–95 were persistently negative."[6]

If all this is true, what of the data that seemed to demonstrate a positive correlation between big government and economic growth in the 1950s and later? In the case of the Soviet Union, most economists now agree that the data were faulty and misleading. In the case of Europe, perhaps the economic incentives of rebuilding after the war overshadowed the growth of the welfare state. In other words, Europe grew in spite of, not because of, government. Once rebuilding was complete by the late 1950s, the weight of government began to be felt.

After 50 years of hard work, it is high time for FEE and the other free-market think-tanks to celebrate their untiring efforts to educate the world about the virtues of liberty. Their work is finally paying off. Let me be one of the first to say congratulations—a job well done!

1. Henry C. Wallich, *The Cost of Freedom* (New York: Collier Books, 1960), p. 146.

2. Paul A. Samuelson and William D. Nordhaus, *Economics,* 12th ed. (New York: McGraw-Hill, 1985), p. 776.

3. Mancur Olson, *How Bright Are the Northern Lights?* (Lund University, 1990), p. 10.

4. Wallich, *The Cost of Freedom,* p. 9.

5. Olson, *How Bright Are the Northern Lights?,* p. 88.

6. James D. Gwartney, Robert A. Lawson, and Walter E. Block, *Economic Freedom of the World: 1975–1995* (Washington, D.C.: Cato Institute, 1996), p. xvii. This survey is updated annually.

It All Started with Adam

"Adam Smith was a radical and a revolutionary in his time—
just as those of us who preach laissez faire are in our time."
—MILTON FRIEDMAN[1]

A dam Smith, that is. Having completed writing a history of economics,[2] I have concluded that, despite the protestations of
Murray Rothbard and other detractors, the eighteenth-century
moral philosopher and celebrated author of *The Wealth of Nations*
deserves to be named the founding father of modern economics.

The reason: Adam Smith is the first major figure to articulate in
a profound way what has become known as the first fundamental
theorem of welfare economics: that the invisible hand of competition automatically transforms self-interest into the common good.
George Stigler rightly labels Smith's model of laissez-faire capitalism (Smith never used the phrase) the "crown jewel" of *The
Wealth of Nations* and "the most important substantive proposition in all of economics." He states, "Smith had one overwhelmingly important triumph: he put into the center of economics the
systematic analysis of the behavior of individuals pursuing their
self-interests under conditions of competition."[3]

In short, Smith's thesis is that a "system of natural liberty," an
economic system that allows individuals to pursue their own self-
interest under conditions of competition and common law, would
be a self-regulating and highly prosperous economy. Eliminating
restrictions on prices, labor, and trade meant that universal prosperity could be maximized through lower prices, higher wages,
and better products. Smith assured the reader that his model

would result in "universal opulence which extends itself to the lowest ranks of the people."[4]

Indeed it has. Published in 1776, *The Wealth of Nations* was the intellectual shot heard around the world, a declaration of economic independence to go along with Thomas Jefferson's declaration of political independence. It was no accident that the industrial revolution and sharply higher economic growth began in earnest shortly after its publication. As Ludwig von Mises declares, "It paved the way for the unprecedented achievements of laissez-faire capitalism."[5]

For or Against Smith

The most amazing discovery I made in researching and writing over the past few years is that every major economic figure— whether Marx, Mises, Keynes, or Friedman—could be judged by his support of or opposition to Adam Smith's invisible-hand doctrine. Karl Marx, Thorstein Veblen, John Maynard Keynes, and even British disciples Thomas Robert Malthus and David Ricardo denigrated Adam Smith's classical model of capitalism, while Alfred Marshall, Irving Fisher, Ludwig von Mises, and Milton Friedman, among others, remodeled and improved on Smithian economics.

For example, Keynes is unsympathetic to Adam Smith's worldview. "It is not true that individuals possess a prescriptive 'natural liberty' in their economic activities. . . . Nor is it true that self-interest generally is enlightening. . . . Experience does not show that individuals, when they make up a social unit, are always less clearsighted than when they act separately."[6] The basic thesis of Keynes's magnum opus, *The General Theory of Employment, Interest, and Money* (1936), is that laissez-faire capitalism is inherently unstable and requires heavy state intervention to survive. Keynesian disciple Paul Samuelson correctly understood the true meaning of Keynes: "With respect to the level of total purchasing power and employment, Keynes denies that there is an invisible hand channeling the self-centered action of each individual to the social optimum."[7] Thus, I conclude that Keynesian economics, rather than its savior, is an enemy of Adam Smith's system of natural liberty.

Karl Marx went even further. Instead of creating a system of natural liberty, Marx set out to destroy it. Modern-day Marxist

John Roemer agrees. The "main difference" between Smith and Marx is: "Smith argues that the individual's pursuit of self-interest would lead to an outcome beneficial to all, whereas Marx argued that the pursuit of self-interest would lead to anarchy, crisis, and the dissolution of the private property-based system itself. . . . Smith spoke of the invisible hand guiding individual, self-interested agents to perform those actions that would be, despite their lack of concern for such an outcome, socially optimal; for Marxism the simile is the iron fist of competition, pulverizing the workers and making them worse off than they would be in another feasible system, namely, one based on the social or public ownership of property."[8]

Adam Smith as a Heroic Figure

By measuring economists against a single standard, Adam Smith's invisible-hand doctrine, I found a fresh way to unite the history of economic thought. Virtually all previous histories of economics, including Robert Heilbroner's popular work, *The Worldly Philosophers*, present the story of economics as one conflicting idea after another without resolution or a running thread of truth. This hodgepodge approach to history leaves the reader confused and unable to separate the wheat from the chaff.

My approach places Adam Smith and his system of natural liberty at the center of the discipline. Think of it as a story of high drama with a singular heroic figure. Adam Smith and his classical model face one battle after another against the mercantilists, socialists, and other enemies of liberty. Sometimes even his "dismal" disciples (Malthus, Ricardo, and Mill) wound him. Marx and the radical socialists attack him with a vengeance and leave him for dead, only to have him resuscitated by the leaders of the marginalist revolution (Menger, Jevons, and Walras) and raised up to become the inspiration of a whole new science.

But the "neoclassical" model of capitalism faced its greatest threat from the Keynesian revolution during the Great Depression and the postwar era. Fortunately, the story has a good ending. Through the untiring efforts of free-market advocates, especially Milton Friedman and F. A. Hayek, Adam Smith's model of capitalism is re-established and in the end triumphs. As Milton Friedman proclaims, "To judge from the climate of opinion, we have won the war of ideas. Everyone—left or right—talks about the virtues of markets, private property, competition, and limited government."[9]

Long live Adam Smith!

1. Quoted in Fred R. Glahe, ed., *Adam Smith and The Wealth of Nations: Bicentennial Essays* (Boulder: Colorado Associated University Press, 1978), p. 7.

2. *The Making of Modern Economics* (Armonk, N.Y.: M. E. Sharpe Publishers, 2001).

3. George Stigler, "The Successes and Failures of Professor Smith," *Journal of Political Economy*, December 1976, p. 1201.

4. Adam Smith, *The Wealth of Nations* (New York: Modern Library, 1965 [1776]), p. 11.

5. Ludwig von Mises, "Why Read Adam Smith Today," in *The Wealth of Nations* (Washington, D.C.: Regnery, 1998), p. xi.

6. John Maynard Keynes, "The End of Laissez-Faire," *Essays in Persuasion* (New York: Norton, 1963 [1931]), p. 312. Keynes's speech was given in 1926, a full decade before *The General Theory* came out.

7. Paul A. Samuelson, "Lord Keynes and the General Theory," *The New Economics*, ed. Seymour Harris (New York: Knopf, 1947), p. 151.

8. John E. Roemer, *Free to Lose* (Cambridge, Mass.: Harvard University Press, 1988), pp. 2–3. Note the title, imitative, albeit negatively, of Milton and Rose Friedman's popular *Free to Choose* (New York: Harcourt Brace Jovanovich, 1980).

9. Milton and Rose Friedman, *Two Lucky People* (Chicago: University of Chicago Press, 1998), p. 582.

Is This the Age of Ignorance— Or Enlightenment?

"I am more and more impressed by my ignorance."
—Herbert Stein, "The Age of Ignorance,"
The Wall Street Journal
(June 11, 1993)

The late Herbert Stein ought to have known better. He was the chairman of President Nixon's Council of Economic Advisers and an economics professor at the University of Virginia. He was a member of the *Wall Street Journal's* board of contributors and an American Enterprise Institute fellow.

Yet here he is filling up a valuable page in the *Wall Street Journal* proclaiming to the entire world that he knows very little, if anything. After reading three daily newspapers and numerous magazines, watching all the talk shows, and talking to dozens of "well-informed" people, he confesses complete ignorance about the budget deficit, taxes, the money supply, the stock market, and the war in Bosnia.

"I don't know whether increasing the budget deficit stimulates or depresses the national income. I don't know whether it is M2 or M1 that controls the level of spending. I don't know how much a 10 percent increase in the top rate of individual income tax will raise the revenue. . . . I do not know how to pick winning stocks."

257

The New Nihilism: The Bankruptcy of the Economics Profession

It wouldn't bother me if one lonely Ph.D. economist claimed ignorance of basic economics, but the amazing thing is that Herbert Stein was not alone. He was representative of a strange new malaise in the economics profession, an eerie complacency about the burning economic issues of the day. Economists all along the political spectrum are eschewing responsibility for policy decisions or forecasting the future. Will interest rates rise or fall? Are we headed for another recession, more inflation, or both? Will the stock market go up or down? The answer is always the same: Who knows?

Robert J. Barro, Harvard economist and exponent of the New Classical School, seemed to take pride in his laid-back attitude about the economy during the 1991–1992 recession: "The questions I am asked most often these days are: Why is the economic recovery weaker than expected? How will the economy do over the next year? What should the government do to help? As a first approximation, the right answers to questions like these are: 'I don't know,' 'I don't know,' and 'nothing.' " (*Wall Street Journal,* November 21, 1991)

Not to be outdone is Paul Krugman, self-proclaimed Keynesian professor at MIT. He asserts that economists, including himself, don't understand why there are business cycles. Furthermore, economists "don't know how to make a poor country rich, or bring back the magic of economic growth when it seems to have gone away. . . . Nobody really knows why the U.S. economy could generate 3 percent annual productivity growth before 1973 and only 1 percent afterward; nobody really knows why Japan surged from defeat to global economic power after World War II, while Britain slid slowly into third-rate status."[1] Really? Mind you, this is the professor who won the John Bates Clark Medal, a prize given every two years to the most promising American economist under the age of forty. According to the dust jacket of Krugman's latest book, *The Economist* called him "the most celebrated economist of his generation." Hmm . . . .

Daniel Hausman, economics professor at the University of Wisconsin at Madison, wrote a massive volume on capital and interest and concluded with a straight face: "Economists do not understand the phenomena of capital and interest. They do not understand why the rate of interest is positive (and thus how it is that capitalism can work). They do not know how large-scale changes in the rate of profit will affect innovation."[2] And he's a specialist!

Economists as ignoramuses can best be summed up by John Maynard Keynes, the economist-king of the twentieth century, who declared in 1937, "The fact that our knowledge of the future is fluctuating, vague and uncertain, renders wealth a peculiarly unsuitable subject for the methods of classical economic theory. . . . There is no scientific basis on which to form any calculable probability whatsoever. We simply do not know."[3]

An Admission of Failure

In some ways, the New Ignorance school of economics is a welcome sign. In the 1960s, it was the New Arrogance school of economics. Forgetting Keynes' admission of 1937, the Keynesian technocrats claimed they had the tools to fine tune the economy, control inflation and ban the business cycle forever. Now, a generation later, the establishment economists are finally admitting that their theories and policies have failed miserably. The profession has had a terrible record in predicting recessions, inflation, and stock prices, and their policy recommendations have made things worse, not better. As Hayek stated when he received his Nobel Prize in 1974: "We have indeed at the moment little cause for pride: as a profession we have made a mess of things."[4] By the 1990s, all the major schools of economics had failed, one way or another—Keynesian, monetarist, and Marxist. Alfred Malabre, Jr., former economics editor of the *Wall Street Journal,* appropriately calls today's economists "Lost Prophets," the title of his new book.

So it is fashionable today to plead naivete. But is ignorance a virtue? St. Paul didn't think so when he warned Timothy about intellectuals who are "ever learning, and never able to come to the knowledge of the truth." (2 Timothy 3:7)

The Standardbearers of Sound Economics

Among the many schools of economics, who carries the banner of truth? I believe that the best and the brightest thinking today is coming from the Austrians, the supply-siders, and other free-market scholars. Although some have fallen into the trap of "radical subjectivism," where everything is uncertain and unpredictable, most free-market economists have established objective principles of economic behavior, and can predict with considerable certainty the benefits of economic liberty and the ill-effects of government intervention, and how certain economic policies will affect output, prices, and stock markets.

Armed with these principles, let us see how well we do with the issues raised by the new nihilists. Herbert Stein says: "I don't know whether increasing the deficit stimulates [p. 322] or depresses the national income." Response: Transfers from the *productive* private sector to the *unproductive* public sector inevitably depress the national income.

Stein admits, "I don't know whether it is M2 or M1 that controls the level of total spending." Didn't he read Adam Smith or Ludwig von Mises? Purchasing power is not determined by the money supply, but by productivity and output.

Stein declares, "I don't know how much a 10 percent increase in the top rate of individual income tax will raise the revenue." Hadn't he read the numerous studies demonstrating that the rich pay fewer taxes when marginal tax rates go up?

Finally, Stein confesses, "I do not know how to pick winning stocks." Instead of watching all those talk shows, why doesn't Stein follow the work of Peter Lynch, Warren Buffett, John Templeton, Value Line, and other analysts who know how to pick winning stocks?

Now onto Professor Barro, who didn't know why the recession hit in the early 1990s and where the economy was headed. The answers are pretty clear: The economic recovery was weaker than expected in 1991 because of a massive tax increase passed in 1990, on top of a tight money policy. The economy began recovering in 1992 due to the Fed's easy money supply. What should the government do to create a permanent recovery? Cut taxes and business regulations immediately, across the board.

Professor Krugman doesn't understand the business cycle? The Mises-Hayek theory is a good starting place, but unfortunately MIT has had a long tradition of ignoring the Austrian school. Daniel Hausman could get some answers there too. Why are interest rates positive? Time preference, declared Menger, Böhm-

Bawerk, and Mises many decades ago. These Austrians specialized in the theory of capital and interest, and the role of the entrepreneur. Technological breakthroughs increase productivity and wages, and higher profits stimulate innovation by providing more capital for research and development.

Paul Krugman doesn't know how poor nations become rich? He should investigate the economic miracles of southeast Asia. The common denominators for Singapore and Hong Kong are a strong, stable, and lean government, low taxation, high levels of saving and investment, open markets, and minimal concern with income distribution (*Forbes*, April 11, 1994). Could these reasons also help explain Japan's post-war success story? Pro-growth government, high saving rates, low taxes on investment, emphasis on training, and quality improvements. Or why Britain stagnated? High taxes, price and exchange controls, excessively powerful labor unions, bureaucracy, and welfarism.

In short, this isn't the Age of Ignorance. It's the Age of Enlightenment, for those who are willing to open their eyes and see. Unfortunately, too many of today's economists are blind guides. "For this people's heart is waxed gross, and their ears are dull of hearing, and their eyes they have closed; lest at any time they should see with their eyes, and hear with their ears, and should understand with their heart, and should be converted, and I should heal them." (Matthew 13:15)

---

1. Paul Krugman, *Peddling Prosperity* (New York: W. W. Norton, 1994), pp. 9, 24. His previous book, *The Age of Diminishing Expectations*, came out in the early 1990s, just when Third World nations began throwing off socialism and Marxism, and sensed rising expectations for the first time.

2. Daniel M. Hausman, *Capital, Profits, and Prices* (New York: Columbia University Press, 1981), p. 190.

3. John Maynard Keynes, "The General Theory of Employment," *Collected Writings of John Maynard Keynes* (London: Macmillan, 1973), p. 114. This essay originally appeared in *The Quarterly Journal of Economics* in 1937.

4. Friedrich A. Hayek, "The Pretence of Knowledge," Nobel Prize Lecture, reprinted in *The Essence of Hayek*, ed. by Chiaki Nishiyama and Kurt R. Leube (Stanford: Hoover Institution Press, 1984), p. 266.

Has Capitalism Failed or Succeeded? The Tale of Two Graphs

"Yet, in the aftermath of the Keynesian revolution, too many economists forgot that classical economics provides the right answers to many fundamental questions.

—N. Gregory Mankiw[1]

The Great Depression of the 1930s brought us Keynesian economics and a broad shift in emphasis from the classical study of economic growth to concern about economic fluctuations and how to subdue the boom-bust business cycle. Postwar textbooks, led by Paul Samuelson's *Economics,* focused primarily on the ups and downs of the capitalist system and how government policy could ameliorate the business cycle. Keynesian economists stressed "countercyclical demand management" and "compensatory fiscal policy" to "iron out the business cycle, with boom surpluses canceling out depression deficits."[2] Economists taught the "New Economics" of "automatic built-in stabilizers," "discretionary fiscal policy," and "fiscal drag." Even free-market economist Milton Friedman focused his research on ways to stabilize the economy through monetary policy.

Indeed, according to the new conventional wisdom, the primary purpose of studying economics was to achieve "short-run stabilization" of the capitalism system. Postwar textbooks abound in the study of cyclical fluctuations, while burying the study of economic growth and development in the back pages.

The Volatility of Capitalism?

If you look at Graph #1 at the top of the next page, you might agree with this focal point: The business cycle appears to be volatile and the primary problem facing the United States. This graph, published in Michael Parkin's popular textbook, shows real GDP fluctuations from 1869 to 1992.

Graph #1 suggests that the U.S. economy has run amok, suffering untold boom and bust over the past century and a half. According to the critics, capitalism has failed and needs to be tamed.

Is this an accurate picture of the U.S. economy? We all know that games can be played with charts and graphs. Darrell Huff, in his classic book, *How to Lie With Statistics* (W. W. Norton, 1993 [1954]), described the distortions that can occur with a one-dimensional picture.

The Long-Term View Favors Economic Growth

Now let's look at Graph #2, which tells quite a different story. This graph highlights real GDP, 1869–1992, rather than changes in real GDP.

Amazingly, Graph #2 also comes from Parkin's textbook. It uses the same statistics, but paints an entirely different picture. Here the overwhelming conclusion is not that the U.S. economy is subject to violent fluctuations, but that it has grown dramatically over the past century or more. In this graph, the periods of inflationary booms and recessions are relatively minor. Even the Great Depression is dwarfed by unrelenting economic progress over the long term. The key point is that Americans have enjoyed a dramatic increase in their standard of living over the past century. Capitalism works!

Graph #1: Real GDP Fluctuations, 1869–1992

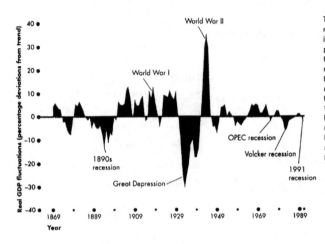

Source: 1869–1929: Christina D. Romer. "The Prewar Business Cycle Reconsidered: New Estimates of Gross National Product, 1869–1908, *Journal of Political Economy* 97. (1989) 1–37; and Nathan S. Balke and Robert J. Gordon, "The Estimation of Prewar Gross National Product: Methodology and New Evidence," *Journal of Political Economy* 97, (1989) 38–92. The data used are an average of the estimates given in these two sources. 1929–1958: *Economic Report of the President,* 1991. 1959–1992: *Economic Report of the President,* 1993. The data for 1869 to 1958 are GNP and those for 1959 to 1992 are GDP. The difference between these two measures is small and is explained in Chaplet 23, pp. 619–520.

The uneven pace of increase of real GDP is illustrated by tracking its fluctuation measured as the percentage deviation of real GDP from trend. Rapid expansion of real GDP, which occurred during both world wars, puts real GDP above trend. Decreases in real GDP, which occurred during the 1890s recession, the Great Depression, and the three most recent recessions, puts real GDP below trend. The real GDP fluctuations describe the course of the business cycle.

Between 1869 and 1992 real GDP grew at an annual average rate of 3.3 percent. But the growth rate was not the same in each year. In some periods, such as the years during World War II, real

Graph #2: Real GDP, 1869–1992

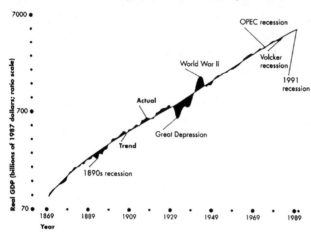

Between 1869 and 1992 real GDP grew at an annual average rate of 3.3 percent. But the growth rate was not the same in each year. In some periods, such as the years during World War II, real GDP expanded quickly. In other periods, such as the Great Depression and, more recently, following the OPEC oil price hikes, the Volcker interest rate increases, and in 1991, real GDP declined. There were several periods of decline in the nineteenth century as well, one of which is marked in the figure.

Source: Michael Parkin, *Economics,* 2nd ed., p 595.

GDP expanded quickly. In other periods, such as the Great Depression and, more recently, following the OPEC oil price hikes, the Volcker interest rate increases, and in 1991, real GDP declined. There were several periods of decline in the nineteenth century as well, one of which is marked in the figure.

The Economics Profession Alters Its Viewpoint

For decades, the American economics profession worried about recession, unemployment, and income inequality. Economists endorsed "compensatory" fiscal policy (deficit spending and government expansion) as a way to tame the business cycle. Meanwhile, economic growth slowed relative to other nations.

Now the pendulum has swung back. More and more economists are recognizing the paramount importance of economic growth and rising standards of living rather than business fluctuations and inequality of income distribution. Greg Mankiw, a New Keynesian at Harvard, is a case in point. He places the classical model of economic growth upfront in his *Macroeconomics* textbook, ahead of Keynesian business-cycle theory. He highlights the success stories of countries that have grown dramatically since the end of World War II. It's another sign that free-market economics has triumphed in the academic world.

---

1. Gregory Mankiw, *Macroeconomics*, 2nd ed. (New York: Worth Publishers, 1994), preface.

2. Paul A. Samuelson, *Economics*, 8th ed. (New York: McGraw-Hill, 1970), p. 337.

Will Keynes Ever Die?

"It was here [The General Theory] that Keynes invented
Keynesianism, disproving the classical laissez-faire theory of
the self-adjusting, self-regulating, self-sufficient market . . ."
— ARTHUR SCHLESINGER, JR.

Keynesian economics should have died long ago. Ludwig von
Mises, one of Keynes's chief critics, thought it was already
dying out in 1948. "What is going on today in the United States is
the final failure of Keynesianism. There is no doubt that the American public is moving away from the Keynesian notions and slo-
gans."[1] Mises, Hayek, and other free-market economists thought
The General Theory was a "tract of the times," not anything revolutionary or permanent. Hence many conservative economists
miscalculated the persistence of Keynesianism.

What's even more strange is that every theoretical tenet of
Keynesianism has now been disproven. The process took decades.
Arthur Pigou first refuted the "liquidity trap" hypothesis by
demonstrating that deflation increases the real value of cash holdings, thus boosting potential demand during a depression. F. A.
Hayek showed that Keynesian economics is based on a "critical
error," namely, that economic activity is solely a function of final
aggregate demand, when the truth is that employment and production are based on a delicate balance between investment and
consumption, where interest rates and entrepreneurship play a
vital role. W. H. Hutt offered a devastating attack on the accelerator principle and also demonstrated that a government-induced
high-wage policy generates significant joblessness.[2]

Henry Hazlitt proved that cutting wages during a slump, a Keynesian bugaboo, could actually *increase* wage income and end the recession if, as a result of a wage cut, more workers are hired or employees work more hours. Murray Rothbard criticized the multiplier, the stagnation thesis, and demonstrated the inherent instability of inflationary measures by government.

Milton Friedman effectively destroyed the Keynesian argument that monetary policy is not effective during a slump. With painstaking research, he showed that the Federal Reserve allowed the money supply to decline by a third during 1929–32, proving conclusively that government, not the free market, was largely responsible for the Great Depression. Friedman also demolished Keynes's "consumption function," which gave theoretical support for progressive taxation, and raised serious doubts about the Phillips curve.

Robert Higgs, in a brilliantly researched study of the American economy during World War II, showed that deficit spending did not have the beneficial effects commonly believed, and that it was only after the war that genuine prosperity returned.[3]

A Persistent Virus

Yet, despite all these attempts to dislodge the "New Economics," Keynesianism survives. Today in academia there are post-Keynesians, neo-Keynesians, and New Keynesians. Most economists and government leaders in the West still maintain that deficit spending is necessary and beneficial during a recession. The media persists in its mistaken notion that consumer spending drives the economy and efforts to save can be debilitating. (The February 14, 1994, issue of *Business Week* contained this comment on the proposed tax cuts in Japan: "The risk is that consumers, still hung over from the go-go-1980s, will just dump their new money into savings accounts and so torpedo a recovery.") The Old Guard, as represented by the statement made by Arthur Schlesinger, Jr., at the beginning of this article, continues to sway the public into believing that big government is essential to stabilize free-market capitalism.[4] They believe that Keynesianism constitutes a "permanent revolution," as Mark Blaug calls it.

The Stability of the Free-Market Economy

But Schlesinger—and Keynes—have been proven wrong. The best and the brightest of economists have demonstrated quite clearly that an economy can function, thrive, and progress without serious unemployment, inflation, and recession if (a) monetary policy is stable and sound, (b) government's role is fiscally responsible and limited to being a referee, not a player, (c) taxes, controls, and regulations are kept to a minimum and (d) people are free to pursue their own self-interest. This free-market counterrevolution has been most popular in emerging markets in Latin America, Asia, Africa, and Europe, where governments are downsizing, privatizing, cutting taxes, and adopting fiscal and monetary restraint. As a result, they are expanding like never before.

Robert Lucas, Jr., sums it up neatly: "The central lesson of economic theory is the proposition that a competitive economy, left to its own devices, will do a good job of allocating resources."[5]

Unfortunately, the Keynesian mystique is an overwhelming temptation to the seekers of power and the politicians of envy. The foundations of the House That Keynes Built are crumbling, but workers are determined to fix it rather than demolish it and replace it with the House That Mises Built. Therefore, I suspect that Keynesianism will be around for many years to come.

Nevertheless, let us not give up. In this new era of political freedom and global markets, there will never be a better opportunity to promote the virtues of free enterprise and to instruct the coming generation that free markets work and big government doesn't. We will know we have won when the Keynesian Cross is replaced with Hayekian Triangles in Econ 101.

---

1. Ludwig von Mises, "Stones into Bread, the Keynesian Miracle," *Planning for Freedom*, 4th ed. (Spring Mills, Pa.: Libertarian Press, 1980 [1952]), p. 62.

2. *Out of Work*, by Richard K. Vedder and Lowell E. Gallaway (New York: Holmes & Meier, 1993), confirms Hutt's thesis in the Great Depression and beyond: Minimum wages, legal privileges for unions, civil rights legislation, unemployment compensation, and welfare have all played significant roles in generating unemployment. See also Hans F. Sennholz, *The Politics of Unemployment* (Spring Mills, Pa.: Libertarian Press, 1987).

3. Robert Higgs, "Wartime Prosperity? A Reassessment of the U.S. Economy in the 1940s," *The Journal of Economic History* (March, 1992), pp. 41–60. For

a review of all the anti-Keynesian arguments, see my edited volume, *Dissent on Keynes: A Critical Appraisal of Keynesian Economics* (New York: Praeger, 1992).

4. Arthur Schlesinger, Jr., *New York Times Book Review*, January 23, 1994.

5. Robert E. Lucas, Jr., "The Death of Keynes," in Halistones, ed., *Viewpoints on Supply-Side Economics* (Richmond: Robert F. Dames, 1982), p. 4.

Pulling Down the
Keynesian Cross

"The circle had come right round; it was as though Keynes
had never been."

—Robert Skidelsky[1]

"Textbooks have to be rewritten in the aftermath of each scientific revolution."

—Thomas S. Kuhn[2]

In his third and final volume on John Maynard Keynes, Robert
Skidelsky comes to the shocking conclusion that the Keynesian
revolution was temporary, that Keynes's *General Theory* was
really only a "special" case, and that "free market liberalism" has
ultimately triumphed. This is all the more amazing given that Lord
Skidelsky has spent the past 20 years of his professional career
studying Keynes and resides in Keynes's old estate, Tilton House.
Few scholars would have the guts to repudiate the theory of the
man they adore.

It's even tougher for old dogs to learn new tricks, and that
refrain applies to Paul Samuelson, the "American Keynes" who
introduced millions of students to the "new economics" of the
master. He continues to hang his hat on the Keynesian cross, even
as he publishes the 17th edition of his world-famous textbook.
The pedagogical paradigm keeps shifting further toward the classical model of Adam Smith, and as each edition of *Economics*

271

moves in that direction, Samuelson resists the change. He cites his mentor more than any other economist; only Keynes, not Adam Smith or Milton Friedman, is measured as a "many-sided genius." His textbook still begins macroeconomics with the Keynesian model, even though most other textbook writers have adopted Greg Mankiw's method of starting with the long-run classical model.[3] According to Samuelson, Adam Smith's invisible-hand doctrine—that laissez-faire behavior maximizes social welfare—"holds only under very limited conditions."[4] On the final page (755) of his massive textbook, he renders "two cheers to the market, but not three."

Two Cheers for Hayek and Friedman

Having reviewed all 17 editions of Samuelson's magnum opus, I conclude that his textbook has gradually shifted, albeit grudgingly, from one cheer to two cheers for the market. Much of this improvement is due to Yale's Bill Nordhaus, his co-author since 1985. (He writes the entire text now, which Samuelson then reviews.)

What's new about the 17th edition? More free-market economists are cited, including Julian Simon, Ronald Coase, James Buchanan, Arthur Laffer, Robert Mundell, and Gary Becker. Samuelson and Nordhaus devote an entire page (41) to F.A. Hayek and Milton Friedman, "guardians of economic freedom." They recommend Hayek's *The Road to Serfdom* and Friedman's *Capitalism and Freedom,* saying, "All thoughtful economists should study his arguments carefully."

In chapter 2, "Markets and Government in a Modern Economy," the authors highlight the benefits of globalization and the importance of property rights, noting that Russia and other former communist nations have suffered because of a failure to enforce "the legal framework."

They also add an entire new page on the issue of lighthouses as public goods. For years Samuelson used the lighthouse as a prime example of market failure; only government could build and operate lighthouses. Several years ago I chided Samuelson for ignoring

Ronald Coase's famous essay, "The Lighthouse in Economics," which proved that the Trinity House and other lighthouses in England were built and owned by private firms that imposed tolls on ships docking at nearby ports.[5]

Now, finally, Samuelson and Nordhaus have responded to Coase's challenge in the 17th edition (pp. 37–38). They admit that privately operated lighthouses existed in England, but then point to the east coast of Florida as a case where "there were no lighthouses until 1825, and no private-sector lighthouses were ever built in this area." According to Nordhaus, the only response to shipwrecks was a thriving private "wrecking" industry that charged high fees for "saving lives and cargo." Nordhaus goes on to note that lighthouses have become obsolete, replaced by the satellite-based Global Positioning System, a service provided by the government.

In sum, the paradigm in economics has definitely shifted from Keynesianism to classical economics, but the case for complete laissez faire is still raging in the halls of academia.

---

1. Robert Skidelsky, *John Maynard Keynes: Fighting for Britain, 1937–1946* (London: Macmillan, 2000), p. 506.

2. Thomas S. Kuhn, *The Structure of Scientific Revolutions*, 2d ed. (Chicago: University of Chicago Press, 1970), p. 137.

3. See N. Gregory Mankiw, *Principles of Economics*, 2d ed. (Ft. Worth, Tex.: Harcourt College Publishers, 2001). I still regard Roy J. Ruffin and Paul R. Gregory, *Principles of Economics*, 7th ed. (Boston: Addison Wesley Longman, 2001) as the best mainstream textbook on the market today.

4. Paul A. Samuelson and William D. Nordhaus, *Economics*, 17th ed. (New York: McGraw-Hill Higher Education, 2001), p. 325.

5. Mark Skousen, "The Perseverance of Paul Samuelson's Economics," *Journal of Economic Perspectives*, Spring 1997, p. 145. Coase's article appeared in the *Journal of Law and Economics*, October 1974, pp. 357–76.

New Keynesians Finally Reject Keynes's "General" Theory

> "When people attempt to save more, the actual result may be only a lower level of output . . ."
>
> —Paul A. Samuelson[1]

> "Higher saving leads to faster growth . . ."
>
> —N. Gregory Mankiw[2]

The two quotations above dramatically demonstrate the stark contrast between the "old" Keynesians and the "new." Samuelson and the old-style Keynesians start with the "general" theory of unemployment equilibrium and end with the classical model of full employment as a "special" case. As long as there are unemployed resources—which, according to the old Keynesians, is most of the time—thriftiness is bad and expansionary monetary and fiscal policy (i.e., inflation and deficit spending) are good. For 50 years, this "demand-management" model has been the standard approach in college economics.

The New Keynesian Revolution

Now along comes a new generation of economists, known as "New" Keynesians, who have wisely changed their way of thinking. In the most popular textbook on macroeconomics, author N. Gregory Mankiw reverses the standard Keynesian pedagogy. Mankiw, you may recall, is the young Harvard economist who was paid a $1.4 million advance in 1995 to write the next "Samuelson" textbook.

His mammoth advance was due, in part, to the success of his previous textbook on macroeconomics. *Macroeconomics* may be a harbinger of what's to come. In a brilliant move, he begins with the classical model and ends with the Keynesian model, just the opposite of Samuelson & Company. Mankiw states in the preface, "in the aftermath of the Keynesian revolution, too many economists forgot that classical economics provides the right answers to many fundamental questions."

Under Mankiw's long-run "general equilibrium" model, what are the effects of an increase in government spending? Crowding out of private capital. "The increase in government purchases must be met by an equal decrease in investment. . . . Government borrowing reduces national saving" (p. 62).

Economic growth is discussed up front, not at the end, as most textbooks do. Using the Solow growth model, Mankiw takes a strong pro-saving approach. He maintains that "the saving rate is a key determinant of the steady-state capital stock. If the saving rate is high, the economy will have a large capital stock and a high level of output. If the saving rate is low, the economy will have a small capital stock and a low level of output" (p. 86). What is the effect of higher savings? It's positive. "An increase in the rate of saving raises growth until the economy reaches the new steady state," although the law of diminishing returns suggests that "it will not maintain a high rate of growth forever" (p. 86). Mankiw writes favorably toward those nations with high rates of saving and capital investment, and even includes a case study on the miracles of Japanese and German growth (examples virtually ignored in Samuelson's textbook). He supports efforts to increase the rate of saving and capital formation in the United States, including the possibility of altering Social Security from a pay-as-you-go system to a fully funded plan, though he does not discuss outright privatization (pp. 103–4).

The cause of unemployment? Relying on the "natural" rate of unemployment hypothesis, Mankiw suggests that unemployment insurance and similar labor legislation reduce incentives for the unemployed to find jobs (pp. 121–5). He provides evidence that unionizing labor and adopting minimum-wage laws increases the unemployment rate (pp. 127–30). He offers a case study on Henry Ford's famous $5 workday as an example of wages determined by productivity.

He approvingly quotes Milton Friedman on monetary theory: "Inflation is always and everywhere a monetary phenomenon." Mankiw uses numerous examples, including hyperinflation in Interwar Germany, to confirm the social costs of inflation (pp. 161–9).

Sins of Omission

Not all is right with Mankiw, however. In Mankiw's model, tax cuts have the same effect as deficit spending—by raising consumption, it "crowds out investment and raises the interest rate," he says (p. 64). However, he fails to realize that tax cuts also stimulate savings, as the graph (below) from Dolan and Lindsey clearly demonstrates. Not all tax cuts will be spent on consumer goods.

Further more, Mankiw apparently assumes that government spending remains the same when tax cuts are put into effect, thus raising the deficit. He repeats the common historical error that the Reagan tax cuts enlarged the deficit, and thereby raised interest rates and lowered national savings (p. 65). In fact, while marginal tax rates declined, tax revenues rose during every year of the Reagan presidency. Tax cuts didn't cause expanding deficits, excessive federal spending did.

The second half of Mankiw's textbook introduces all the standard tools of Keynesian modeling—aggregate supply (AS) and aggregate demand (AD), the multiplier and accelerator, and IS-LM model. The author presents real business cycle theory, wage rigidity, money neutrality, and the Ricardian Equivalence Theorem, all in a bewildering effort to explain economic fluctuations "in the short run." Although he includes a section on Robert Lucas, Jr., and the Rational Expectations School, he has virtually nothing to say about the supply-siders and the Austrians, a major omission. These two schools could have cleared up a lot of confusion about macroeconomic theory and policy.

Still, free-market economists should celebrate in knowing that the profession is slowly moving in the right direction—toward fundamentally sound economics.

That's quite a feat for a man (Mankiw) who named his dog "Keynes."

1. Paul A. Samuelson and William D. Nordhaus, *Economics,* 15th ed. (New York: McGraw Hill, 1995), p. 357. Similar anti-saving statements have existed in all previous editions of Samuelson's *Economics.*

2. N. Gregory Mankiw, *Macroeconomics,* 2nd ed. (New: York: Worth Publishers, 1994), p. 86.

FIGURE 13–5
Inverse Relationship between Taxes and Savings

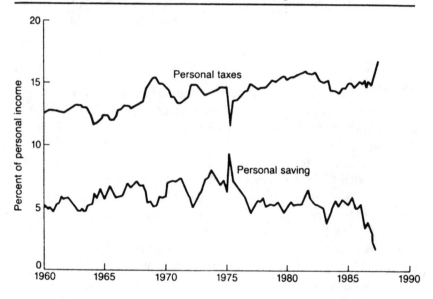

Source: Edwin G. Dolan and David E. Lindsey, *Economics* (The Dryden Press, 1988, Perspective 11).

Another Shocking Reversal in Macroeconomics

"The potency of fiscal policy—both good and bad—has been demonstrated time and again in the past couple of decades."
—WALTER HELLER, 1968[1]

W ho wrote this? "Fiscal policy is no longer a major tool of stabilization policy in the United States. Over the foreseeable
future, stabilization policy will be performed by Federal Reserve
monetary policy."

Milton Friedman? No, it was not a monetarist.

I met with Milton Friedman a few years ago in his home in San
Francisco, and asked him who he thought wrote the above state-
ment. "Alan Greenspan?" he queried. No, it wasn't a Federal
Reserve official.

The author is none other than Paul Samuelson! Starting in his
15th edition of *Economics,* co-authored by William D. Nordhaus,
the premier Keynesian economist admits defeat for fiscal policy as
an effective countercyclical tool.[2] This is truly an amazing confes-
sion, a shocking reversal of his long-standing bias of yesteryear.

It was Samuelson who wrote in his first edition (1948) of his
famous textbook, "Today few economists regard Federal Reserve
monetary policy as a panacea for controlling the business cycle"
(1st ed., p. 353). Only fiscal policy mattered. His pivotal chapter,
"Fiscal Policy and Full Employment Without Inflation," totally
ignored the role of money in the economy.

278

By the ninth edition (1973), his views had shifted to a middle ground. After labeling monetarism "an extreme view," he declared, "*both* fiscal and monetary policies matter much" (9th ed., p. 329). However, Samuelson stood squarely in the fiscal camp. The title of his chapter, "Fiscal Policy and Full Employment Without Inflation," remained the same from the first edition until the eleventh edition (1980), the last written solely by Samuelson.

Finally, in the 1995 edition, Samuelson has thrown in the towel, as if to admit, "We are all monetarists now." According to the MIT professor, running a federal deficit to jump start the economy "has lost much of its attractiveness to policymakers and macro-economists" (15th ed., p. 644). His concluding chapter on government economic policy is now entitled, "Policies for Growth and Stability."

Why Fiscal Policy Has Become Impotent

In the late 1960s, economists debated the merits of fiscal policy (spending and tax changes) vs. monetary policy (the money supply and interest rates). The Keynesians argued that fiscal policy was the most powerful tool, the monetarists defended monetary policy as the most influential.

Now the debate is over: the monetarists have won.

Under the influence of new theories in economics (especially public choice and rational expectations), Samuelson offers several reasons for an impotent fiscal policy today: increasing delays (a year or more) between changes in the economy and Congressional action on the budget; ineffectiveness of deficits or tax cuts to stimulate consumer spending; and the enormity of the national debt, which severely limits the ability of lawmakers to run higher deficits to fight recession. In sum, declares Samuelson, fiscal policy has become "useless" (15th ed., p. 644).

Artificial Stimulants Don't Work

Samuelson's amazing change of heart reflects a growing realism in the economics profession. It never did make sense to artificially stimulate the economy through makework projects, war production, and other spendthrift programs, as Keynes suggested. But running a deliberate deficit is not only "useless," it is harmful to the economy. It discourages private saving and forces lawmakers to raise taxes in the future. Indeed, that has been the trend: higher deficits and higher taxes.

The lesson is clear: government needs to move in the opposite direction if it truly wants to stabilize the economy and permanently increase economic growth. By cutting out wasteful spending, it can turn the deficit into a surplus, and reduce taxes sharply.

Monetary Policy Is Useless, Too

Paul Samuelson needs to learn another lesson: Efforts to stimulate the economy through "easy money" Federal Reserve monetary policy are useless, too. If the Fed artificially lowers interest rates and expands the money supply, it can only cause an unsustainable boom-bust cycle. History has demonstrated this "Austrian" insight time and time again. Easy credit may provide temporary recovery, but the long-term effects are serious—more unemployment and recession in the future. In short, there is no free lunch. Active government intervention in the macroeconomy, whether in the form of deficit spending or easy money, is harmful to long-term growth.

Returning to the Classical Model

The best policy is non-interventionism. Taxes should stay low. Government budgets should be limited to essential services, and regularly balanced. The money supply should be stable and non-inflationary. Interest rates should not be manipulated.

There is nothing new about this non-interventionist approach. It represents the old classical school of Adam Smith (balanced budgets, low taxes, sound money, laissez faire).

What is noteworthy is the economics profession's gradual shift away from Keynesian economics toward the classical position. An examination of all editions of Samuelson's *Economics* reveals that he has slowly but surely abandoned the tenets of Keynesianism. In the past, he favored deficit spending; now he's opposed to it. He denigrated savings; now he promotes it. He condoned central planning; now he supports market reforms. Might we see a total conversion to laissez faire by the next edition? We can only hope.

---

1. Walter W. Heller, "Is Monetary Policy Being Oversold?" in *Monetary Policy vs. Fiscal Policy,* by Milton Friedman and Walter W. Heller (New York: Norton, 1969), p. 31.

2. Paul A. Samuelson and William D. Nordhaus, *Economics,* 15th ed. (New York: McGraw-Hill, 1995), p. 644–45.

Free Marketers Miss
Opportunity at
AEA Meetings

"People saved more and we had a recession in 1990."
—OLIVIER BLANCHARD

"A reduction in the federal deficit is short-term expansionary."
—ALAN BLINDER

The two statements above, made on January 7, 1997, at the American Economic Association meetings in New Orleans, contrast the "old" and the "new" visions of economic policy.

MIT professor Olivier Blanchard, reflecting old-style Keynesian thinking, blamed the 1990–1991 recession on excessive saving instead of higher taxes and tight money.

Alan Blinder, Princeton economist and former Fed official, represented new classical thinking when he declared that increased deficit spending was bad for the economy and that a deliberate policy of cutting the deficit was expansionary because it would mean a decline in interest rates. Keynes must be turning over in his grave!

Both statements were made at a well-attended meeting titled, "Is there a core of practical macroeconomics that we should all believe?" The participants were all mainstream economists from established institutions, yet they could not agree on many fundamental issues. Blanchard (MIT) was anti-saving and John Taylor (Stanford) was pro-saving. Some said the Phillips trade-off between inflation and unemployment was real, others said it was chimera. Supply-side economics was not represented. No one advocated tax reduction in an age of high tax burdens.

The debate could have been much more lively if the organizers had invited economists from outside the mainstream, such as Marxists and Austrians. But in most cases unorthodox thinkers are not invited to the sessions sponsored by the AEA. What to do? Most outcasts offer their own programs, side by side with the regular AEA sessions.

Where Were the Free-Market Advocates?

The Marxists are particularly well organized—the Union for Radical Political Economists sponsored over 30 sessions of their own. The "Growth and Gender" session was especially unprecedented: All five members of the panel were from the University of Utah's economics department, which has apparently been taken over by Marxists. Imagine, a Marxist revolution in the center of conservative Utah!

Why the free-market schools don't offer their own agenda at these national meetings is a mystery. The Society for the Development of Austrian Economics has its own program at the annual meetings of the Southern Economic Association; why not sponsor sessions at the annual AEA meetings? In the exhibit hall, where thousands of academic economists mingle and search for alternative books and materials, there were hardly any representatives of free-market economics. The American Enterprise Institute was there, but that was about it.

My Debate with Paul Samuelson

Quite by accident, I ran into Paul Samuelson, the famed MIT economist and Nobel Prize winner. We had recently been corresponding over an article I wrote entitled, "The Perseverance of Paul Samuelson's *Economics*." It is a rather unfriendly review of the first 15 editions of Samuelson's famed textbook. (The article, along with a rebuttal by Samuelson, appears in the Spring 1997 issue of *The Journal of Economic Perspectives.*) I accuse Samuelson of, among other things, an anti-saving mentality. But Samuelson denied the charge, saying that he regularly appeared before Congressional committees advocating a higher saving rate to stimulate economic growth. In response, I said it was too bad he didn't inform his students of his views in his textbook. Instead they got the "paradox of thrift."

What Will Stimulate Long-Term Growth?

One of the more interesting sessions I attended was a discussion about the 50th anniversary of the Employment Act of 1946. Murray Weidenbaum (Washington University) and Martin Feldstein (Harvard) represented the free-market viewpoint, while Robert Eisner (Northwestern) represented the Keynesian approach. Andrew Brimmer, a former Fed official, chaired the panel.

The Employment Act of 1946 established three economic policy goals: full employment, stable purchasing power of money, and economic growth. Most of the panel agreed that all three policies had been achieved in the 1990s—employment was dynamic and growing, inflation was low, and recession had been avoided. However, there was an uneasy feeling that economic growth could be substantially higher than the current 2–3 percent rate. In a recent *Business Week* column (September 2, 1996), MIT professor Rudi Dorbusch advocated two structural reforms in the United States that would substantially increase economic growth: privatize Social Security and privatize education. I asked the panelists what they thought of these proposals. Surprisingly, everyone on the panel except Eisner endorsed them.

The Dismal Science Comes to China

Most of the agenda at AEA meetings is pretty plain fare, although I encountered a few exceptions. One was a paper presented by K. K. Fung, who teaches at the University of Memphis. "Dying for Children" advocates the buying and selling of "birth rights" as a way of solving China's population problem. Each Chinese married couple would have the right to one child, plus an additional child if a parent or grandparent died. Or they could buy a birth right in the marketplace from an elderly Chinese who chooses to "exit early" (commit suicide). Accordingly, "hopelessly ill" grandparents would be encouraged to exit early in order to create another grandchild. According to Fung, suicide would then be viewed as beneficial—allowing a child to be born! Brigham Young University's Larry Wimmer, who presided over the session, called the paper "grim," a proposal that "sets families against parents and grandparents." It amounts to a "social program of euthanasia."

Apparently the dismal science has a long way to go before solving the world's problems.

Heilbroner's
One-Armed Philosophers

"Without the government, the market as a system would not last two minutes."

—ROBERT HEILBRONER[1]

The May-June 1999 issue of *Challenge* magazine highlighted Robert Heilbroner, perhaps the best-selling economics author of all time. This year he published the seventh edition of his celebrated work, *The Worldly Philosophers* (Simon & Schuster, 1999), which has now sold over three million copies.

I am not surprised that *The Worldly Philosophers* has gone through multiple editions since 1953. Heilbroner has written a colorful and entertaining masterpiece. And no one has come up with a better title about the lives and ideas of the great economic thinkers.

Challenge also interviewed the 70-year-old professor. One question they failed to ask, however, is, "Why have you doggedly refused to acknowledge the success of twentieth-century free-market schools of economics?"

Heilbroner's Bias

Yes, it's a sad commentary: Robert Heilbroner, the masterful stylist, suffers from one serious defect—a highly prejudicial, unbalanced view of economics. After revising and updating his

286

book seven times, he still never mentions the Chicago school of Milton Friedman and the Austrian school of Ludwig von Mises and F. A. Hayek (although he does have a chapter on Joseph Schumpeter, the *enfant terrible* of the Austrians).

Heilbroner's resolve is a tragic reminder of the one-sided way economics was taught a generation ago: Give Adam Smith his due, and then spend the rest of the time patronizing Keynes, Marx, Veblen, and the socialists. Meanwhile, the Chicago school, the Austrians, the supply-siders, the public-choice school, and other free-market proponents are poured down an Orwellian memory hole.

Heilbroner's bias reminds me of Stalin's rewriting of history when he would have his enemies' pictures erased from official photographs. In Heilbroner's photograph of the "great economic thinkers," he has erased men like J. B. Say, Carl Menger, Eugen Böhm-Bawerk, Knut Wicksell, Irving Fisher, Frank H. Knight, Henry Simons, Mises, Hayek, Friedman, Robert Lucas, and James Buchanan, among others. Heilbroner writes as if the Nobel Prize in economics hadn't existed for the past 25 years! Both Mark Blaug and James Tobin regard Irving Fisher as the greatest American economist. A year ago, *Time* magazine's editor-in-chief, Norman Pearlstine, named Milton Friedman "economist of the century," ahead of Keynes.[2] Daniel Yergin and Joseph Stanislaw wrote in *The Commanding Heights:* "In the postwar years, Keynes's theory of government management of the economy appeared unassailable. But a half century later, it is Keynes who has been toppled and Hayek, the fierce advocate of free markets, who is preeminent."[3] Yet you wouldn't know anything about Fisher, Friedman, or Hayek after reading *The Worldly Philosophers.*

No one is objecting to Heilbroner's right to favor Keynes over Friedman, but to ignore Friedman (whose name does not even appear in the seventh edition) is a travesty.

Why the Sins of Omission?

All editions of *The Worldly Philosophers* have purposely hid the background of the author, and with good reason. His mentors are Marxists Paul Sweezy at Harvard and Adolph Lowe at the

New School for Social Research. No wonder he wrote so sympathetically toward Marx.[4] Heilbroner has been a dedicated "democratic socialist" for most of his life and was for many years the Norman Thomas Professor of Economics at the New School. He is perhaps the only economist in the United States who holds a chair named after a socialist political leader. He has long favored a large public sector and Keynesian deficit spending. He hates the term "free market," adding, "Markets aren't free. They depend on government."[5] He prefers the Marxian term "capitalism."

Several years ago, I met Bob Heilbroner in his New York apartment and asked him why he ignored Friedman and Hayek. He felt that Friedman had not advanced economics beyond Adam Smith, and as for Hayek, he said, "I tried reading Hayek but could never follow him." Yet I give Heilbroner high marks for condemning abstract mathematical modeling in economics as generating "rigor, but, alas, also rigor mortis," and for being the only socialist to publicly give credit to Mises and Hayek for correctly anticipating the collapse of Soviet central planning.[6]

Galbraith and Buchholz: More Balanced Views

Heilbroner could learn a lot from his friend John Kenneth Galbraith. Although Galbraith's title isn't as dramatic, *Economics in Perspective* (Houghton Mifflin, 1987) bends over backwards to be fair to free-market economists. Sure, Galbraith gives full space to his favorite writers (Keynes, Veblen, Marx), but he also devotes major portions of his book to Say's law and the French laissez-faire school, the Austrians' critique of socialism, Fisher's quantity theory of money, and Friedman's monetary counterrevolution to Keynesian economics.

Heilbroner's rewriting of history is one reason more and more instructors are turning to more balanced histories of economic thought such as Todd Buchholz's *New Ideas from Dead Economists* (Penguin, 1989 and revised in 1999). Like Heilbroner, Buchholz has chapters on Smith, Marx, Veblen, and Keynes, but then gives equal time to Alfred Marshall and the marginalist revolution and the twentieth-century counterrevolution of Friedman and Buchanan. Buchholz leaves out the Austrians because, he says, he was never taught anything about Mises or Hayek when he attended Harvard.

---

1. Interview with Robert Heilbroner, *Challenge*, May-June 1999, p. 62.

2. *Time*, December 7, 1998, p. 35. However, when *Time* published its "The Century's Greatest Minds" special issue, the editors gave top billing to Keynes. Pearlstine acknowledged a disagreement between him and his editors. "This is not the first time that the editors of *Time* have chosen to disagree with me. . . . I still think Friedman is the economist of the century." (Private correspondence, April 20, 1999.)

3. Daniel Yergin and Joseph Stanislaw, *The Commanding Heights* (New York: Simon & Schuster, 1998), pp. 14–15.

4. In the 1961 edition I used in college, Heilbroner wrote that Marx was a "devoted husband and father" (p. 124), but after it was revealed that he had an illegitimate son from his housemaid, Heilbroner dropped the approving reference.

5. *Challenge* interview, p. 61.

6. Robert Heilbroner, "The Triumph of Capitalism," *The New Yorker*, January 23, 1989, and "Reflections After Communism," *The New Yorker*, September 10, 1990.

I Like Hayek

"Half a century later, it is Keynes who has been toppled and Hayek, the fierce advocate of free markets, who is pre-eminent."

—DANIEL YERGIN AND JOSEPH STANISLAW[1]

In 2000 *Time* magazine named John Maynard Keynes the economist of the twentieth century for his countercyclical demand-management thesis—that big government is necessary to stabilize an inherently shaky capitalist system. But in the latest biography of Keynes, Robert Skidelsky declares that arch-critic Milton Friedman disproved Keynes's theory by demonstrating with convincing empirical evidence that market economies were far more stable than Keynes believed, and that government—particularly central-bank monetary policy—is the real source of the boom-bust cycle. "It was as though Keynes had never been," Skidelsky pronounced solemnly.[2]

Who should take the place of Keynes to lead economics into the 21st century? Should it be the economics of Friedman, Ludwig von Mises, Joseph Schumpeter, or F. A. Hayek? While all four have much to offer, I favor Hayek. I am not alone. Lately there has been a plethora of books and articles about Hayek, so extensive that an entire website, maintained by Professor Gregory Ransom, is devoted to this eminent economist and philosopher. (See www.hayekcenter.org.) For the past dozen years, the University of Chicago Press has published the collected works of Hayek up to volume ten, with another ten expected.

In addition, an excellent biography has just been released, *Friedrich Hayek: A Biography*, by Alan Ebenstein. It offers a comprehensive look at Hayek's life and ideas, and even includes some surprises, such as his controversial divorce and remarriage; how his bestseller, *The Road to Serfdom*, may have cost Sir Winston Churchill re-election in 1945; and the remarkable similarities between Hayek's and Marx's theories of crises.[3]

Hayek's Political Contributions

What do I like about Hayek? First, Hayek advanced the case for an institutional framework for liberty. In his classic work *The Constitution of Liberty*, he set out the legal and constitutional system needed to create the delicate balance between liberty and law in a liberal society.[4] Hayek rejected central planning by technocrats and emphasized the "spontaneous order" and prosperity generated by individuals using their own specialized knowledge and pursuing their own self-interest. According to Hayek, intervention could only lead down "the road to serfdom," the title of his most famous book. This book was written during World War II and reflected his pessimism about the future of government and Western civilization. When he wrote chapter 10, "Why the Worst Get on Top," he had in mind Hitler, Stalin, and Mussolini.

In 1976 he was even more dejected: "Both the influence of socialist ideas and the naive trust in the good intentions of the holders of totalitarian power have markedly increased."[5] Yet, only a few years later, Margaret Thatcher and Ronald Reagan appeared on the scene and under the influence of Hayek and other free-market economists, reversed the tide of socialism and inflation. The worst don't always get on top!

New Advances in Hayek's Economics

Hayek's economics has been both lauded and attacked by his colleagues. Economists have readily incorporated his concept of prices and profits as essential communicators of critical information. They signal where scarce resources should be allocated in the economy, thus creating "order without command."

But it's another story when it comes to the "Austrian" theory of capital, the business cycle, and monetary policy. "I am an enormous admirer of Hayek, but not for his economics," confesses Milton Friedman, "His writings in [political theory] are magnificent . . . [but] . . . I think his capital theory is unreadable. . . . There hasn't been an iota of progress."[6]

But Friedman spoke prematurely. There has been considerable progress in Austrian capital theory. Recent advancements in theoretical Austrian macroeconomics include Roger Garrison's *Time and Money,* which deftly compares the flawed models of Keynesian and monetarist theory with the more advanced Austrian theory, and Steve Horwitz's *Microfoundations and Macroeconomics.* Both books were published in the past year by Routledge.

On the statistical side, U. S. Department of Commerce's Bureau of Economic Analysis has begun to measure Hayek's triangle; that is, the total amount of annual spending at all stages of production. This new national statistic, called "Gross Output," is based on my original work *The Structure of Production,* an updated vision of Hayekian macroeconomics.[7]

The Austrian Business Cycle and NASDAQ

The Hayek-Mises theory of the business cycle is also relevant to today's business cycle and financial markets. Indeed, the most recent boom-bust in technology stocks and the NASDAQ is a perfect example of Hayekian economic behavior. Hayek's theory predicts that an easy credit policy will create an artificial inflationary boom in the earlier stages of capital and technological development that will eventually and inevitably collapse. "Every period of inflation ends with a crash," he said. Indeed, that is precisely what has occurred in the past few years on the technology-weighted NASDAQ. The 1997–99 easy-credit policies by the Federal Reserve pushed the NASDAQ index far above its natural level, and when the Fed stopped inflating, the bubble burst. What goes up must come down.

On a personal note, I had the opportunity to meet Nobel-laureate Hayek twice, once in the late 1970s at the New Orleans Investment Conference and again in the mid-1980s, when Gary North and I visited him at his summer home in the Austrian Alps and conducted what turned out to be his last interview. Even at the

age of 86, he greeted us warmly and for three hours spoke masterfully of his career and his contributions to economics. His biggest
regret was that his theory of capital had not been pursued. Now all
that is changing.

Yesterday's heresy is tomorrow's dogma!

---

1. Daniel Yergin and Joseph Stanislaw, *The Commanding Heights* (New
York: Simon and Schuster, 1998), p. 431.

2. Robert Skidelsky, *John Maynard Keynes: Fighting for Britain, 1937–1946*
(London: Macmillan, 2000), p. 506.

3. Alan Ebenstein, *Friedrich Hayek: A Biography* (New York: Palgrave/St.
Martin's Press, 2001).

4. F.A. Hayek, *The Constitution of Liberty* (Chicago: University of Chicago
Press, 1960).

5. F.A. Hayek, *The Road to Serfdom* (Chicago: University of Chicago Press,
1976 [1944]), p. xxi.

6. Quoted in Ebenstein, pp. 81, 273.

7. Mark Skousen, *The Structure of Production* (New York: New York University Press, 1990).

A Much-Deserved Triumph in Supply-Side Economics

"After occupying center stage during the 1980s, the supply-side approach to economics disappeared when Ronald Reagan left office."

—PAUL SAMUELSON[1]

Until Robert Mundell won the Nobel Prize in 1999, supply-side economics had been a school without honor among professional economists. Established textbook writers such as Paul Samuelson (MIT), Greg Mankiw (Harvard), and Alan Blinder (Princeton) frequently condemned the supply-side idea that marginal tax cuts increase labor productivity, or that tax cuts stimulate the economy sufficiently to increase government revenues.

The Laffer Curve—the theory that when taxes are too high, reducing them would actually raise tax revenue—is dismissed. "When Reagan cut taxes after he was elected, the result was less revenue, not more," reports Mankiw in his popular textbook.[2] Never mind that tax revenues actually rose significantly every year of the Reagan administration; the perception is that supply-side economics has been discredited. Arthur Laffer isn't even listed in the 1999 edition of *Who's Who in Economics*, although the Laffer Curve is frequently discussed in college textbooks.[3]

That is all changed with Columbia University economist Robert A. Mundell's Nobel Prize in economics. According to Jude Wanniski, Mundell is the theoretical founder of the Laffer Curve.[4] In the early 1970s he told Wanniski, "The level of U.S. taxes has become a drag on economic growth in the United States. The national economy is being choked by taxes—asphyxiated."[5]

Mundell offered a creative solution to stagflation (inflationary recession) of the 1970s: impose a tight-money, high-interest rate policy to curb inflation and strengthen the dollar, and slash marginal tax rates to fight recession. Mundell's prescription was adopted by Reagan and Fed chairman Paul Volcker in the early 1980s. "There's been no downside to tax cuts," he told reporters recently.

Yet, oddly enough, Mundell hasn't been accorded much attention compared to supply-siders Laffer, Paul Craig Roberts, and Martin Anderson. In their histories of Reaganomics, Roberts and Anderson mention Mundell only once.[6]

Two major studies of supply-side economics in 1982 don't cite his works at all.

Nevertheless, Mundell accomplished a great deal worth lauding. In fact, he is considered the most professional scholar of the supply-siders.

Robert Mundell has had an amazing professional career. A Canadian by birth, he has attended, taught, or worked at over a dozen universities and organizations, including MIT, University of Washington, Chicago, Stanford, Johns Hopkins, the Brookings Institution, Graduate Institute of International Studies in Geneva, Remnin University of China (Beijing), and the IMF. Before going to Columbia in 1974, he was a professor at the University of Chicago and editor of *The Journal of Political Economy*. Thus the Chicago school once again claimed a Nobel, although Mundell differs markedly from the monetarist school.

Monetary vs. Fiscal Policy

Famed monetarist Milton Friedman said, "I have never believed that fiscal policy, given monetary policy, is an important influence on the ups and downs of the economy."[7] Supply-siders strongly disagree. Cutting marginal tax rates and slowing government spending can reduce the deficit, lower interest rates, and stimulate long-term economic growth. Mundell counters, "Monetary policy cannot be the engine of higher noninflationary growth. But fiscal policy—both levers of it—can be. . . . The U.S. tax-and-spend system reduces potential growth because it penalizes success and rewards failure."

Mundell favored spending on education, research and development, and infrastructure rather than government welfare programs. He advocates reducing top marginal income tax rates, slashing the capital gains tax, and cutting the corporate income tax. Such policies would sharply raise saving rates and economic growth—"an increase in the rate of saving by 5% of income (GDP), say from 10% of income to 15%, would increase the rate of [economic] growth by 50%, i.e., from 2.5% to 3.75%."[8]

Mundell as Gold Bug

Supply-siders also take a different approach to monetary policy. They go beyond the monetarist policy of controlling the growth of the money supply. Unlike the monetarists, supply-siders like Mundell resolutely favor increasing the role of gold in international monetary affairs. "Gold provides a stabilizing effect in a world of entirely flexible currencies," he told a group of reporters in New York in November 1999. According to Mundell, gold plays an essential role as a hedge against a return of inflation. He predicted that the price of gold could skyrocket in the next decade, to as high as $6,000 an ounce, if G7 central banks continue to expand the money supply at 6 percent a year. "I do not think this an outlandish figure. Gold is a good investment for central bankers." He did not foresee central banks selling any more gold. "Gold will stay at center stage in the world's central banking system," he said.

In awarding Mundell the prize, the Bank of Sweden recognized him as the chief intellectual proponent of the euro, the new currency of the European Community. He considers the euro a super-currency of continental dimensions that will challenge the dollar as the dominant currency. The benefits of a single currency include lower transaction costs, greater monetary stability, and a common monetary policy. Mundell advocates an open global economy, expanded foreign trade, and fewer national currencies. Ultimately, he envisions a universal currency backed by gold as the ideal world monetary system. Under a strict gold standard, "real liquidity balances are generated during recessions and constrained during inflations."[9] Mundell is an optimist as we enter a new century. He's bullish on the global stock markets, the gold standard, globalization, and downsized government. He's my kind of economist.

1. Paul Samuelson and William D. Nordhaus, *Economics,* 16th ed. (Boston: Irwin/McGraw-Hill, 1998), p. 640.

2. N. Gregory Mankiw, *Principles of Economics* (Fort Worth, Tex.: Harcourt/Dryden Press, 1998), p. 166.

3. Mark Blaug, compiler of *Who's Who in Economics* (Northampton, Mass.: Edward Elgar, 1999), determines the top 1,000 names in the book based on frequency of citation in scholarly journals. Among the famous economists missing the cut are Arthur Laffer, Paul Craig Roberts, and Murray N. Rothbard.

4. Jude Wanniski, The *Way the World Works,* rev. and updated (New York: Simon and Schuster, 1983), p. x.

5. Wanniski, "It's Time to Cut Taxes," *Wall Street Journal,* December 11, 1974.

6. Paul Craig Roberts, *The Supply-Side Revolution* (Cambridge, Mass.: Harvard University Press, 1984) and Martin Anderson, *Revolution* (Stanford, Calif.: Hoover Institution Press, 1990).

7. Milton Friedman, "Supply-Side Policies: Where Do We Go from Here?" *Supply-Side Economics in the 1980s Conference Proceedings* (Federal Reserve Bank of Atlanta, 1982), p. 53.

8. Robert A. Mundell, "A Progrowth Fiscal System," The *Rising Tide,* ed. Jerry J. Jasinowski (New York: Wiley, 1998), pp. 198, 203–204.

9. Mundell, The *New International Monetary System* (New York: Columbia University Press, 1977), p. 242.

"They Were Right"

"Americans need to know the history of American anti-communism if they are to understand the great role they have played in ridding the world of the most murderous of the twentieth century totalitarians."

—RICHARD GID POWERS[1]

On October 16, 1961, thousands of people packed the Hollywood Bowl. The occasion was not a rock concert or a sporting event but the biggest anticommunist rally in the country. "Hollywood's Answer to Communism" was carried on nationwide television. Actor George Murphy was the master of ceremonies and other speakers included Herb Philbrick, Congressman Walter Judd, Dr. Fred Schwarz, Senator Thomas Dodd, and my uncle, W. Cleon Skousen, a former special assistant to J. Edgar Hoover and author of the bestseller *The Naked Communist*.

I was in my early teens when the anticommunist movement was at its zenith and remember seeing my uncle on TV. I watched shows like *I Led Three Lives* and read books like John Stormer's *None Dare Call It Treason*, J. Edgar Hoover's *Masters of Deceit*, and Whittaker Chambers's *Witness*.

But despite this groundswell of concern over the threat of communism, communist sympathizers at high levels combined with media forces to ridicule and vilify patriotic conservatives. Most historians deplored the anticommunist movement of the 1950s and 1960s as "extremist," "paranoid," "right-wing" hysteria. Accordingly, there was little credence given to this alleged vast

298

communist conspiracy; reaction went rarely beyond references to McCarthyism, redbaiting, and blacklisting. They challenged the anti-communists' claims that the Soviets had planted numerous agents in government, that Stalin had infiltrated the film industry as a means of promoting communist propaganda, that the Communist Party USA was a pawn of Moscow, and that the Soviet Union was a serious military threat.

They depicted the anticommunist era as an unwarranted "witch hunt" against liberal progressives and idealistic movie stars and a groundless attack on patriotic government officials who they say were falsely accused of espionage. They carried on a 40-year campaign to prove Alger Hiss and Julius and Ethel Rosenberg innocent. My uncle's book so angered members of the political science and history departments at Brigham Young University that Richard D. Poll, a history professor, wrote a scathing critique of his "extremist" views on Karl Marx and communism.

Mises and Socialism

In those days, the economics profession also cast doubt on free-market criticisms of socialism and the Soviet economy. Half a century earlier, Ludwig von Mises and F. A. Hayek were lone voices in charging that socialist central planning could not work. According to conventional wisdom, Mises and Hayek had lost the debate with the socialists in the 1930s, and in 1985 Paul Samuelson reported in his popular textbook that the Soviet Union had grown faster than any other industrial economy since the 1920s. As late as 1989, Samuelson claimed that "The Soviet economy is proof that, contrary to what many skeptics had earlier believed, a socialist command economy can function and even thrive."[2]

But then, following the collapse of the Berlin Wall and Soviet communism in 1989–90, economist Robert Heilbroner shocked his colleagues in the socialist world by boldly declaring that the long-standing debate between capitalism and socialism was over. "Capitalism has won," he confessed. "Socialism has been a great tragedy this century." Furthermore, Heilbroner was forced to change his mind about Mises and the debate over socialism. Following the unexpected collapse of communism, Heilbroner admitted, "It turns out, of course, that Mises was right."[3] And it wasn't long before Paul Samuelson did an about-face in his textbook, labeling Soviet central planning "the failed model."

Revelations from the Soviet Archives

The fall of the Soviet Union brought about another dramatic outcome that would have far-reaching effects on modern history. The Russian government opened up thousands of secret KGB files in Moscow, revealing what one historian called "stunning revelations" about espionage and the Soviet economy under Stalin. This new information has sparked a harsh reevaluation of the anticommunist movement by historians and the media. As one reviewer put it, "It's like looking into the new edition of a book from which half the pages had previously been torn out."[4]

The KGB files prove beyond doubt that Alger Hiss, the Rosenbergs, and numerous other Americans accused of spying for the Soviets were guilty. They confirm what J. Edgar Hoover and the House Un-American Activities Committee were saying all along: that spies reached the highest levels of the State and Treasury departments, the White House, and the Manhattan Project, and that the Communist Party USA (which had 50,000 members in World War II) got its marching orders from Moscow.[5]

Stalin's Economic Disaster

Based on research at the Soviet archives, historian Sheila Fitzpatrick has written a pioneering account of everyday Russian life in the 1930s: "With the abolition of the market, shortages of food, clothing, and all kinds of consumer goods became endemic. As peasants fled the collectivized villages, major cities were soon in the grip of an acute housing crisis, with families jammed for decades in tiny single rooms in communal apartments. . . . It was a world of privation, overcrowding, endless queues, and broken families, in which the regime's promises of future socialist abundance rang hollow. . . . Government bureaucracy often turned everyday life into a nightmare."[6] What a sharp contrast to Samuelson's glowing account of the Soviet economy.

After writing three books on the Soviet archives, historians John

Earl Haynes and Harvey Klehr summed it up this way about the anticommunists: "They were right."

And being right, they deserve our praise and gratitude.

---

1. Richard Gid Powers, *Not Without Honor: The History of American Anticommunism* (New York: Free Press, 1995), p. 428.

2. Paul A. Samuelson and William D. Nordhaus, *Economics,* 13th ed. (New York: McGraw-Hill, 1989), p. 837.

3. Robert Heilbroner, "Reflections After Communism," *The New Yorker,* September 10, 1990, and "The Triumph of Capitalism," *The New Yorker,* January 23, 1989.

4. Joseph E. Persico, "The Kremlin Connection," review of *The Haunted Wood: Soviet Espionage in America,* by Allen Weinstein and Alexander Vassiliev, *New York Times Book Review,* January 3, 1999.

5. Several books have been published detailing new findings from the Russian archives, including John Earl Haynes and Harvey Klehr's *Venona: Decoding Soviet Espionage in America* (New Haven: Yale University Press, 1999) and *The Soviet World of American Communism* (New Haven: Yale, 1998).

6. Sheila Fitzpatrick, *Everyday Stalinism* (Oxford University Press, 1999), flyleaf.

Predicting the Future

Economics for the
21ˢᵗ Century

"Nature has set no limit to the realization of our hopes."
—Marquis de Condorcet

Recently I came across the extraordinary writings of the Marquis de Condorcet (1743–94), a mathematician with an amazing gift of prophecy in *l'age des lumières*. Robert Malthus
(1766–1834) ridiculed Condorcet's optimism in his famous *Essay
on Population* (1798). Today Malthus is well known and Condorcet is forgotten. Yet it is Condorcet who has proven to be far
more prescient.

In an essay written over 200 years ago, translated as "The
Future Progress of the Mind," Condorcet foresaw the agricultural
revolution, gigantic leaps in labor productivity, a reduced work
week, the consumer society, a dramatic rise in the average life
span, medical breakthroughs, cures for common diseases, and an
explosion in the world's population.

Condorcet concluded his essay with a statement that accurately
describes the two major forces of the twentieth century—the
destructive force of war and crimes against humanity, and the creative force of global free-market capitalism. He wrote eloquently
of "the errors, the crimes, the injustices which still pollute the
earth," while at the same time celebrating our being "emancipated
from its shackles, released from the empire of fate and from that of

the enemies of its progress, advancing with a firm and sure step along the path of truth, virtue and happiness!"[1]

In the early 21st century, the public has focused on the history of the twentieth century. Condorcet's essay reflects two characteristics of this incredible period. First, the misery and vicious injustices of the past hundred years, and second, the incredible economic and technological advances during the same time.

The Crimes of the Twentieth Century

Paul Johnson's *Modern Times,* by far the best twentieth-century history of the world, demonstrates powerfully that this century has been the bloodiest of all world history.[2] Here is a breakdown of the carnage:

Civilians Killed by Governments (in millions)

Soviet Union	62 (1917–91)
China (communist)	35 (1949-　)
Germany	21 (1933–45)
China (Kuomintang)	10 (1928–49)
Japan	6 (1936–45)
Other	36 (1900-　)
Total	**170 million**

Deaths in War (in millions)

International wars	30
Civil wars	7
Total	**37 million**

Economists use a statistic to measure what national output could exist under conditions of full employment, called Potential GDP. Imagine the Potential GDP if the communists, Nazis, and other despots hadn't used government power to commit those hateful crimes against humanity.

Another great French writer, Frédéric Bastiat (1801–50), wrote an essay in 1850 on "What Is Seen and What Is Not Seen."[3] We do not see the art, literature, inventions, music, books, charity, and good works of the millions who lost their lives in the Soviet gulags, Nazi concentration camps, and Pol Pot's killing fields.

The Economic Miracle of the Twentieth Century

Yet the twentieth century was also the best of times, for those who survived the wars and repression. Millions of Americans, Europeans, and Asians were emancipated from the drudgery of all-day work by miraculous technological advances in telecommunications, agriculture, transportation, energy, and medicine. The best book describing this economic miracle is Stanley Lebergott's *Pursuing Happiness: American Consumers in the Twentieth Century* (Princeton University Press, 1993). Focusing on trends in food, tobacco and alcohol, clothing, housing, fuel, housework, health, transportation, recreation, and religion, he demonstrates powerfully how "consumers have sought to make an uncertain and often cruel world into a pleasanter and more convenient place." As a result, Americans have increased their standard of living at least tenfold in the past 100 years.

What should be the goal of the economist in the 21st century? Certainly not to repeat the blunders of the past. In the halls of Congress, the White House, and academia, we need to reject the brutality of Marxism, the weight of Keynesian big government, and the debauchery of sound currency by interventionist central banks. Most important, ivory-tower economists need to concentrate more on applied economics (like the work of Lebergott) instead of high mathematical modeling.

As far as a positive program is concerned, the right direction can be found in an essay on the "next economics" written by the great Austrian-born management guru Peter F. Drucker almost 20 years ago: "Capital is the future . . . the Next Economics will have to be again micro-economic and centered on supply." Drucker demanded an economic theory aiming at "optimizing productivity" that would benefit all workers and consumers.[4] Interestingly, Drucker cited approvingly from the work of Robert Mundell, the 1999 Nobel Prize winner in economics, who is famed for his advocacy of supply-side economics and a gold-backed international currency.

Beware the Enemy

Market forces are on the march. The collapse of Soviet communism has, in the words of Milton Friedman, turned "creeping socialism" into "crumbling socialism." But let us not be deluded. Bad policies, socialistic thinking, and class hatred die slowly. Unless we are vigilant, natural liberty and universal prosperity will be on the defensive once again.

We need to deregulate, privatize, cut taxes, open borders, stop inflating, balance the budget, and limit government to its proper constitutional authority. We need to teach, write, and speak out for economic liberalization as never before. Let our goal for the coming era be: freedom in our time for all peoples!

---

1. Marquis de Condorcet, "The Future Progress of the Human Mind," *The Portable Enlightenment Reader,* ed. Isaac Kramnick (New York: Penguin Books, 1995), p. 38. Several of Condorcet's writings can be found in this excellent anthology.

2. Paul Johnson, *Modern Times: The World from the Twenties to the Nineties,* rev. ed. (New York: Harper, 1992). The best survey of the horrors of communism is *The Black Book of Communism: Crimes, Terror, Repression* (Cambridge, Mass.: Harvard University Press, 1999), written by six French scholars, some of whom are former communists.

3. Frédéric Bastiat, *Selected Essays on Political Economy* (Irvington-on-Hudson, N.Y.: Foundation for Economic Education, 1995 [1964]).

4. Peter F. Drucker, *Toward the Next Economics, and Other Essays* (New York: Harper & Row, 1981), pp. 1–21.

America Is Number 1 Again

"By the year 2000 Japan may well be enjoying the highest
standard of living of any industrialized country."

—ECONOMICS TEXTBOOK, 1987[1]

In 1991, I prepared an advertising campaign for my book *Economics on Trial* (Irwin). The headline was: "Japan and Germany Win World War III," followed by the subtitle, "Their formula multiplies wealth so rapidly that they will achieve their goal of world domination by the year 2000." In this ad, I referenced the sound economic model that had transformed war-torn Germany and Japan into economic powerhouses in one generation and vulcanized their stock markets. These principles were high savings rates, low taxes on capital and investment, low inflation, balanced budgets, and free markets.

Friedman Sets Me Straight

I sent a copy of my ad to the Nobel laureate economist Milton Friedman, who wasted no time debunking it: "This prediction is a bunch of nonsense," he wrote to me. "I will not live long enough to see it falsified, but you will. In the [year 2000] as in 1991, the U.S. standard of living will be higher than the Japanese."

It wasn't long before Professor Friedman was proven right. (He has set me straight on a number of occasions.) My prediction of German and Japanese dominance went awry. Not because the market formula for growth is wrong, but because Germany and Japan abandoned their model of success. Germany adopted high-cost labor-union controls, imposed anti-business regulations, and dramatically increased taxes to pay for a unified Germany. Japan exacted substantial tax increases (including a capital gains tax), propped up inefficient banks, and imposed a severe tight money policy in the early 1990s (following an excessive liberal monetary policy in the 1980s that created a bubble in real estate and stocks). Japan is still trying to recover from these devastating anti-market measures. Easier money and a higher national sales tax haven't helped. If Japan and Germany want to regain their fast-track status, they need to embrace a healthy dose of supply-side tax cuts and deregulation (known as Reaganomics in this country). Meanwhile, the good ol' USA is rolling right along. The tax increases in the early 1990s are being reversed (long-term capital gains are now taxed at only 20 percent). Corporations have downsized and labor remains wage-flexible and productive. We lead the world in technology and employment creation, among other categories.

Friedman (and others)' convinced me to turn bullish on the U.S. economy and stock market in the early 1990s. In January 1995, I made a major prediction in *Forecasts & Strategies,* arguing that America was on the comeback, and would lead the world in stock market performance. It did, although Wall Street turned severely bearish in the early 2000s.

How Does the U.S. Rank?

Recently I came across a delightful book that confirms my view that America is once again on top of the world: the fourth edition of *The Illustrated Book of World Rankings,* edited and compiled by George Thomas Kurian.[2] Out of some 100 positive listings, the United States received top billing in 33 categories. Among them:

- Most powerful nation (based on military manpower and economic capacity), way ahead of number 2 Russia.
- Largest gross domestic product (GDP), way ahead of number 2 Japan and number 3 Germany.
- World's highest per capita income based on purchasing power parity (though number 6 based on exchange rates), ahead of number 2 Switzerland.
- World's biggest exporter and importer, ahead of number 2 Germany and number 3 Japan.

- World's leader in retail sales.
- Leader in production of electricity, timber, and milk.
- Number 1 in airline travel, passenger cars, and commercial vehicles.
- Primary country of destination based on tourist expenditures.
- Number 1 in mail, telephones, faxes, and e-mail addresses.
- Tops in number of scientists and engineers, patents in force, and Nobel Prize winners (three times more than number 2 United Kingdom).
- Number 1 in televisions and radios per capita, number of movie theaters, museums, botanical gardens, and zoos. (India produces more films per year, but the United States dominates in movie revenues.)

The United States was edged out by Canada for number 1 in the Human Development Index (longevity, educational achievement, and standard of living). Japan is number 3. Lest you think America can do no wrong, the United States is also ranked number 1 in several negative categories: teen pregnancies, divorce rate (among industrial nations), sulfur and carbon emissions and nuclear wastes, AIDS cases, and number of prisoners. However, it is way down the list in several crime statistics.

Debunking the Pessimists

A wonderful book confirms America's lead in the world. In *Myths of Rich and Poor,* Michael Cox and Richard Alm highlight a slew of facts demonstrating American prowess and denying economic decay since the mid-1970s: real wealth has skyrocketed, the poor have not gotten poorer, corporate downsizing has created jobs, and the trade deficit suggests the United States is the "best place to invest."[3]

What about the future? Another fascinating book argues that the United States has a monopoly position on future technology. In *Probable Tomorrows: How Science and Technology Will Transform Our Lives in the Next Twenty Years,* Marvin Cetron and Owen L. Davies compile an exhaustive list of possible technological breakthroughs in engineering, manufacturing, computers, communications, energy, space, and medicine, noting which countries are likely to produce these innovations.[4] The United States was named the likely choice in 95 percent of the cases.

No wonder so many people from abroad want to come here. Their best alternative: invest in U.S. stocks, businesses, and real estate.

---

1. Richard G. Lipsey, Peter O. Steiner, and Douglas R. Purvis, *Economics*, 8th ed. (New York: Harper & Row, 1987), p. 735.

2. Sharpe Reference, 1997.

3. See chapter 5, "Still on Top of the World," *Myths of Rich and Poor* (New York: Basic Books, 1999), pp. 91–108.

4. St. Martin's Press, 1997.

What Do You Make
of This Graph?

"It was felt that if the policy prescriptions of the New Economics were applied, business cycles as they had been known
would be a thing of the past."

—HYMAN P. MINSKY, 1968[1]

In the 1960s, the heyday of Keynesian economics, economists
spoke optimistically of an end to the dreaded business cycle.
Then came the stagflationary jolt of the 1970s, the credit crunch
and banking crisis of the 1980s, and Japan's depression of the
1990s. In short, the business cycle seems alive and kicking.

Now, however, comes a graph published by the National
Bureau of Economic Research (NBER) showing that the cycle has
been tamed since World War II, resurrecting the "business cycle is
dead" thesis. The graph is printed below.

*Source: Victor Zarnowitz, Business Cycles (NBER and University of Chicago Press, 1995), reprinted in The
Economist, Oct. 28, 1995.*

313

According to these GDP statistics, the American economy has become more stable since World War II. Expansions are longer and slumps are milder. Moreover, the trend appears to be improving, and some economists are once again predicting that recessions will disappear altogther.

Big Government: Boom or Bane?

So what do we make of this graph? I asked an MIT economist, who immediately responded, "Keynesianism works!" Then I asked a Chicago professor, who exclaimed, "Monetarism works!"

Can we surmise from this graph that big government, as reflected in activist fiscal and monetary policy, has permanently reversed the prewar ups and downs of America's GDP?

Granted, there have been significant increases in the size and scope of government policy since the 1940s—the introduction of so-called automatic stabilizers (unemployment compensation, federal deposit insurance, Social Security), the increase in total government spending to over 40 percent of GDP, and a resolve by federal authorities to inflate in the face of any sign of economic downturn or crisis. All these policy changes have created an environment that errs on the side of inflation, rather than deflation. And an inflation-biased economy is likely to give you more boom than bust over the long term.

Of course, there could be other explanations for a milder and less frequent postwar business cycle:

—no world war since 1945;
—expanding free trade and globalization, which tend to ameliorate economic ups and downs;
—improved methods of inventory control, thus minimizing fluctuations in industrial output; and
—shifts in the economy away from volatile agricultural markets toward more stable manufacturing and service industries.[2]

The Cost of Artificial Stability: Less Growth

But there is no free lunch. Interestingly, greater stability in the business cycle has also coincided with less growth in the postwar

U.S. economy. There has clearly been a secular decline in the economic growth rate, particularly the late 1960s when the size of government began to explode upward. According to real growth rates provided by Milton Friedman, the U.S. economy grew between 3 and 4 percent a year in inflation-adjusted terms between 1869 and 1969, except during the 1929–39 depression. However, since 1969, the annual real growth rate fell to only 2.4 percent, and lately, in the 1990s, the real growth rate declined even further.

What is the cause of this malaise? A ubiquitous and unproductive state has clearly left a huge and growing burden on society. Government at all levels is strangling business and individual initiative through excessive taxation and regulation. Not surprisingly, most federal regulatory agencies (EPA, OHSA, FDA, etc.) burgeoned in the late 1960s and early 1970s—the same time the growth rate began falling. It was also the time that the government broke the last link to sound money (the gold standard).

In sum, we must not fall into the trap of supporting big government because of its allure of economic stability and a safety net. For stability may simply be a camouflage for economic lethargy and a declining standard of living. As Ben Franklin remarked, "Those who would give up essential liberty to purchase a little temporary safety, deserve neither liberty nor safety."

Leviathan Is Not Benign

Before we join the "business cycle is dead" school, let us not forget that Leviathan is not benign. More than likely, it will blunder again in the face of a world crisis—whether it be a financial panic, a natural disaster, or a war. As Adam Smith once remarked, "There is much ruin in a nation." According to the Austrian theory of the business cycle, as developed by Ludwig von Mises and Friedrich Hayek, monetary inflation does not simply raise prices, but also de-stablizes the economy. In a world of fiat money inflation and fractional reserve banking, business cycles are inevitable.

Just because we have avoided another Great Depression over the past 50 years does not guarantee that we will avoid it in the next 50 years. The U.S. economy may be Depression-resistant, but it is not Depression-proof.

1. Quoted in Martin Bronfenbrenner, ed., *Is the Business Cycle Obsolete?* (New York: Wiley, 1969), p. vi.

2. Some economists, especially Berkeley economist Christina Romer, emphasize this point and question whether there has been much improvement in postwar business cycles. See "The Postwar Business Cycle Reconsidered," *Journal of Political Economy,* February 1989. However, even accepting Romer's revised GDP figures, a huge difference exists between prewar and postwar business cycles.

"An Enemy Hath Done This"

> "Government measures . . . give individuals an incentive to
> misuse and misdirect resources and distort the investment of
> new savings."
>
> —MILTON FRIEDMAN[1]

A couple of years ago, I had the opportunity of speaking before
a Miami chapter of Legatus, a group of Catholic business
leaders organized originally by Tom Monaghan, founder of
Domino's Pizza. The topic was the outlook for the stock market,
which had reached sky-high levels and by any traditional measurement appeared extremely overvalued. Even many experienced
Wall Street analysts recognized that a bear-market correction or
crash was inevitable and necessary. As the old Wall Street saying
goes, "Trees don't grow to the sky." Indeed, in the spring the stock
market took a well-deserved tumble.

What is the cause of this boom-bust cycle in the stock market?
Does capitalism inherently create unsustainable growth? Is the
bull market on Wall Street real or a bubble?

The Parable of the Wheat and the Tares

To answer these questions, I applied Jesus' parable of the wheat
and the tares (Matthew 13:24–30) to today's financial situation.

Jesus tells the story of a wheat farmer whose crop comes under
attack by an unknown assailant. In the middle of the night this
enemy sows tares (weeds) in his wheat fields. Soon the farmer's

servants discover that the farmer's crop appears to be twice the normal size. Yet the master realizes that half the crop is fake—weeds instead of wheat. But he warns his servants not to tear out the weeds for fear of uprooting the good shoots; they must wait and let the wheat and the tares grow up together until harvest time. Months later, the wheat produces good grain, while the tares are merely weeds and provide no fruit. The servants pull out the weeds and burn them, and store the grain in the barn.

The parable is imminently applicable to the recent wild ride on Wall Street. In today's robust global economy, the wheat represents genuine prosperity—the new products, technologies, and productivity generated by capitalists and entrepreneurs. It represents real economic growth and when harvested, reflects a true higher standard of living for everyone. Under such conditions, stock prices are likely to rise.

On the other hand, the tares represent artificial prosperity that bears no fruit in the end and must be burned at harvest time. Where does this artificial growth come from? The central bank's "easy money" policies! The Fed artificially lowers interest rates and creates new money out of thin air (through open-market operations). This new money, like regular savings, is invested in the economy and stimulates more growth and higher stock prices—higher than sustainable over the long run.

Who is the Enemy? The Fed!

Who is the enemy who sows artificial prosperity? Alan Greenspan! (Or, to be more accurate, central bankers.) The money supply—which is controlled by the Fed—has been growing by leaps and bounds, especially since the 1997 Asian crisis.

But there is no free lunch, as sound economists have warned repeatedly. At some point, the harvest time comes and the wheat must be separated from the tares. This is the crisis stage, where the boom turns into the bust. Harvest time in wheat is fairly easy to predict, but not so in the economy. Clearly the U.S. economy became overheated in the 1990s, as measured by asset inflation, real estate prices, the art market, and the Consumer Price Index. By the year 2000, a "burning" of excessive asset values in the financial markets was inevitable. As Ludwig von Mises stated long ago, "if a brake is thus put on the boom, it will quickly be seen that the false impression of 'profitability' created by the credit expansion has led to unjustified investments."[2]

Lesson: Globalization and supply-side free-market policies have justified genuine economic growth and higher stock prices over the past two decades, but "easy money" policies created an artificial boom and "irrational exuberance" on Wall Street that had to end. Ignore this lesson at your own peril. Remember the parable of the wheat and the tares!

---

1. Milton Friedman, *Capitalism and Freedom* (Chicago: University of Chicago Press, 1962), p. 38.

2. Ludwig von Mises, "The 'Austrian' Theory of the Trade Cycle," in *The Austrian Theory of the Trade Cycle and Other Essays,* compiled by Richard M. Ebeling (Auburn, Ala.: Ludwig von Mises Institute, 1996), p. 30.

Forecasting Elections:
Economists Do It Better!

"It is the competition of profit-seeking entrepreneurs that
does not tolerate the preservation of *false* prices..."
—LUDWIG VON MISES[1]

In the spring of 1988, three economists at the University Iowa—
Forrest Nelson, Robert Forsythe, and George Newmann—were
having lunch together and the subject of the Michigan Democratic
Primary came up. The polls had shown Michael Dukakis ahead in
the primary, but Jesse Jackson turned out to be the surprise winner
the night before. "How could the pollsters be so wrong?" asked
one of the economists. "If traders on the COMEX in Chicago set
the November price of corn that badly, they would be out of a
job!" said another. It was the last comment that got the economists thinking. Could there be a futures market in political races
where traders might do a better job of forecasting elections than
the pollsters?

Thus began the Iowa Electronic Markets program. Since 1988,
the economics faculty at the Henry B. Tippie College of Business at
the University of Iowa, steeped in statistics and economic analysis
more than political science, has offered its own version of predicting elections. IEM offers futures contracts on the outcome of presidential and congressional elections, and occasionally important
senate races. Traders bet money (up to $500 per person) on who is

going to win the presidential race and whether Republicans or Democrats will control Capitol Hill.

The economics profession has invaded the pollster's territory. The imperial economist is at it again.

Which Is a Better Forecaster: Gallup or IEM?

What have been the results? So far the evidence is clear that IEM traders do a far better job than professional pollsters in predicting election outcomes, and at far less expense. Summarizing the evidence from 49 IEM election markets between 1988 and 2000, financial economists from Iowa concluded that (a) election-eve prediction errors by IEM traders averaged less than 2 percent, (b) polling proved far more volatile during the election campaign, and (c) approximately 70 percent of the time, IEM traders bettered the pollsters in predicting the percentage outcome of each election during the campaign period. "The market [IEM] appears to forecast the election outcomes more closely than polls months in advance," they state.[2] And this despite the fact that IEM traders differ greatly from a representative sample of voters.[3]

Who Won in 2000: Bush or Gore?

The IEM has run markets in four U. S. presidential elections. The political futures market predicted with great accuracy the election of George Bush in 1988, and Bill Clinton in 1992 and 1996. The Iowa futures market also predicted an extremely close race in 2000. According to the futures market, George W. Bush and Al Gore were neck-and-neck from May until September, when Gore opened a slight lead. Through the debates, Gore's lead evaporated and Bush pulled ahead slightly. But two days before the election, the lead switched to Gore. Then, finally, on election eve, it barely switched back to Bush. In contrast, the polls showed Bush with large leads from April through mid-August, a relatively large Gore surge (the traditional "convention" bounce) until mid-September, and a relatively large Bush resurgence into the election night. "Thus, throughout the election, the IEM showed a close race in absolute terms and a closer race than polls did."[4] However, IEM traders still predicted a slight victory in the popular vote for

Bush on election day, when in fact Gore won by 0.2 percent while still losing the electoral college by one vote. Thus, interestingly, traders who paid approximately $510 on election eve betting that Bush would win, lost their entire investment, while those who paid approximately $480 betting that Gore would win, earned a $1,000 payoff. The "winner-take-all" market for president was based on plurality of votes, not electoral college votes. For both Republican and Democratic traders, the 2000 election was a bittersweet experience.

Like the futures markets in Chicago and New York, IEM speculators can still be on the wrong side of the trade, and the overall market consensus can, like the pollsters, still make mistakes. What we can say is that the futures markets do tend to minimize error—they are right most of the time. But so are the polls.

Why Speculators Outperform Pollsters

The more interesting question is: Why are futures traders better forecasters of elections than professional pollsters? Is it luck or do they have some economic advantages? Economists give two basic reasons. First, traders appear to have a stronger profit motive in predicting the outcome of an election. Because they are putting their own money at risk, they tend to be more confident in their predictions. Admittedly, Gallup and other professional pollsters also have a financial interest the making accurate forecasts of elections, but they are at a decided disadvantage. The establishment media poll potential voters with the question, "If the election were held today, who would you vote for?" Voters are not asked to put up their own money and bet on who they think will really win. Consequently, the public has less of a vested interest in taking the question seriously. Their answers can be fickle and sometimes they may even lie. As a result, published polls vary significantly over time and between polling services. Sometimes the polls are downright wrong, the most famous being the Truman-Dewey election of 1948.

Second, the market aggregates the diverse information of traders in a more dynamic, efficient manner. The Austrian economist F. A. Hayek suggested this point years ago when he noted that markets have a dual role. They allocate resources to their most productive use and, through the process of price discovery, they aggregate information about the values of these resources.[5]

Traditional methods of predicting elections, such as polling, have some difficulty in estimating the dynamic forces at work during an election, while IEM traders incorporate polls, marketing surveys, economic data, charismatic appeal, and other information to improve their predictive power. Individual voters have little incentive to become experts on the outcome of an election—they tend to vote their conscience or vested interest—while the speculator needs to take into account as much relevant information as possible to be successful in the marketplace.

Want to know who is likely to win control of the House and Senate in November? Check out *www.biz.uiowa.edu/iem*. You can watch the results without betting.

---

1. Ludwig von Mises, *Human Action,* 3rd ed. (Chicago: Regnery, 1966), pp. 337–38.

2. Joyce Berg, Forrest Nelson, and Thomas Rietz, "Accuracy and Forecast Standard Error of Prediction Markets," University of Iowa Working Draft, November 2001, p. 15. Go to *www.biz.uiowa.edu/iem/archive/BNR_2001.pdf*.

3. In 2000, 20 percent of the traders were from Iowa while Iowa accounted for only 1 percent of the nation's population in 2000. Men constituted 75 percent of the active traders but only 49 percent of the overall population. IEM traders are "typically young, white, well educated, and have high family incomes." Ibid., p. 10.

4. Ibid., p. 13.

5. Friedrich Hayek, "The Use of Knowledge in Society," *American Economic Review* (1945) 35, pp. 519–30.

New Possibilities for Our Grandchildren

"It would not be foolish to contemplate the possibility of a far greater progress still."

—John Maynard Keynes[1]

In 1930, after the Roaring Twenties, John Maynard Keynes wrote an optimistic essay titled "Economic Possibilities for our Grandchildren." After lambasting his disciples who predicted never-ending depression and permanent stagnation, Keynes foresaw a bright future. Through technological improvements and capital accumulation, mankind could virtually solve its economic problem within the next hundred years, he said. Goods and services would become so abundant and cheap that leisure would be the biggest challenge. According to Keynes, capital could become so inexpensive that interest rates might fall to zero.

Interest rates have not fallen to zero, but our standard of living has advanced remarkably since the Great Depression. In fact, we have probably already fulfilled Keynes's prediction that "the standard of living in progressive countries one hundred years hence will be between four and eight times as high as to-day."[2]

Can We Grow Faster?

Today's economists don't appear to be as optimistic as Keynes, even as we enter another year of a dynamic, full-employment

324

economy. I asked several well-known economists for recommendations that would give us sustained (long-term, not short-term) economic growth rates of 6, 7, or maybe even 10 percent a year, eventually fulfilling Keynes's economic nirvana.

"Not possible!" most of them exclaimed. "I think it's impossible to double the long-term growth rate in the U.S.," answered Harvard economist Robert Barro. David Colander of Middlebury College agreed. "The idea of doubling economic growth in ten years sounds very much like a central planning goal of the former Soviet system." He quoted Herbert Stein: "Economic policy is random with respect to the performance of the American economy, but thank God there isn't much of it."

Recently a whole book of essays was devoted to charting a course toward higher growth rates. In the foreword to *The Rising Tide,* Dana Mead, CEO of Tenneco and former chairman of the National Association of Manufacturers, rejects the notion that the U.S. economy can't exceed its secular long-term growth pattern of around 3 percent a year. He argues that faster economic growth is achievable without creating shortages, rising labor costs, and higher interest rates. As Jack Kemp states, "We can raise the ceiling on growth by judicious changes in policy."[3] Of course, not all the economists in the book agree with Mead and Kemp. James Tobin, Yale professor and Nobel laureate, declares, "Although politicians freely promise faster growth, governments have no handy set of tools for effecting it."[4] Apparently he hasn't found the formula to fulfill his mentor Keynes's dream of universal opulence.

Despite their skepticism of substantially higher growth rates, major economists do offer several ways to improve long-term prospects. Rudi Dornbusch of MIT recommends privatizing Social Security and education. Robert Barro urges a flat-rate consumption tax, exemption of savings from taxation, deregulation of labor and business, and a 10 percent cut in the size of government. Robert Mundell warns against inflating the money supply as a growth tool and instead favors slashing capital gains and income tax rates to encourage entrepreneurship and investing. "A lower level of government spending would make more of the surplus of society available for capital formation and growth. A shift in government priorities from consumption and redistribution to social overhead capital, improved education, and investment in scientific and medical research would go far in raising the productivity of capital with a permanent effect on growth."[5]

The Future Is Boundless

My own view is that we are selling our country short by thinking that super-growth cannot be sustained over the long run. Imagine how much advanced our standards of living could become if we

- slashed government spending to its legitimate functions, which undoubtedly means less than 10 percent of GDP;
- replaced the current tax code with a simplified 10 percent flat tax;
- privatized Social Security, or better yet, let Americans make their own plans for retirement;
- established a sound money standard that discouraged malinvestment and the boom-bust business cycle;
- established a fair system of justice that freed 90 percent of the lawyers in this country to become productive citizens; and
- stopped interfering in foreign military affairs.

Imagine the breakthroughs in medicine, transportation, housing, telecommunications, and science that could take place by adopting this laissez-faire program. It boggles the mind to think that we could double or triple our living standards in a short time. To quote Keynes: "Thus for the first time since his creation man will be faced with . . . how to use his freedom from pressing economic cares, how to occupy his leisure, which science and compound interest will have won for him, to live wisely and agreeably and well."[6]

---

1. John Maynard Keynes, "Economic Possibilities for Our Grandchildren," *Essays in Persuasion* (New York: Norton, 1963), p. 365.
2. Ibid.
3. Quoted in Jerry J. Jasinowski, ed., *The Rising Tide* (New York: John Wiley & Sons, 1998), p. xxi.
4. James Tobin, "Can We Grow Faster?," in ibid., p. 44.
5. Robert A. Mundell, "A Progrowth Fiscal System," in ibid., pp. 203–04.
6. *Essays in Persuasion*, p 367.

Index

About the Author

Mark Skousen is the president of the Foundation for Economic Education (FEE), the granddaddy of free-market educational foundations. Founded by Leonard Read in 1946, FEE publishes *Ideas on Liberty*, conducts seminars, and sells books on liberty (it recently acquired Laissez Faire Books, the largest distributor of books on liberty in the world).

For the past 23 years, Skousen has edited his own investment advisory newsletter, *Forecasts & Strategies*, published by Phillips Publishing International in Potomac, Maryland. He is also an occasional columnist for *Forbes*, the premier business magazine in the United States. He has also written for the *Wall Street Journal, Reason, Liberty*, and *The Journal of Economic Perspectives*. For further information about his writing, see his website, www.mskousen.com.

He earned his B.A. and M.S. in economics from Brigham Young University in 1971 and 1972. He received his Ph.D. in economics from George Washington University in 1977. He was an economic analyst for the Central Intelligence Agency, 1972-75. For sixteen years (1986-2001), he taught economics and finance at Rollins College in Winter Park, Florida.

Mark Skousen is the author of twenty books. His economics books include *The Structure of Production* (New York University Press, 1990), *Economics on Trial* (Irwin, 1991, 1993), *Dissent on Keynes* (Praeger, 1992), *Puzzles and Paradoxes in Economics* (Edward Elgar, 1997), *Economic Logic* (Capital Press, 2000), and *The Making of Modern Economics* (M. E. Sharpe, 2001). His latest book is *The Power of Economic Thinking* (Foundation for Economic Education, 2002).

His investment books include *The Complete Guide to Financial Privacy* (Simon & Schuster, 1983), *High Finance on a Low Budget*, co-authored with his wife Jo Ann (Bantam, 1981, Dearborn, 1993), and *Scrooge Investing* (McGraw Hill, 2000).

Skousen has lived in eight nations, and traveled and lectured throughout the United States and in 64 countries. He and his wife and five children have lived in Washington, D.C.; Nassau, the Bahamas; London, England; Orlando, Florida; and now Irvington-on-Hudson, New York.

About the Publisher

Founded in 1946 by Leonard E. Read, the Foundation for Economic Education (FEE) is one of the oldest free-market organizations in the world. FEE is devoted to teaching the principles of economics and liberty to students, teachers, business people, and the general public through seminars, books, and its award-winning monthly publication, *Ideas on Liberty*. FEE also recently acquired Laissez Faire Books, the largest distributor of books on liberty in the world (with book buyers in 90 countries).

FEE headquarters are located in a 35-room mansion on a six-acre estate in Irvington-on-Hudson, New York (just 22 miles north of Manhattan). Visitors are welcome.

Published since 1955, *Ideas on Liberty* offers the best in book reviews, columns by top libertarian thinkers, and features on history, economics, philosophy, technology, and public policies.

FEE seminars and lectures are held throughout the year at FEE headquarters and around the world. It holds an annual national convention known as FEE Fest every May (for details, go to www.FEEnationalconvention.org).

FEE publishes a variety of books on economics and liberty, such as *The Law*, by Frederic Bastiat; *Anything That's Peaceful*, by Leonard E. Read; and *The Mainspring of Human Progress*, by Henry Grady Weaver.

FEE is a non-political, non-profit 501(c)(3) tax-exempt organization, supported solely by private contributions and sales of its literature.

For more information about FEE, contact:

Foundation for Economic Education
30 South Broadway
Irvington-on-Hudson, New York 10533
Telephone: Toll free 1-800-USA-1776 (U. S. and Canada)
914-591-7230
914-591-8910 (fax)
E-mail: fee@fee.org
FEE home page: www.FEE.org
Daily news service: www.FEEnews.org